Trinitarian Doxology

*T. F. and J. B. Torrance's Theology
of Worship as Participation by the Spirit
in the Son's Communion with the Father*

Kevin J. Navarro

Foreword by Thomas A. Noble

◆PICKWICK *Publications* • Eugene, Oregon

TRINITARIAN DOXOLOGY
T. F. and J. B. Torrance's Theology of Worship as Participation by the Spirit in the Son's Communion with the Father

Copyright © 2020 Kevin J. Navarro. All rights reserved. Except for brief quotations in critical publications or reviews, no part of this book may be reproduced in any manner without prior written permission from the publisher. Write: Permissions, Wipf and Stock Publishers, 199 W. 8th Ave., Suite 3, Eugene, OR 97401.

Pickwick Publications
An Imprint of Wipf and Stock Publishers
199 W. 8th Ave., Suite 3
Eugene, OR 97401

www.wipfandstock.com

PAPERBACK ISBN: 978-1-7252-5098-7
HARDCOVER ISBN: 978-1-7252-5099-4
EBOOK ISBN: 978-1-7252-5100-7

Cataloguing-in-Publication data:

Names: Navarro, Kevin J., author. | Noble, Thomas A., foreword writer

Title: Trinitarian doxology : T. F. and J. B. Torrance's theology of worship as participation by the Spirit in the Son's communion with the Father / Kevin J. Navarro with a foreword by Thomas A. Noble.

Description: Eugene, OR: Pickwick Publications, 2020 | Includes bibliographical references.

Identifiers: ISBN 978-1-7252-5098-7 (paperback) | ISBN 978-1-7252-5099-4 (hardcover) | ISBN 978-1-7252-5100-7 (ebook)

Subjects: LCSH: Torrance, Thomas F. (Thomas Forsyth), 1913–2007 | Torrance, James | Trinity | Public worship | Liturgics

Classification: BV10.2 N38 2020 (print) | BV10.2 (ebook)

OCTOBER 15, 2020

"Too much Christian worship showcases our own feelings and performance rather than Christ, the perfect Worship Leader. Pastor and musician Kevin Navarro finds a vibrant counterpoint in T. F. and J. B. Torrance's theology of worship. An informative, judicious, and ultimately worship-inspiring study!"
—Jerome Van Kuiken, Dean, School of Ministry
and Christian Thought, Oklahoma Wesleyan University

"If you think theology is irrelevant to the lived life of Christian worship, think again! In this book, Kevin Navarro explains with care and clarity the powerful difference one's thinking about Jesus and God makes to the understanding and practice of prayer and worship."
—Robin A. Parry, author of *Worshipping Trinity:
Coming Back to the Heart of Worship*

"A thoroughly informed, articulate, and well-documented exposition of and engagement with the theology and practice of Christian worship as understood and propounded by Thomas F. and James B. Torrance. . . . An indispensable resource for anyone who believes that Christian worship needs to be continually renewed by returning to the breadth and depth of the gospel of the Triune God revealed in Jesus Christ according to his word and empowered by the Holy Spirit."
—Gary W. Deddo, President, Grace Communion Seminary

"There is general agreement that worship is for God, and the purpose of worship services is to glorify God and gratefully remember all that God has done for us. But many continue to view worship simplistically as something that people do to honor God. Missing from this common attitude are the deeper and richer trinitarian dimensions of worship that Scottish theologians Thomas and James Torrance highlighted throughout their many writings. Navarro helpfully presents the worship theology of the Torrances against the background of their distinctive trinitarian theology, making their positions much clearer and more understandable. Along the way, Navarro also addresses several misperceptions and distortions of the Torrances' views and points out the practical significance of their liturgical theology for our understanding and practice of worship. Students of the Torrances and all who care about our understanding of worship will find much to reflect upon and much to rejoice about."
—Robert R. Redman Jr., Professor and Director of Ministry Programs,
South College, Knoxville, Tennessee

Trinitarian Doxology

To my father, Ruben D. Navarro (1943–2013),
who exemplified the love of God.

"The church which takes her eyes off Jesus Christ, the only Mediator of worship, is on the road to becoming apostate. There is no more urgent need in our churches today than to recover the Trinitarian nature of grace—that it is by grace alone, through the gift of Jesus Christ in the Spirit that we can enter into and live a life of communion with God our Father."
—James B. Torrance

Table of Contents

Foreword by Thomas A. Noble xi
Preface xiii
Acknowledgments xv

Introduction: The Doxological Theology of T. F. and J. B. Torrance xvii

Chapter 1: The Biographical Background of T. F. and J. B. Torrance 1
Chapter 2: Unitarian or Trinitarian Worship? 20
Chapter 3: The Trinitarian Faith and Worship 40
Chapter 4: The Mediation of Christ 62
Chapter 5: The Place of Jesus Christ in Liturgical Prayer and Worship 87
Chapter 6: Thomas F. Torrance and Preaching 113
Chapter 7: The Sacraments of Incorporation and Renewal 142

Conclusion 175

Bibliography 191

Foreword

As JAMES B. TORRANCE used to insist, dogmatics arises out of doxology. It is not surprising therefore that there should be contemporary interest in this connection between theology and worship. Indeed, for some decades now there has been renewed interest in worship across many churches, a new interest too in the doctrine of the Trinity, and great interest in linking the two. But one key aspect of that has not always been fully appreciated or investigated. That is the role of Christ as the One who, being truly human, leads us in his priestly role in our worship of God. True Christian worship is therefore to be understood our participation by the Spirit in the Son's communion with the Father.

Kevin J. Navarro is a both a musician and a theologian. As an experienced pastor he has been deeply interested in worship that is truly God-centred. But a new and deeper understanding of worship came to him through the writings of the Scottish theologians Thomas F. and James B. Torrance. The brothers taught together at New College in the University of Edinburgh where I was privileged to be taught by both. Thomas Torrance "retired" soon afterwards to devote the next decades to writing and publishing many of his most profound works. His younger brother James went on to become Professor of Theology at the University of Aberdeen. J. B.'s Didsbury Lectures, *Worship, Community and the Triune God of Grace*, published in 1996, have been widely influential as an introduction to their shared theology of worship. T. F. was the major theologian who published numerous influential works on Christology, theology, and science, the doctrine of the Trinity and much more. Their shared theology of worship, presented so compellingly by J. B., himself a gifted teacher and theologian, was given an immense theological foundation in the published works of T. F.

If I were asked to put into a nutshell their perspective on the theology of worship, I could do so by employing the two forms of the doxology defended by Basil of Caesarea in his treatise, *On the Holy Spirit*. Basil had been challenged to defend his use of the doxology, *Glory be to the Father with the Son together with the Holy Spirit*. His critics, who were not very sure about attributing full deity explicitly to the Holy Spirit, preferred the other form, *Glory be to the Father through the Son by the Holy Spirit*. Basil insisted on both, and it has been held that whereas in the latter, "through" and "by" express the economic Trinity, our understanding of God active in his world, in the former, "with" and "together with," express the equality of the persons emphasized in the immanent or ontological Trinity—that God is in himself eternally a communion of the three Persons. Some theologians in recent decades have suggested that during centuries of focusing on the ontological Trinity, we lost hold of the economic Trinity—God active in salvation in his world. The doctrine of the Trinity was thus made to appear remote and irrelevant.

What Thomas and James Torrance have done in their theology of worship is to make the economic Trinity a vital part of our understanding of worship. It is of course true that in Christian worship we adore Father, Son and Holy Spirit, co-equal in the Holy Trinity world without end. T. F. Torrance's theology of the Trinity considers that profoundly. But what the brothers have done is to illuminate the significance of the economic Trinity for our worship. We are only able to join in the worship of heaven adoring Father, Son, and Holy Spirit, because the Spirit unites us to the Son, our ascended human brother, so that we may participate in his communion with the Father.

In this book, a revised form of his doctoral thesis completed at the University of Manchester through Nazarene Theological College, Dr Navarro takes us into the theology of worship articulated by the Torrance brothers. He brings together material from across the writings of T. F. to demonstrate the deep foundations of the doctrine so winningly and creatively presented by J. B. Everyone who leads Christian congregations in worship will find this book deepens their understanding of their calling. All thoughtful Christians will find their experience of Christian worship deepened.

Thomas A. Noble,
Research Professor of Theology,
Nazarene Theological Seminary, Kansas City, MO
Senior Research Fellow in Theology,
Nazarene Theological College, Manchester, UK

Preface

MOST APPROACHES TO LITURGICAL theology are anthropocentric: the study of liturgy is primarily focused on what *we*, the worshipers, do. While some have attempted to offer a more theological approach to the subject of worship, they still have not gone far enough. Thomas F. Torrance and James B. Torrance offer a trinitarian and christocentric approach. This informs not only the *why* of worship and not simply the *what* or *how* of worship, but centers on the One whom we worship. Most significantly, it fully recognizes the key role of the humanity of Christ as the ascended High Priest who alone offers the perfect worship and through whom alone we are enabled by the Spirit to worship God.

In order to arrive at a theology of worship informed by T. F. and J. B. Torrance, doxological themes in their writings were collated and are examined in this book. With the exception of two theses (one focused exclusively on the eucharistic theology of T. F. Torrance and another on the Ascended Christ as the leader of our worship), most secondary sources focus on the Torrances' approach to science, epistemology, soteriology, and trinitarian theology. All of these themes are critical to understanding their theology. But this work attempts to offer unique scholarship highlighting the doxological themes that emerge from their writings. This is the first comprehensive theology of worship of the Torrances. This work also provides a lens for a deeper understanding of their theology.

The findings of this research are that the Torrances' own background provides insight into their concern about the worship of the Living God (chapter 1). Regarding the anthropocentric approaches, the Torrances explicitly confront unitarian and existential theologies of worship and present their incarnational-trinitarian alternative (chapter 2). They emphasize that the trinitarian faith of the Nicene-Constantinopolitan Creed is the way back to a trinitarian doxology (chapter 3). They focus on the mediation of Christ (chapter 4) and the place of Jesus Christ in liturgical prayer and worship (chapter 5). They also have a theological understanding of the role of preaching (chapter 6) and the sacraments (chapter 7) with a vibrant Christology that once again, articulates and informs Christian worship.

This book presents this unique and needed theological perspective on Christian worship. It is all too common when discussing the subject of worship to discuss praxis exclusively. But for a subject as central to the Christian faith as worship, a vibrant trinitarian theology of worship is imperative. This work, aims to make a significant contribution to that.

Acknowledgements

I WANT TO THANK my father, Ruben D. Navarro, who went home to be with the Lord on January 26th, 2013. I was born under a lucky star to have a dad who exemplified the love of God by how he treated others. He was replete with kindness, goodness, and grace. He was also my greatest advocate. After my dad passed away, my mom, Velma Navarro, stepped right in continuing to support my dad's advocacy.

I want to thank my wife. Susan was an immense source of encouragement. During the challenging times (and we had quite a few with an extended season of loss), she encouraged me to stay the course and reminded me of the importance of the doxological theology of the Torrances. It was her gentle voice that inspired me to keep on keeping on. I also want to thank our sons and daughter (Timothy, Matthew, Joshua, Aaron, and Naomi) and our two daughters-in-law (Nikaela and Hawa) for their encouragement.

I want to thank those who provided friendship and emotional support over the last decade: Doug Feil, Steve Logan, David Wilks, Randy Rothwell, Mike Wearsch, Penny Wilkinson, Dale Pierce, Brian Thompson, John Roberts, Jeff Foote, Jake Fierberg, Will Burger, Dave Ahlman, Michael Eckelkamp, Roy Graham, Tim Musslewhite, John Pyrc, Bill O'Byrne, and our *Imago Christi* Community. A special thanks to Bethany Evangelical Free Church who graciously gave me a study leave each summer for my NTC residencies while I served as their senior pastor. I am grateful for the twenty-three years I had to serve as their pastor.

I am grateful for Dr. Thomas A. Noble who served as my PhD supervisor at the University of Manchester, UK. Dr. Noble was such a gracious man. I cherished the many opportunities to hear him tell stories about his days as a student of T. F. and J. B. Torrance. I also want to thank Dr. Peter Rae who was always hospitable and gave me several opportunities to teach at the Nazarene Theological College, Manchester. Finally, I want to thank Dr. Robert T. Walker for the Torrance Retreats at the Firbush Retreat Centre in Killin, Scotland. Bob graciously invited me to stay with him and his wife, Mioko, in Edinburgh, the summer of 2015. He was also extremely helpful answering my questions through email correspondence. He was always eager to help me appreciate the theology of his uncle, T. F. Torrance.

Introduction

The Doxological Theology of T. F. and J. B. Torrance

"True theology is done in the presence of God in the midst
of the worshipping community."
—J. B. Torrance[1]

The Collect for Trinity by T. F. Torrance

Almighty and everlasting God, who hast revealed thyself as Father, Son,
and Holy Spirit, and dost ever live and reign in the perfect unity of love:
Grant that we may always hold firmly and joyfully to this faith, and,
living in the praise of thy divine majesty, may finally be one in thee; who
art three Persons in one God, world without end.[2]

A Case for a "Theological" Approach to Worship and Liturgy

ONE OF THE PRIMARY ways we know what Christians have believed is by looking at how Christians have worshiped. Liturgy exposes theology. But it is also true that liturgy shapes and forms theology. In the worshiping community, the Word of God is proclaimed, prayers are offered, and the desired outcome is the praise of God.[3] The subject of congregational worship is consequently essential for the study of theology. To contribute to this discussion, Thomas F. Torrance and James B. Torrance offer an

---

1. J. B. Torrance, *Worship, Community, and the Triune God of Grace*, ix.
2. Torrance, *The Trinitarian Faith*, 340.
3. Bromiley, "Theology as Service in Karl Barth" in Hart and Thimell, *Christ in Our Place*, 145.

important christological perspective, which is an important alternative to the more common "anthropocentric" approaches that abound within worship studies, theory, and praxis. Furthermore, they offer reflection going beyond the theologies that reference the Trinity but do not expound the priesthood of Christ or his vicarious humanity. This book will explore the way in which the Torrances' scientific trinitarian theology can shape and form a more trinitarian approach to Christian liturgy.

The unique contribution of this work is to introduce this particular *theological* perspective from the doxological theology of T. F. and J. B. Torrance. These two theologians emphasize that Christian worship is not something *we* primarily do at all but rather it is something that has been done and is being done on our behalf and that whatever we are doing in worship, it is participation by the Spirit in the Son's communion with the Father. T. F. and J. B. Torrance emphasize that Christian worship is something that happens vicariously through the worship of Jesus Christ, the High Priest of all creation. It is the intent of this work to offer a comprehensive exposition of this unique doxological theological perspective as well as a critical analysis.

This more theological approach to the subject of worship is exemplified through their writings such as the article by James Torrance, "The Place of Jesus Christ in Worship."[4] James Torrance, in that article, emphasizes that the person of Jesus Christ came to do for humanity what it could not do effectively for itself, namely, offer acceptable worship to the Living God. He states, "Here lies the mystery, the wonder, the glory of the Gospel, that He who is God, the Creator of all things, and worthy of the worship and praises of all creation, should become man and *as a man worship God*, and as a man lead us in our worship of God, that we might become the sons of God we are meant to be."[5]

Other works by J. B. Torrance, such as *Worship, Community, and the Triune God of Grace*, as well as the prolific writings of T. F. Torrance, point to an awareness of a theological orientation with an emphasis on the objective revelation of God in the incarnation of Jesus Christ as well as a theological emphasis on the active obedience of Christ. This emphasis on the vicarious humanity of Christ has implications not only for soteriology but also for the theology of worship. T. F. Torrance writes, "Christian

---

4. J. B. Torrance, "The Place of Jesus Christ in Worship" in Anderson's, *Theological Foundations for Ministry*, 348–69.

5. J. B. Torrance, "The Place of Jesus Christ in Worship," in Anderson's, *Theological Foundations for Ministry*, 351. cf. Calvin, *Institutes of the Christian Religion*, 464–74.

worship is properly a form of the life of Jesus Christ ascending to the Father in the life of those who are so intimately related to him through the Spirit, that when they pray to the Father through Christ, it is Christ the Incarnate Son who honors, worships, and glorifies the Father in them."[6]

The repeated refrain in the writings of the Torrances is that the worship of all humanity was purified and made perfect through the worship of Jesus Christ. The emphasis should not be on our prayers, sermons, and songs but on the faithful worship by Christ as he lived in perfect obedience to God the Father. It is only because of the faithfulness of Jesus Christ that human beings can approach God the Father, with their liturgies and their worship and do so with confidence that it will be embraced within the worship of Christ. J. B. Torrance states, "It can never be too strongly stressed that worship is our response to objective realities, to Jesus Christ and all that He has done for us."[7]

In light of this emphasis on the faithfulness of Christ, a critical question that must be answered is, "Is all of humanity included in the worship of Christ?" In that the Torrances' believed that Jesus Christ in his incarnation, both in his active and passive obedience, worshiped perfectly on behalf of humanity, is all of humankind included in the faithfulness of Christ? The correlated soteriological question is, "Will all of humanity be saved?" This issue must be addressed. The Torrances seem to reject both universalism and limited atonement. But does their emphasis on the vicarious humanity of Christ make these denials incoherent? In the conclusion, a summary will be made that articulates the charges against the Torrances, their rebuttal, and a judgment regarding this concern. Even though this book is focused on their theology of worship, one cannot help but address this charge of universal atonement as it relates to their theology of worship. This question will be addressed in this work.

Anthropocentric Approaches to Worship and the Liturgy

In contrast to the emphasis on the vicarious humanity of Christ, in the theology of the Torrances, many approaches to the subject of worship are more "anthropocentric." The focus of these approaches is on what human beings do. It may be asked, for example, how we can improve

---

6. Torrance, *Theology in Reconciliation*, 139.

7. J. B. Torrance, "The Place of Jesus Christ in Worship" in Anderson's, *Theological Foundations for Ministry*, 368.

congregational prayer. What could we do better to make it more effective? Or, the focus may be on homiletics. How can the ministers improve their preaching? In the contemporary worship context, the focus is usually about how to improve "the flow" of the praise music (the praise band, a worship set, a worship choir, design of the worship service)? However, what is common to these approaches is they are "anthropocentric," meaning that the focus is on what we do when we worship. David Peterson is correct when he states, "We have enough how-to-do-it books and not enough reflection on worship as a total biblical idea."[8]

Contemporary worship studies became popular during the charismatic renewal movement of the late sixties and early seventies. Out of the Jesus Movement in Southern California, Maranatha Music, affiliated with Pastor Chuck Smith and Calvary Chapel, captured a new sound of worship music associated with those coming to faith in Christ out of the Hippie Counter-Cultural Movement in Southern California. Praise choruses captured the voice of a new generation of worshipers who were new converts to Christianity and who were writing their testimonies into the new worship choruses and writing folk music to Scripture verses as a way of expressing adoration, confession, thanksgiving, and supplication. With those praise and worship recordings, books and conferences followed.

A decade later, The Vineyard Movement, founded by John Wimber, created a whole new music worship culture that spread throughout the United States, Canada, New Zealand, Australia, and the United Kingdom. Vineyard Music International (the music distribution for Vineyard Music) focused on the creation of praise choruses that promoted a sense of intimacy with God. Robb Redman writes,

> In many Vineyard churches, songs rich in biblical and non-biblical anthropomorphic language predominate; many songs describe a relationship with God in physical terms (seeing, hearing, touching, holding, kissing). As biblical justification for this, Vineyard worship leaders emphasize a meaning of a New Testament Greek word for worship (*proskuneo*), "to turn toward to kiss," which they take to mean intimacy or closeness to God.[9]

The lyrics of these songs could be summed up by "the Father loves us," "Jesus loves us" and "I/we love the Father and Jesus." Robin Parry states,

---

8. Peterson, *Engaging with God*, 21.
9. Redman, *The Great Worship Awakening*, 35–36.

"If there is a problem with Christian worship songs, it is more a failure to bring out the Trinitarian dimensions of the God we worship than a problem of violating Trinitarian faith."[10] Along with reinforcing a new worship music culture, a distinctive Vineyard theology of worship and ministry was promoted (particularly the New Testament Theology of George Ladd: "The Kingdom is here but not yet"). This orientation was introduced to discuss worship as a way of experiencing the rule and reign of Jesus Christ.[11]

Looking at the conversions and the church planting these movements brought about, it would be difficult for the Christian theologian to argue that this music was not used by God to promote renewal in many local churches and in many English-speaking countries. A whole new generation was praising God. Young people were giving thanks with a grateful heart. Robb Redman states, "Christians raised on Jesus music learned how to praise. Despite what its critics have said about it, early CWM (Contemporary Worship Music) was, for the most part, both God-centered and biblical in content. They also stressed a variety of worship themes (adoration, praise, confession, humility before God)."[12] Yet some, while appreciative of this new worship music were asking other liturgical questions. Hughes Oliphant Old states, "A worshiping assembly is very different from a theatre crowd or a lecture audience. A worshiping assembly interacts. We sing praises together, and of the very essence of that act of worship is the way the singing of others lifts us up to join in the song. We gather around the Lord's Table one with another to share the loaf and the cup."[13] Robert E. Webber was another who was advocating a worship culture that honored the liturgical values of the ancient church.

Approaches that Attempted to Be Theological

Robert Webber began to look back into history at liturgical structures to point out that Christians have had some kind of liturgical *ordo* to their corporate worship practices, whether that was a four-fold worship pattern in a Sunday service (Gathering, Word, Table, Dismissal), or a Church Year Rhythm (Advent, Christmas, Epiphany, Ordinary Time, Lent, Holy

10. Parry, *Worshipping Trinity*, 133.
11. Ladd, *The Gospel of the Kingdom*; Wimber, *Power Evangelism*.
12. Redman, *The Great Worship Awakening*, 54.
13. Old, *Themes and Variations of a Christian Doxology*, 133–34.

Week, Easter, Ascension, Pentecost, Ordinary Time). Many of Robert E. Webber's books were focused on how to reintroduce liturgical rhythm in Evangelical worship practices.[14]

Another critical contribution from the work of Robert E. Webber was that he made a compelling case to reinstate the Jesus story back into the center of Christian worship. He stated, "One of the greatest discoveries of my Christian pilgrimage has come with the realization that the primary importance in worship is not what I do, but what God is doing."[15] This was the reason that Robert Webber was so adamant that we need to re-introduce the Church Year into Christian worship.[16] The Church Year, he argued, kept the birth, life, death, resurrection, and ascension at the center of the church's worship practices instead of mere aesthetic considerations. "Worship tells and acts out the Christ-event."[17]

Marva Dawn was another theologian who addressed the subject of worship from a theological perspective. However, Dawn was primarily concerned with how the church had been influenced by the surrounding culture. She examined the subject of worship from an ethical and anthropological perspective. One of her primary influences was Jacques Ellul and his critique of technology. Her suggested response, to what she saw as narcissism in corporate worship, was to structure the worship service so that it was God-centered yet promoting character development and biblical community. What made Marva Dawn an important voice in the worship discussion was that she offered a prophetic voice to the contemporary church.[18]

Others who made significant contributions to worship literature were biblical scholars such as Ralph Martin (*The Worship of God, Worship and the Early Church*), David Peterson (*Engaging with God*), Timothy Pierce (*Enthroned on Our Praise*), Larry Hurtado (*At the Origins of Christian Worship*), Gerard Borchert (*Worship in the New Testament: Divine Mystery and Human Response*), and Daniel I. Block (*For the Glory of God:*

---

14. See the following books by Webber, *Ancient-Future Worship*; *Evangelicals on the Canterbury Trail*; *Ancient Future Time*.

15. Webber, *Worship Is a Verb*, 66. Yet, it is worth noting that earlier in his book, he states, "Worship is a verb. It is not something done to us or for us, but by us." Webber, *Worship is a Verb*, 2. J. B. Torrance would describe this statement as unitarian.

16. See the argument that worship has become secular in his book, Webber, *Worship Is a Verb*, 6–7.

17. Webber, *Worship Is a Verb*, 45.

18. Dawn, *Reaching out without Dumbing Down*; *A Royal Waste of Time*.

Recovering a Biblical Theology of Worship).[19] David Peterson's *Engaging with God* was an exceptional biblical theology of worship with a chapter on the book of Hebrews and the worship of Jesus and thus touching briefly on the subject of the priesthood of Christ.[20] Liturgical scholars such as James F. White (*Protestant Worship, Introduction to Christian Worship, A Brief History of Christian Worship*), Paul Bradshaw (*Early Christian Worship*), and Geoffrey Wainwright (*Doxology: The Praise of God in Worship, Doctrine and Life*) also had influence on the academic community as to how they perceived the centrality of liturgy in the local church.[21] Furthermore, there have been many recent books addressing the subject of worship theology such as Maeve Louise Heaney's *Music as Theology: What Music Says about the Word,* with its emphasis on aesthetics and its ethnomusicology considerations.[22]

What must be said however is that, although all of these movements, scholars, and literature made important contributions to how the local church conceptualized worship, they did not go far enough. They did not adequately reflect on the priesthood of Jesus Christ or his vicarious humanity. The term "Christ-centered worship" meant that Christ was a reference point in the liturgy. However, Jesus is not only the *object* of our worship, he is the *subject* of our worship. The Torrances made the case that what makes worship trinitarian and thus evangelical is that Christ in his incarnation not only revealed the Father but in his humanity, offered the perfect worship to the Father on behalf of humanity.

In summary, this work will examine the theological basis and implications of the Torrances' view that Christian worship is participating by the Spirit in the Son's communion with the Father. Throughout the book the case will be made, that whether one agrees with the Torrances or not, to appreciate the writings of T. F. and J. B. Torrance fully, one should consider reading their theology from a liturgical perspective with

19. Martin, *The Worship of God*; *Worship in the Early Church*; Peterson, *Engaging with God*; Pierce, *Enthroned on Our Praise*; Hurtado, *At The Origins of Christian Worship*; Borchert, *Worship in the New Testament;* Block, *For the Glory of God.*

20. David Peterson states, "Hebrews presents the most complete and fully integrated theology of worship in the New Testament. All the important categories of Old Testament thinking on this subject—sanctuary, sacrifice, altar, priesthood, and covenant—are taken up and related to the person and work of Jesus Christ." Peterson, *Engaging with God*, 228.

21. White, *Protestant Worship*; *Introduction to Christian Worship*; *A Brief History of Christian Worship*; Bradshaw, *Early Christian Worship*; Wainwright, *Doxology*.

22. Heaney, *Music as Theology.*

an awareness of the doxological foundation of their theological agenda. Following a biographical chapter of the Torrances, the themes that will be addressed, as the theological basis for the Torrances' theology of worship, are: unitarian or trinitarian worship, the trinitarian faith and worship, the mediation of Christ, the place of Jesus Christ in liturgical prayer and worship, preaching, and the sacraments of incorporation and renewal.

1

The Biographical Background of T. F. and J. B. Torrance

Introduction

THE PURPOSE OF THIS chapter is to highlight the doxological nature of the Torrances' biographies. Many have written about their backgrounds, but this chapter exists to emphasize that the Torrances' theological program was undergirded by doxological influences. What is worth noting is how much the subject of worship comes up in their upbringing, education, pastoral ministry, and academic calling.

Biography of Thomas F. Torrance

Thomas Forsyth Torrance (born 30th August 1913) and James Bruce Torrance (born 3rd February 1923) along with their other siblings (Mary, Grace, Margaret, and David) were born in Chengdu, China and raised by parents who were British missionaries serving with the American Bible Society. Growing up in that context established the framework for mission and evangelism that provided the groundwork for later theological pursuits. T. F. Torrance's writings reveal the heart of an evangelist who had a passion for the mission of God.

It was customary for the Torrance family to read three chapters of the Bible a day and five chapters each Sundays for their family devotions. Elmer Colyer states, "Torrance describes his mother as a 'woman of the greatest spiritual depth, prayer life and theological insight,' and the real theologian of the family. Being raised in a Christian and missionary home meant that 'belief in God simply pervaded everything' and so belief in God 'always seemed so natural' to Torrance."[1] This appreciation of the Scriptures provided the foundation for loving Jesus Christ, the Living Word of God. Geoffrey W. Bromiley asserts, "Theological reflection on the gracious ways and works of God should constantly lead to prayers of gratitude and praise."[2] A similar perspective is that the economy of God prompts praise and thanksgiving from those who understand and appreciate what God has done for them in Christ Jesus. This is what was instilled in the Torrance home. Here is how T. F. Torrance described that upbringing:

> Through my missionary parents I was imbued from my earliest days with a vivid belief in God. Belief in God was so natural that I could no more doubt the existence of God than the existence of my parents or the world around me. I cannot remember ever having had any doubts about God. Moreover, as long as I can recall my religious outlook was essentially biblical and evangelical, and indeed evangelistic. I used to read three chapters of the Bible every day and five on Sundays, which meant reading through the whole Bible each year. My father who could repeat by heart the Psalms and some of the books of the New Testament (the Epistle to the Romans, for example) encouraged us children to memorize many passages of the Holy Scriptures, which I greatly appreciated later in life. Family prayers led by my father on his knees and the evangelical hymns he taught us to sing nourished our spiritual understanding and growth in faith. I can still repeat in Chinese, "Jesus loves me, this I know; for the Bible tells me so." I was deeply conscious of the task to which my parents had been called by God to preach the Gospel to heathen people and win them for Christ. This orientation to mission was built into the fabric of my mind, and has never faded—by its essential nature Christian theology has always had for me an evangelistic thrust.[3]

Both T. F. Torrance and J. B. Torrance often referred to their upbringing as the foundation of their theological pursuits and interests. It was also their missionary context that gave meaning to their theological

---

1. Colyer, *How to Read T. F. Torrance*, 36.
2. Bromiley, *Participatio*, Vol 1, 14.
3. McGrath, *T. F. Torrance*, 13.

pursuits. Theology was never a mere academic exercise for either T. F. or J. B. Torrance. It was a matter of heralding the mighty acts of God.[4] Theology existed to speak of the Triune God and the incarnation and what God had done for men and women in the saving humanity of Jesus Christ. Both T. F. Torrance and J. B. Torrance honored both their parents and their upbringing frequently throughout their life.

Theological Education[5]

Between 1927 and 1931, T. F. Torrance focused his attention on the academic subjects that would prepare him for Christian ministry in preparation for becoming a missionary. While at Bellshill Academy, a senior secondary school in Lanarkshire, he focused on Greek, Latin, History, English, and Mathematics.[6] This prepared him well for his studies at the University of Edinburgh. There, Torrance studied philosophy and classical languages for the next three years having enrolled for the three-year ordinary degree instead of the four-year honors degree owing to family financial challenges. He studied metaphysics under Norman Kemp Smith, and moral philosophy under Edward Alfred Taylor. Alister McGrath writes, "Although Torrance did not begin the formal study of theology until he entered New College in October 1934, it is clear that his theological development proceeded apace at this earlier stage in his studies."[7]

When T. F. Torrance began his studies at New College, Edinburgh in October of 1934, New College was a worshiping community. Some historical background will help us appreciate the context in which both of the Torrances had their theological education. The Free Church of Scotland, for the preparation of its ministers, had built New College as a church college. In 1843, the Free Church of Scotland had broken away from the established Church of Scotland (the "Auld Kirk"). The division was between what had been the "Evangelical" and "Moderate" wings of the Kirk. The evangelical wing formed the "Free Church of Scotland"

---

4. Stewart, *Heralds of God*.

5. McGrath has described T. F. Torrance's theological education, in great detail. I have attempted to summarize McGrath's history of this period, in this section. McGrath, *T. F. Torrance*, 19–46.

6. A Scottish senior secondary was the equivalent of an English grammar school.

7. McGrath, *T. F. Torrance*, 24.

and built three colleges to prepare its ministers (including New College). They also built a church building in every parish and sent out missionaries to India and Africa. The ministers for the old established Church of Scotland studied under the Divinity Faculty of Edinburgh University. The "Auld Kirk" had no missionaries and the Torrances' father, the Rev. Thomas Torrance, who had grown up in the "Auld Kirk", had gone to China with the China Inland Mission, and later, with the American Bible Society. In 1900, the Free Church united with the United Presbyterians to form the United Free Church of Scotland, and in 1929, they were reunited with the "Auld Kirk." T. F. Torrance began his studies at New College five years later.

The institution in which T. F. Torrance studied was therefore a union of the Divinity Faculty of Edinburgh University and at the same time a church college. While New College was part of the university, it was at the same time a Christian college. The impressive assembly hall for the General Assembly of the Kirk was part of the college building. All of the professors were ordained ministers in the newly united Church of Scotland. They wore their clerical dress and academic gowns. A committee represented by both the university and the church appointed them. Most of the students were preparing for the ministry in the Church of Scotland, in a country that was predominately Christian. New College was therefore a worshiping community with daily prayers, prayer prior to each lecture and a service of the Lord's Supper each term. A verse of a psalm (unaccompanied in the Presbyterian tradition) was sung each weekday at the conclusion of the college lunch. It was in this worshiping, Christian community that the Torrances received their theological education.[8]

Between 1934 and 1937, Torrance pursued what was sometimes referred to as a "second first degree," the Bachelor of Divinity (now known as the Master of Divinity in North America) at the University of Edinburgh. Hugh Ross Mackintosh, Professor of Christian Dogmatics, without doubt was one of two professors who had a lasting influence on him. Mackintosh was passionate about the subject of the atoning love of God and was the leading advocate for the centrality of Jesus Christ for the doctrine of revelation and salvation. He insisted that preachers be

---

8. Cheyne, "New College, Edinburgh, 1846–1996," in *Studies in Scottish Church History*, 287–312. T. A. Noble was also very helpful with Cheyne's history of New College, Edinburgh University. A. C. Cheyne was T. F. Torrance's successor as Professor of Ecclesiastical History at New College.

evangelistic, "preaching for a verdict." Mackintosh's lectures, in particular, had a tremendous influence on Torrance as evidenced by Torrance's meticulous notes.[9]

The second professor who influenced Torrance during this period was Daniel Lamont who lectured in apologetic and pastoral theology. It was Daniel Lamont who contributed to Torrance's interest in a scientific approach to Christian Dogmatics.[10]

A doctrinal dispute worth noting was Torrance's disagreement with John Baillie who became Professor of Divinity in 1934.[11] While he respected Baillie's teaching on prayer, he disagreed with Baillie's criticism of Barth. Alister McGrath states, "He believed that he could discern a deep-seated epistemological dualism behind Baillie's thinking, deriving from nineteenth century philosophy of religion."[12] McGrath provides an example of this from T. F. Torrance's own writing:

> On the one hand in Kantian fashion he [John Baillie] sought first to establish a method of inquiry apart from the subject-matter of his inquiry, and on the other hand he worked out a theory of religion from its roots in the human soul and the moral claims of God upon it, without really taking divine revelation into account. I found this epistemologically untenable, not least in the light of the overthrow by general relativity of a dualist Kantian approach to knowledge, of which we learned from Lamont, and also found its rather stand-off relation divine revelation theologically unacceptable—it certainly conflicted very sharply with the primary place given to revelation by Lamont in *Christ and the World of Thought* and by Mackintosh in *Immortality and the Future*, *The Originality of the Christian Message*, the *Divine Initiative*, the *Doctrine of the Person of Jesus Christ*, *Some Aspects of Christian Belief*, the *Christian Apprehension of God*, or *Types of Modern Theology*! I recall an occasion in *Interpretation of Religion* one of his lectures when Professor Mackintosh, after referring to John Baillie's *Interpretation of Religion*, paused to say, "But, gentlemen, is that really religion?" His own exhaustive study of Hegelian philosophy of religion convinced him that it is

---

9. Mackintosh, *The Doctrine of the Person of Jesus Christ*; *Immortality and the Future*; *The Christian Experience of Forgiveness*; *The Christian Apprehension of God*.

10. Lamont, *Christ and the World of Thought*, 199–265.

11. On John and Donald Baillie, see Cheyne, *Studies in Scottish Church History*, 287–312.

12. McGrath, *T. F. Torrance*, 37.

impossible for man to gain knowledge of God "by digging into himself."[13]

Following six months in the Middle East in 1936 in which Torrance was the recipient of the Blackie Fellowship (a year fellowship but Torrance was only granted six months owing to exams), he returned home to Scotland under great distress after learning about the death of H. R. Mackintosh. Torrance finished his exams for his Bachelor of Divinity and graduated *summa cum laude*. While still interested in missionary work, under the influence of H. R. Mackintosh, Torrance began to perceive a calling to theology for the sake of the gospel. Because of his examination success, he was granted the Aitken Fellowship, which allowed him to pursue postgraduate studies at a location of his choice. He chose to study with Karl Barth in Basel.

T. F. Torrance had already been familiar with Barth's theology during his time at Edinburgh University, as Barth's ideas had been influencing if not dominating the theological discourse as early as 1926. Prior to arriving in Basel, Torrance needed to acquire a good knowledge of the German language. He moved to Berlin in 1937, which he found to be very difficult. McGrath states:

> Torrance found the Nazification of German culture as ridiculous as it was oppressive, and began to get himself into trouble. Wandering down Berlin's *Unter den Linden*, he was greeted with a "*Heil Hitler!*" from everyone he passed. Irritated by this, he responded to one such greeting with "*Heil deinen Grossmutter!*"; fortunately, he was able to slip away before anyone could react.[14]

Torrance left Berlin and moved to Marburg where he secured lodging with the Heintzmann family who spoke English yet restricted the conversation to German to help him develop a working knowledge of the German language. During this time, Torrance read through Barth's *Credo* in the original German edition and began to process the language and theology of early editions of the *Church Dogmatics*.[15] After Marburg and then a short visit to Heidelberg, Torrance finally arrived in Basel.

Barth's 1937–38 seminar consisted of approximately fifty students. He had a smaller group called the *Sozietat* which met at his home. The

---

13. Torrance, "*Itinerarium mentis in Deum*," 14. Quoted in McGrath, *T. F. Torrance*, 37.

14. McGrath, *T. F. Torrance*, 43.

15. McGrath, *T. F. Torrance*, 43.

process for being accepted into this home group consisted of translating a Latin text and an exam on the topic, "Who is the Holy Spirit?" Torrance chose to write on the *communio quaedam consubstantialis*, which Barth had addressed in the first half volume of the *Church Dogmatics*. Regarding the Latin oral exam, Torrance found it very difficult primarily because of Barth's pronunciation. In the end, Torrance was accepted into the *Sozietat* and Barth was very pleased with the "Scotlander."[16]

In addition to Barth's ideas, as communicated through his dogmatic lectures, Torrance was fascinated with the way in which he led his seminars and the smaller group in his home. Torrance was also impressed with the great respect he had for his theological opponents. The one time Torrance saw Barth extremely angered was when a student disrespected the bust of Schleiermacher. Although he disagreed with him, Barth declared that he was a great Reformed theologian and that he needed to be treated with respect.[17]

When Barth and Torrance discussed what Torrance would write his thesis on, Torrance suggested that he would like to write on the scientific structure of Christian dogmatics. Barth replied that he was too young to write on that subject. He suggested that Torrance write on "the doctrine of grace in the second-century fathers." Torrance had completed everything except the *Rigorosum*, the doctoral examination that was part of the German and Swiss theological final requirement for the graduation with the doctorate.[18]

However, a change of plans quickly developed. Owing to encouragement from John Baillie, Torrance was invited to lecture at Auburn Theological Seminary in New York from 1938–39. This was a decision he never regretted. His lectures on the incarnation of Jesus Christ were meticulously written during this time. These years were formational for Torrance. However, war was looming in Europe and it was critical for Torrance to return home to Scotland. He even declined an offer to teach at Princeton, which was one of the most difficult decisions he ever had to make.

Because of what was now developing in Europe, it was unthinkable for Torrance to return to Basel. In the autumn of 1939, he enrolled as a post-graduate student at Oriel College, Oxford. His supervisor was

---

16. McGrath, *T. F. Torrance*, 43–44.
17. McGrath, *T. F. Torrance*, 45.
18. McGrath, *T. F. Torrance*, 45–46.

Marcus Niebuhr Todd. While Oxford was a good experience, he would be called away from Oxford to his first parish ministry. It was not until 1946, following the war, that Torrance finally graduated with his Dr. Theol. from the University of Basel. Barth had a lasting influence on the doxological theology of T. F. Torrance.

The Doxological Influence of T. F. Torrance's Parish and Chaplaincy Ministry (1940–50)

In addition to T. F. Torrance's upbringing and education, his time serving as a chaplain and parish minister in the thirties and forties proved to be significant for the ecclesiastical orientation of his theological vocation. He was not only a theologian; he was a churchman and would remain a churchman his whole life, eventually serving as the Moderator of the General Assembly of the Church of Scotland. Ironically, he never considered himself primarily an academician. This of course is a statement of either humility or illusion as T. F. Torrance had a penetrating mind, was erudite in historical and dogmatic theology, philosophy, and also within the sciences. He was a prolific author with much influence yet not universally accepted. Again, T. F. Torrance was not primarily out to pursue an academic career. Jock Stein in his introduction to a series of essays entitled, *Gospel, Church, and Ministry*, states: "In his student days he was preparing to serve as a missionary, and his work as a parish minister and later in academic positions was undertaken within that frame of reference."[19] To separate dogmatics from the mission of God was inconceivable for T. F. Torrance.

Applying the mission of Christ to the local church, when Torrance was serving the two parishes in the forties in Alyth and Beechgrove, he followed Calvin's pastoral theology and practice of preaching the gospel corporately and personally. He believed, following Calvin's influence, that he should not only preach the gospel on Sundays but from house to house with each of the families in his parish. He wrote, "During those pastoral visits I used to recall the statement of John Calvin that the gospel should be preached *privatim et domatim*, privately and from house to house, and made that a major part of my ministry. I found that after I had visited people two or three times and read the Bible to them and prayed

---

19. Torrance, *Gospel, Church, and Ministry*, 2.

with them, they often opened their hearts to me."[20] In the chapter entitled "My Parish Ministry: Alyth, 1940–43," Torrance told a story about the importance of personal visitation, prayer and the ministry of the word:

> I must record another pastoral experience, which left me with a vivid recollection. I learned of a former deacon of the Barony Kirk who had for some reason quarreled with the minister and had become very bitter and hostile to the Faith. When I said I would visit him, I was urged not to do so, but of course I went. When I knocked at his door it was opened by his daughter who was half-blind and unkempt, and I told her who I was and that I had come to visit her father. She told me he would not see me—he heard and shouted at me from within telling me to go away. But I insisted, and when I went in I found him lying on this bed, which was rather filthy—he was clearly very ill. When he knew who I was and why I had come he shouted fiercely at me, but I told him I was a messenger from the Lord and had come to read the Bible and pray with him. In spite of his foul mouth objections I began to read the 51st Psalm, but he kept shouting at me all the way through. When I had finished he told me that now I could go, but I said that I would now pray, at which he objected vehemently. I prayed for him and his daughter, and asked the Lord to forgive his sins. In spite of his attempts to stop me I kept on and prayed through the 51st Psalm applying it directly to him and at length he grew quiet. When I opened my eyes, he was quite calm, an entirely different person. I realized that it was a kind of exorcism, and now the poor man was restored to his right mind, and at peace with God. When I went away to the war, I asked my brother-in-law, Kenneth MacKenzie, who had come to take services in Alyth for a few weeks before he left as a missionary for Central Africa, to visit the old man, which he did and found him quite changed as I related. He had not long to live and died soon afterwards. What impressed me was the wonderful power of the Word of God, which I read in that ancient Psalm, and the power of the gospel of the Lord Jesus. The congregation soon knew what had happened, and welcomed my pastoral visits even more than before. That was an unusual incident and an extreme case, but it reminded me of what happened in the mission field when my father prayed and spoke to people, which sometimes provoked bitter, even demonic, opposition,

---

20. Torrance, *Gospel, Church, and Ministry*, 34.

but when again and again the grace of the Lord Jesus triumphed over opposition and when even the most hostile were saved.[21]

This narrative reveals Torrance's faith in the power of prayer, Scripture, and the gospel of Jesus Christ. Torrance states, "We have to recover a theology that will invigorate us to preach the truth about who Jesus is."[22] Torrance believed that the parish minister was ordained for word and sacrament.[23] This belief and practice was significant to Torrance's parish ministry and to his theology. It would be helpful to stop at this point and ask, is it really necessary to commit to the mission of preaching Christ as the outcome of the study of dogmatics? It is certainly plausible (and we know this has happened in colleges, seminaries, and divinity schools around the world) to engage in theological discipline yet to maintain a discipleship distance. However, for T. F. Torrance, dogmatics was for the purpose of discovering the God who is there and who has revealed himself in Christ Jesus. To engage in the discipline of theology without a doxological disposition (studying in prayer and worship), was unthinkable to T. F. Torrance. Karl Barth said, "Theological study must be permeated by the attitude of prayer if it is to be genuinely free to respond to the living word of God. . . . Without the attitude of prayer, theology quickly becomes captive to forces alien to its subject matter."[24] Humility must accompany the study of God.

Regarding Torrance's service as a chaplain, he told the story of being on the frontline in Italy during the war. When asked, what is God like? Torrance's response was, "There is no God except the God who has come and meets us in Jesus. When we look into the face of Jesus Christ and see there the very face of God, we know we have not seen and cannot see God anywhere else or in any other way but in him, for he is God himself come among us."[25] Torrance told the story as follows:

> When daylight filtered through, I came across a young soldier (Private Philips), scarcely twenty years old, lying mortally

21. Torrance, *Gospel, Church, and Ministry*, 34–35.

22. Thomas F. Torrance, James B. Torrance, and David W. Torrance, *A Passion for Christ*, Dawson and Stein (eds.), 3.

23. Torrance states, "Ordination means ordination to the ministry of the Word and Sacraments, that is to dispensing Word and Sacraments. Strictly, therefore, 'ordination' should be used only for the order of those who dispense the Word and Sacrament." Torrance, *Gospel, Church, and Ministry*, 132.

24. Barth, *Prayer*, 104–5.

25. Torrance, *A Passion for Christ*, 5.

wounded on the ground, who clearly had not long to live. As I knelt down and bent over him, he said: "Padre, is God really like Jesus?" I assured him that he was—the only God that there is, the God who had come to us in Jesus, shown his face to us, and poured out his love to us as our Savior. As I prayed and commended him to the Lord Jesus, he passed away.[26]

Torrance's chaplaincy experience forced him to address the most important issues of life. For him, helping people understand the grace of the Lord and Savior, Jesus Christ, was both a theological and missionary privilege. Torrance believed that preaching the gospel took place in the pulpit and on the battlefield. Praying and commending a brother to the Lord Jesus was not only the pastoral care of a chaplain but also the doxological instinct of a theologian. It is this pastoral and doxological experience and background that T. F. Torrance brought with him as a theologian and which emerged within his writings even if it is at times written for the academic community and very dense. The objectivity of Christ coming in human flesh for humanity was the good news in the theology of T. F. Torrance.

Biography of James B. Torrance

James B. Torrance served as his brother's colleague at New College, Edinburgh and then as the Professor of Systematic Theology at the University of Aberdeen. Regarding his philosophical and theological training, J. B. Torrance also studied at the University Edinburgh. "He took a four-year honors degree in philosophy under two of the greatest Scottish philosophers of the twentieth century—Norman Kemp Smith and John MacMurray. Both considered JB the brightest student they had ever taught."[27] He continued his studies at Marburg and Basel where he studied under Karl Barth. Finally, he studied at Oxford University.

J. B. Torrance was focused on proclaiming the risen, ascended Lord who he believed was sovereign over every aspect of reality. He frequently would remind his students that the important question in theology is the "*who* question" rather than the "*how* question." This emphasis would play a significant role in his liturgical theology. He asserts:

---

26. McGrath, *Torrance*, 74.
27. Alan Torrance, *Participatio*, Supplement to Volume 3 (2014) 5.

> In Jesus Christ each and every one of us finds our worship, prayers, and intercessions lifted up, sanctified and presented by the one who is the sole Priest and Representative of each of us. The very nature of our ongoing life of worship and, indeed, ethics (worth-ship) is to be conceived, therefore, in terms of this very concrete participation, by the Spirit, in our sole priest, intercessor and *leitourgos*. In worship we are not "turned back upon ourselves" to try and generate what God requires of us. Worship and, indeed, every facet of our response (all that is required of us by the *torah*) is to be conceived as participation, by grace, in Christ's fulfillment of these *dikaiomata*, in his Amen, in his "Yes" to the Father, and in his worship. In the Eucharist and in prayer and, indeed, in every facet of the Christian life the Spirit seeks to lift us up to share in his perfect response and ongoing worship offered on our behalf.[28]

For J. B. Torrance, the doctrine of the Trinity was the heart of the Christian faith. And at the heart of the doctrine of the Trinity was the doctrine of the incarnation. This led him to emphasize the vicarious humanity of Jesus Christ in which, as High Priest, he came to represent humanity before the Father. And behind this God-humanward and human-Godward movement was an emphasis upon the covenant. J. B. Torrance maintained that there was a difference between a unilateral covenant (*diatheke*) and a bi-lateral contract (*suntheke*) even though the two terms are often employed synonymously. He emphasized a unilateral covenant as a legal agreement made by one party and a bi-lateral contract as an agreement made by two parties. He argued that the gospel was centered in "a covenant God" and not a "contract God." J. B. Torrance argues, "The important thing is that God's dealings with men in Creation and Redemption—in grace—are those of Covenant and not of contract. This was at the heart of the rediscovery of the Reformation (and is also the thesis of Martin Buber's *Moses*). Divine covenants have their source in the divine initiative, in the loving heart of God."[29] Torrance's point was that this covenant of love is not conditioned by anything in our response. Rather, God's covenant, while soliciting a response, is satisfied in the human response from Christ. J. B. Torrance states:

> Two things must be held together on this understanding of grace in worship, (i) It is unconditioned—by any considerations of

---

28. J. B. Torrance, *Participatio*, Supplement to Volume 3 (2014) 9–10.
29. J. B. Torrance, "Covenant or Contract?" 54–55.

worth in man, i.e. it is free, (ii) It is unconditional in the claims it makes upon us, i.e. it is costly. No doubt Lutheranism stressed free grace, and puritan Calvinism stressed the costly claims of grace. But something goes wrong if we stress one at the expense of the other. If, as Bonhoeffer has urged, Lutheranism can sometimes turn free grace into cheap grace, Puritan Calvinism can sometimes turn costly grace into conditional grace.[30]

J. B. Torrance's emphasis on the Father's covenant love for humanity led him to oppose Federal Scholastic Calvinism. Paul Molnar states, "His main objection to Federal theology is to the idea that Christ died only for the elect and not for the whole human race and that salvation is conditional on our observance of the law."[31] He believed that Jesus Christ lived, died, and rose not just for a select group but for *all* of humanity, including his enemies. Atonement was never merely judicial but filial. Men and women through the vicarious humanity of Jesus Christ have been adopted into the family of God.[32] This theological emphasis inspired J. B. Torrance to speak against sectarianism and racism. He was a voice of reconciliation, from a theological perspective, in South Africa where apartheid had theological underpinnings in addition to nationalistic tendencies. By understanding that Christ reconciled even his enemies, the message of reconciliation was predominately an outworking of the gospel.

These were the issues that were near to the heart of J. B. Torrance and that he passed on to his students. And at the center of these concerns was a Savior, Jesus Christ the Son of God who lived, died, rose, and ascended so that humanity might participate by the Spirit in the Son's communion with the Father. For J. B. Torrance, the emphasis on what Christ has done for us in his humanity was central to his theology of worship. This will be explored more in the next chapter.

While James Torrance explicitly focused on the subject of worship in several of his lectures, his brother, T. F. Torrance was also keenly aware of the doxological aspects of his own theology. T. F. Torrance focused on the subject of worship as well but in a more nuanced way. In particular,

---

30. J. B. Torrance, "Covenant or Contract?" 56.

31. Molnar, *Thomas F. Torrance*, 181. For an account of a debate between James Torrance and John Murray on the same issue, see Noble, *Tyndale House and Fellowship*, 76.

32. For the influence of earlier Scottish theologians regarding this, see Torrance, *Scottish Theology*, 287–317.

he focused on the sacraments in several of his essays. This too will be addressed later in this book.

Theological Method and Scientific Thinking

In order to understand T. F. Torrance's view of worship, it is important to examine not only his wider theology, but also his theological method. Torrance argued that theological method must begin with the revelation of God if its methodology is to remain objective. Paul Molnar writes, "It is certainly not too much to say that Torrance became a lifelong opponent of subjectivism because such an approach to objective knowledge essentially cut one off from the truth as it exists independent of the subject."[33]

Unlike F. D. E. Schleiermacher's *The Christian Faith*, which he said lacked a "scientific structure," Torrance argued that we must always begin our theological inquiry from what God has objectively revealed about himself. The only way to know Jesus Christ, the Living Word of God, is to know what God has revealed about his one and only Son in the Holy Scripture. Torrance's view of the Scriptures held a historical and theological depth missing from both fundamentalism on the one hand and narrative theology on the other. Colyer writes:

> Here we see another point of difference between Torrance and fundamentalism (and some strands of evangelicalism) and also some forms of narrative theology, for they both view the character of the Scripture in primarily literary terms. Fundamentalism construes the character of the Bible on the basis of its verbal inspiration and identifies the words of the Bible with the Word of God. Certain strands of narrative theology speak of the Bible projecting a "followable world" that is rendered through the literary devices of narrative depiction, but the ontological reference of the narrative remains obscure or eschatological, as in the case of Ronald Thiemann who thinks that theology should dispense with the category of revelation altogether.[34] Both are attempts to overcome the problems posed for Christian faith and scripture by modern natural science and historiography, though the attempts are very different from one another in detail. In a sense, they both represent a retreat from science and history into the literary character of the Bible. Torrance's view

---

33. Molnar, *Thomas F. Torrance*, 5.
34. Thiemann, *Revelation and Theology*, 47–71, 141–55.

has a theological and historical depth missing in these other perspectives.³⁵

This "theological and historical depth" that Colyer referred to can once again be attributed to Torrance's upbringing. Torrance claimed that his mother had an objective hermeneutical approach to the Bible that she passed down to him. She encouraged her son to have a christological approach when reading the Bible. Torrance states:

> So far as my view of Holy Scripture was concerned, I had been brought up to believe in its verbal inspiration, but my mother taught me to have an objective and not a subjective understanding of the Word of God. This did not lessen but rather deepened my sense of the divine authority and verbal inspiration of the Bible, which mediated to us the Gospel of salvation. She taught us to adopt a Christ-centered approach to the Holy Scriptures, for Christ was the Word of God made flesh.³⁶

When Torrance entered New College, Edinburgh University, his mother gave him a copy of *Credo* by Karl Barth. Torrance stated that he found himself in conflict "not only with the rationalistic liberalism of some of his teachers, but with the rather rationalistic and fundamentalistic way of interpreting the Bible being advocated in Inter-Varsity Fellowship circles together with a rather deterministic Calvinism which was then mistakenly being imported into the thinking of the Christian Unions."³⁷

Torrance's theological orientation was also inspired by what has been central in liturgy, the historical confessions. Later in his tenure at Edinburgh University, Torrance required all theological students to read the catechisms of the Reformed church, which he published in *The School of Faith* as a starting point for theological reflection. Included in this collection were: Calvin's Geneva Catechism (1541), The Heidelberg Catechism (1563), Craig's Catechism (1581), The New Catechism (1644), The Larger Catechism (1648). In Part II, there are the shorter catechisms.

---

35. Colyer, *How to Read T. F. Torrance*, 107.

36. McGrath, *Torrance*, 25. While T. F. Torrance had a love for the Scriptures, his understanding of verbal inspiration was very different than those of the Calvinists within the J. I. Packer School. The term "verbal inspiration" was associated with inerrancy and fundamentalism. Torrance's description of his mother teaching him to have an objective instead of a subjective understanding of the Bible clarifies his understanding of inspiration. He was taught to have a Christ-centred approach to the Scriptures.

37. Torrance, "*Itinerarium mentis Deum*," 9. McGrath, *Torrance*, 25.

Torrance's introduction is invaluable to understanding his doxological orientation. He writes:

> While each Church provides this instruction in responsible fulfillment of its mission in its own place and time in history, the Catechism is designed, not for the self-expression and self-culture of a particular Church, but to serve the Communion of Saints, so that all who use it may worship one God, Father, Son, and Holy Spirit, and be schooled in one Faith in the unity of the whole Church of God past and present. It is for that reason that the common basis of the Catechisms has traditionally been the Apostles Creed, the Ten Commandments, and the Lord's Prayer, and these have been expounded as far as possible in the universal language of the Church, and apart from the particular characteristic of any one Church and age.[38]

In one of Torrance's lectures, he talked about having a theological instinct.[39] The basis for this idea was Einstein's concept of scientific instinct. Einstein believed that as one is exposed to nature, the laws and ways of nature infused their realities into one's being. Likewise, Torrance argued that it was imperative to cultivate a theological instinct, which was only possible as the result of saturating oneself in the Scriptures as well as the creeds.[40] As one allows God's precepts to infuse one's being, God's ways start to become the compass for an internal theological orientation. This private approach to reading the Scriptures and this cultivation of a theological instinct complements the public reading, preaching and teaching of the Scriptures historically common in the worshiping community. McGrath writes:

> Through participation in the worship of the Christian community and engaging with the Scriptures (Torrance occasionally speaks of "indwelling" scripture, thereby stressing the personal engagement he envisages), the "Trinitarian pattern of God's self-revelation implicit in them becomes stamped on our minds." This pattern is more appreciated or intuited than subjected to rigorous analysis—yet the intuitive apprehension of the ordering of the Christian *kerygma* and *didache* must be regarded as

---

38. Torrance, *The School of Faith*, xi.

39. A lecture entitled "Theological Instinct" by T. F. Torrance was recorded by Regent College, October 2002. http://www.regentaudio.com/products/theological-instinct

40. Torrance speaks of saturation in the Scriptures. However, his interest in the historic creeds for theological formulation for the worshiping community is undeniable. See the introduction to *The School of Faith: The Catechisms of the Reformed Church*.

the essential foundation for the process of theological reflection which will follow.[41]

James Torrance also believed that the Bible was to be central in the worshiping community. The written word points to the Living Word and without an emphasis on reading the Bible or the teaching of Christ, the worshiping community will not be exposed to the fundamental doctrines central to historic Christianity. J. B. Torrance communicated the value of reading Scripture for the purpose of informing the doxological life of the church when he asserted:

> The Bible is supremely a manual of worship, but too often it has been treated, particularly in Protestantism, as a manual of ethics, or moral values, of religious ideas, or even of sound doctrine. When we see that the worship and mission of the Church are the gift of participating through the Holy Spirit in the incarnate Son's communion with the Father and the Son's mission from the Father to the world, that the unique center of the Bible is Jesus Christ, "the apostle and high priest whom we confess" (Heb. 3:1), then the doctrines of the Trinity, the incarnation, the atonement, the ministry of the Spirit, Church and sacraments, our understanding of the kingdom, our anthropology and eschatology, all unfold from that center.[42]

In addition to the attention given to the reading of the Scriptures, T. F. Torrance dedicated entire essays to the subject of worship notably the collection of essays in *Theology in Reconciliation: Essays Towards Evangelical and Catholic Unity in East and West*.[43] Three essays in particular stand out revealing liturgical/doxological themes: "The One Baptism Common to Christ and His Church," "The Paschal Mystery of Christ and the Eucharist" and "The Mind of Christ in Worship: The Problem of Apollinarianism in the Liturgy." The emphases of doxological themes in the theological works of the Torrances' are explicit. For example, in his work, *The Mediation of Christ*, T. F. Torrance writes:

> In worship and prayer Jesus Christ acts in our place and on our behalf in both a representative and substitutionary way so that what he does in our stead is nevertheless effected as our very own, issuing freely and spontaneously out of ourselves.

---

41. McGrath, *Torrance*, 170.
42. J. B. Torrance, *Worship, Community and the Triune God of Grace*, ix.
43. Torrance, *Theology in Reconciliation*.

> Through his incarnational and atoning union Jesus Christ has united himself with us in such a reconciling and sanctifying way that he interpenetrates and gathers all of our faltering, unclean worship and prayer into himself, assimilates them into his one self-oblation to God, so that when he presents himself as the worship and prayer of all creation, our worship and prayer are presented there also. When the Father accepts us in Jesus Christ his beloved Son, who then can distinguish our worship and prayer from Jesus' worship and prayer, for they are one and the same, wholly his and wholly ours in him?[44]

The assertion that our worship and prayer cannot be distinguished from the worship and prayer of Christ, because of our union with him, is certainly not universally held within Christianity. The idea that Christ has worshiped on behalf of humanity can appear to leave no room for our human response. This is a common critique of the Torrances' theology of worship.

T. F. Torrance emphasized that Jesus Christ was the Messiah for Israel within Israel's liturgical structure thus serving as its ultimate High Priest.[45] The implication of this for Israel and for all people is that the life, death, resurrection, and ascension of Jesus Christ is sufficient for encouraging all liturgical practices to be lived out vicariously through him. Christian worship is a recapitulation of the worship of Christ and a participation in the worship of Christ. This interest in the God of Israel, later taken up by his brother, David Torrance, placed T. F. Torrance's theology within a larger context—from within Jewish liturgy.[46] T. F. Torrance writes, "Because his passion is related to the Old Testament and he deliberately laid down his life in such a way as to take upon himself the burden of the servant of which the Old Testament spoke, it is only in the context of the Old Testament revelation that we can rightly appreciate and understand his teaching."[47] In his lectures to his divinity students at the University of Edinburgh, Torrance expounded what atonement meant first and foremost for Israel.[48] The emphasis on Old Testament history was significant for understanding atonement biblically and liturgically for T. F. Torrance.

---

44. Torrance, *The Mediation of Christ*, 88.

45. See the chapter entitled "The Priesthood of Christ" in Torrance's *Atonement* edited by Robert T. Walker.

46. See, David Torrance, *The Witness of the Jews to God* and *Israel God's Servant*.

47. Torrance, *Atonement: The Person and Work of Christ*, 25.

48. Torrance, *Atonement: The Person and Work of Christ*, 25–60.

The book of Hebrews, an epistle interpreting the thematic material of the Old Testament liturgy, was and is critical for understanding mediation and the vicarious humanity of Jesus Christ.

The Sacramental Emphasis of T. F. and J. B. Torrance

Both T. F. and J. B. Torrance also discussed the importance of baptism and the Lord's Supper as indicative signs of a trinitarian approach to worship. James Torrance writes, "Christ baptizes us by the Spirit that we might participate in his cleansing of our humanity and enter into his Body, the communion of saints. At the Lord's Supper, he brings his passion to our remembrance and draws us into wonderful communion—Holy Communion—with the Father, with himself and with one another, proleptic of our life in the kingdom of God, nourishing our faith 'till he come.'"[49] The Torrances have much to say regarding the sacraments, both of them being influenced by Calvin's view of the sacraments. Robert Bruce's sermons preached on the sacraments in the High Kirk of Edinburgh in A.D. 1589 also influenced T. F. Torrance. He states, "This [reading of these sermons] also had the effect of deepening my concern for more liturgical worship and for more attention to the celebration of Holy Communion. In a lax or dying church it is the evangelical and sacramental liturgy that keeps alive and deepens the beliefs and spiritual life of people."[50] This subject will be addressed in chapter seven, as an entire chapter is needed to cover their rich appreciation of the sacraments.

Conclusion

In glancing at the biographical sketches of both of the Torrances, whether their upbringing, education, or pastoral ministry, they were both influenced to be concerned about the state of Christian worship. Consequently, many doxological themes arise within their writings. The first of the themes to be explored in the next chapter is the contrast between unitarian worship and trinitarian worship. Let us turn our attention there.

---

49. J. B. Torrance, *Worship, Community and the Triune God of Grace*, 63.
50. Torrance, *Gospel, Church and Ministry*, 60.

2

Unitarian or Trinitarian Worship?

Introduction

IT IS IMPORTANT AT this point to reflect on the concern that J. B. Torrance had regarding what he called unitarian and existential views in worship. By understanding his concern about the way in which body/soul or body/mind dualism had influenced theology, including liturgical theology, one will better understand J. B. Torrance's passion for a vibrant trinitarian-incarnational theology for corporate worship.[1] T. F. Torrance also had concern regarding dualism in both theology and liturgy. He defined dualism and the under-emphasis of the saving humanity of Jesus Christ with what he called the influence of Apollinarianism in modern liturgy.[2]

Unitarian and Existential Tendencies and Practices in Corporate Worship

Both T. F. and J. B. Torrance believed that there had been a shift in the modern era from a theological center to an anthropological focus in theological discourse. This misplaced emphasis, according to the Torrances, removed theology from its objectivity and thus, its scientific nature. James Torrance argued that this shift from theology to anthropology

---

1. Robert T. Walker defines "dualism" as any way of thinking that rigidly separates entities, which should be seen in relation to each other. Torrance, *Atonement*, 456.

2. Torrance, *Theology in Reconciliation*, 139–214.

had devastating consequences within the liturgy of the church. In the 1994 Didsbury Lectures, he defined worship as our participation by the Spirit in the Son's communion with the Father. These lectures gave him the opportunity to expose what he believed was a wrong emphasis in worship. Emphasizing the work of Jesus the High Priest of all creation, he immediately began to place the focus on Christ. He began with the thesis that the real agent of all true worship is Jesus Christ. It is because of what Christ has done that humanity can approach God by the power of the Spirit. As the result of the incarnation and Christ's perfect obedience to the Father, humanity can live vicariously through the faithfulness of Jesus Christ. James Torrance argues, "He is our great High Priest and ascended Lord, the one true worshiper who unites us to himself by the Spirit in an act of memory and in a life of communion, as he lifts us up by word and sacrament into the very triune life of God."[3] Jesus Christ was the one true worshiper. He did for humanity what humanity failed to do for itself—offer unadulterated worship to the Father. However, if Jesus is the one true worshiper, what is the point of the rest of humanity responding to the revelation of God? Worship is typically thought of as *our* response to the revelation of God. Is this not needed from human beings today? Anthropocentric worship does not only refer to human beings initiating worship in the theology of the Torrances. Responsive worship is equally criticized by the Torrances if the emphasis is put back on our shoulders. When the term anthropocentric worship is employed in this work, it refers to both initiated *and* responsive worship when it does not factor in the mediation of Christ. Torrance addressed this concern in his lectures and his answer was affirmatively, yes, that worship is response but that the agent of true worship is the One who reveals *and* responds perfectly on our behalf: Jesus the Messiah. Whatever the response of human beings is, it is purified through the perfect response of Jesus Christ. In order to arrive at his thesis, James Torrance allocated one of his Didsbury sessions to addressing a concern: Why has evangelical worship lost its focus on Jesus Christ? He described the common assumption: "Worship is something which we, religious people, do—mainly in church on Sunday. We

---

3. J. B. Torrance, *Worship, Community, and the Triune God of Grace*, 5. James M. Houston writes about James Torrance, "His further emphasis on worship as the gift of participation through the Spirit in the Son's communion with the Father renews the focus of the church today on the teachings of the early Church Fathers." Houston, "Spirituality and the Doctrine of the Trinity" in Hart and Thimell, *Christ in Our Place*, 48.

go to church, we sing our psalms and hymns to God, we intercede for the world, we listen to the sermon (too often simply an exhortation), we offer our money, time and talents to God."[4] This is a common viewpoint regarding worship and liturgy. It is something that religious people do during religious occasions, in religious time, in religious places. This perspective that worship is something that religious people do is not limited to a particular movement or denomination. Many would understand worship to be something religious people *do*—the response of the faithful community. Again, it would be typical to understand initiated worship as something that is done by God and responsive worship as something that is done by us. In other words, God reveals himself and we respond to his revelation. And while yes, liturgy by definition is the work of the people, James Torrance argued that there must be a larger framework in which the work of the people is made efficacious, namely the work of Christ. J. B. Torrance asserted that to neglect the high priestly ministry of Jesus Christ in worship is to throw human beings back upon themselves. He states:

> Indeed this view of worship is in practice Unitarian, has no doctrine of the Mediator or sole priesthood of Christ, is human-centered, has no proper doctrine of the Holy Spirit, is too often non-sacramental, and can engender weariness. We sit in the pew watching the minister "doing his thing," exhorting us "to do our thing," until we go home thinking we have done our duty for another week! This kind of do-it-yourself-with-the help-of the-minister worship is what our forefathers would have called Arian or Pelagian and not truly catholic. It is not Trinitarian. Bishop Lesslie Newbigin has commented that when the average Christian in this country hears the name of God, he or she does not think of the Trinity. After many years of missionary work in India among Eastern religions, he returned to find that much worship in the West is in practice, if not in theory, Unitarian.[5]

Notice the emphasis on what James Torrance defines as unitarian worship. It is exclusively anthropocentric. It is focused on what *human beings* do, not on what *Christ* has done. It is also focused on the "what" of worship not the "who" of worship. In other words, it is focused on the specific liturgical responses: the prayers of the people, the creeds of the church, the sermons of the ministers, and the response of the "faithful."

---

4. J. B. Torrance, *Worship, Community, and the Triune God of Grace*, 7.
5. J. B. Torrance, *Worship, Community, and the Triune God of Grace*, 7.

Torrance argued that this is humanistic in its orientation, placing the activity of human beings at the center of worship. According to this view, there is no need for a vibrant Christology or pneumatology of worship if worship is merely something that human beings do. Furthermore, Torrance argued that this approach is often non-sacramental. Baptism and the Lord's Supper are neglected or ignored. Baptism can tend to be seen as an exclusively missiological emphasis (one aspect of disciple making according to Matthew 28:19–20) instead of a sacrament of incorporation into the death and resurrection of Jesus Christ by the power of the Spirit, which is another way of saying a participation in the work of the Triune God. The Lord's Supper can be merely an ordinance (something that the *ecclesia does*) and not a sacrament of renewal (something the *ecclesia receives* by the grace of God). And if the sacraments are primarily about what the local church does, the local church can also negotiate the frequency of the sacraments, particularly how often the Lord's Supper should not be celebrated. This is what he means by non-sacramental. What is important at this point is what Torrance is stating about the emphasis; it is human-centered. "In theological language, this means that the only priesthood is our priesthood, the only offering our offering, the only intercessions our intercessions."[6] It must be noted that what Torrance refers to as unitarian is not necessarily how unitarians employ this term. When James Torrance referred to the term "unitarian," what he meant was that this approach does not factor in the doctrine of the mediation of Jesus Christ or the doctrine of the Triune God of Grace. There is no need for a High Priest, mediator, or advocate. There is also no need for the activity of the Holy Spirit. What is interesting about James Torrance's argument is that one could argue that most of the liturgical systems in world religions are unitarian if examined by their practices for how humanity relates to God (or the gods in a pantheistic religion). The emphasis is exclusively on the sacrifices, prayers, and actions of human beings. There is no need of mediation from God himself. The activity that

---

6. J. B. Torrance, *Worship, Community, and the Triune God of Grace*, 8. Alan E Lewis states, "True prayer and praise are possibilities of grace: participations in the prayer and praise of God's own Son. It is not that in the church we offer worship to Christ in grateful response to his salvation, but that he himself made once, and continues to make, the full, perfect response of human faith, as our sole Savior, Priest and Representative, empowering us by his Spirit to share in movements of adoration, confession and intercession toward the Father which are uniquely his." Lewis, "Kenosis and Kerygma: The Realism and the Risk of Preaching" in Hart and Thimell, *Christ in Our Place*, 73.

is central to the worshiping individual or community is what they bring to the altar.

Unitarian Tendencies (The Harnack/Hick Model)

James Torrance offered two models to describe what he called a "unitarian" view. The first model comes from nineteenth-century Protestant liberalism. He credited two theologians for this view: Adolf Harnack in his 1900 Berlin lectures *Das Wesen des Christentums* (What is Christianity?) and John Hick, who according to James Torrance revived Harnack's theological views in the twentieth century. James Torrance argues:

> According to this, the heart of religion is the soul's immediate relationship to God. What God the Father was to Old Testament Israel, he was to Jesus, and what he was to Jesus, he was to Paul and still is the same to us and all men and women today. We, with Jesus, stand as men and women, as brothers and sisters, worshiping the one Father but not worshiping any incarnate Son. Jesus is man but not God. We do not need any mediator, or "myth of God incarnate."[7]

Likewise Rudolf Bultmann's perspective on the resurrection was that the resurrection of Jesus Christ was less of a historical event and more of an event exemplifying the resurrection of the faith of the disciples.[8] One of the problems with this unitarian view according to James Torrance is that it is replaces Jesus Christ as High Priest with a Jesus that is predominately an ethical example. Adolf Von Harnack would have argued that this theological criticism was simply a corruption to historical Christianity and one that is meant to distort the Fatherhood of God and the brotherhood of mankind. Yet, James Torrance argues such a mindset, exemplified by Von Harnack, is sub-gospel since Jesus the Messiah did not come from heaven to earth simply to provide a moral example. This unitarian emphasis, according the perspective of the Torrances, shifted the focus away from the economy of the Triune God. "In Harnack's own words: 'The Gospel, as Jesus proclaimed it, has to do with the Father only and not with the Son.' Jesus' purpose was to confront men and women with the Father, not with himself."[9] According to the Torrances, when the

---

7. J. B. Torrance, *Worship, Community, and the Triune God of Grace*, 12.
8. Bawulski and Holmes, *Christian Theology*, 208.
9. J. B. Torrance, *Worship, Community, and the Triune God of Grace*, 12.

emphasis is placed on what human beings do, there is nothing trinitarian about worship and consequently, nothing Christian.

Existential Tendencies
(The Present-Day Experience Model)

James Torrance employed a second model (a related subcategory of unitarian worship) for contrast to the trinitarian-incarnational model: the existential, present-day experience approach. James Torrance writes, "Here again faith means contemporary immediacy. God gives himself to us in grace in the present moment of encounter as we respond in faith, in repentance and decision."[10] The way this could be communicated in a corporate worship service is emphasizing the need to please God through the *faithful obedient actions* of *devoted* followers of Jesus Christ. Blessings from God are anticipated if humans are obedient, faithful, and invoking the presence of God. This existential disposition that the Torrances referred to could be exposed today through variations of the "name it and claim it" theology. In the vernacular, this has been criticized by some as a vending machine theology where a certain currency is put into the machine and the desired product is received in exchange. This has been expressed in modern times, by the prosperity gospel movement, as the choice (faith) of a believer obligating God to respond with a correlated blessing. J. B. Torrance labeled this as existentialism and existentialism as a sub-category of unitarian worship.

James Torrance states, "The pragmatic problem-centered preoccupation with the question of 'how' in our Western culture can so readily reduce the gospel to the category of means and ends."[11] It was common for him to quote Bonhoeffer's emphasis in his *Christology* giving priority to the *who* over the *what* and *how* of worship.[12] James Torrance writes:

> We can also understand why Bonhoeffer in his Christology criticized the attempt to reconstruct theology from the starting point of "religious experience," as pioneered by Schleiermacher, Ritschl, Herrmann, Harnack and Bousset. He pleaded for following the biblical pattern of giving priority to the question of

10. J. B. Torrance, *Worship, Community, and the Triune God of Grace*, 15–16.

11. J. B. Torrance, *Worship, Community, and the Triune God of Grace*, 17.

12. See "The Unfolding Christological Question in Dietrich Bonhoeffer," *Christ the Center*, 27–39. *Christ the Center* is the American reprint of Bonhoeffer's Christology.

who over *what* and *how*—that we interpret the atonement and personal faith in terms of the incarnation (the triune God of grace) and not the other way around. The pragmatic, problem-centered preoccupation with the question of *how* in our Western culture can so readily reduce the gospel to the category of means and ends. Bonhoeffer saw this in Ritschlian thought, and we see it often today in an over-concern for "relevance." The culture of Protestantism sees religion as the means to realize the ends of culture.[13]

James Torrance asserts, "To reduce worship to this two-dimensional thing—God and ourselves, today—is to imply that God throws us back upon ourselves to make our response. It ignores the fact that God has already provided for us that Response which alone is acceptable to him—the offering made for the whole human race in the life, obedience and passion of Jesus Christ."[14] The theological point that he was making was that humanity is not its own mediator. Jesus Christ and Christ alone is our mediator. And without proper mediation, Torrance argued it is impossible to approach the living God. He writes:

> It seems to me that in a pastoral situation, our first task is . . . to direct people to the gospel of grace—to Jesus Christ, that they might look to him to lead them, open their hearts in faith and in prayer, and draw them by the Spirit into his eternal life of communion with the Father. The Christian doctrine of the Trinity is the grammar of Romans ch. 8–the grammar of grace, the grammar of our pastoral work.[15]

T. F. Torrance, addressing a similar concern about liturgy having an anthropocentric, unitarian, and an existential orientation, gave an example of this very problem in the liturgy of the Israelites:

> The Old Testament tells us, and this is one of its recurring themes, that sin is so deeply ingrained in humanity that it seeks to erect the divine ordinances of worship into liturgy that stands by itself independently of the mediation of the word. That was a persistent sin of Israel. It sought to make the temple and its liturgy independent of God's intervening will as manifested through the law and as continually interpreted and revealed through the ministry of the prophets. They sought to make the temple

---

13. J. B. Torrance, *Worship, Community, and the Triune God of Grace*, 17.
14. J. B. Torrance, *Worship, Community, and the Triune God of Grace*, 18.
15. J. B. Torrance, *Worship, Community, and the Triune God of Grace*, 34.

and its worship a sphere of liturgical action bound up with the natural desires of Israel and to make it operate as action upon God, as manipulation of God's will. In that way it was looked upon as giving Israel security before God, while behind that security Israel sought to go the way of its own desires. But against that independence of the liturgy and priesthood, God sent the prophets, most of them apparently out of the priesthood itself, to protest against the falsification of the cult. However when the priesthood became so very corrupt, God raised up prophets like Amos who had no relation to the priesthood and who came voicing the word of God in criticism of cultic performances. In this prophetic ministry, there was evident an attack upon the independence of the cult, a prophetic and eschatological suspension of liturgy in the demand for obedience to the will of God rather than ceremonial ritual. Hence at last when the prophets were spurned, God promised he would destroy the temple and its liturgy and so over throw the false security of Israel which rested upon a sinful perversion of holy liturgy.[16]

One must ask, "How then should the people of God worship?" In today's liturgy, what is the place of invocations, corporate singing, prayers, reading of Scripture, sermons, the celebration of the Lord's Supper, offerings, and benedictions? Is this liturgical activity anthropocentric in that this is simply done by human beings? Is there not a place for "corporate worship" that involves community participation? What about the role of the minister? What role does the prayer of intercession have in the worshiping community? What role does the sermon play, for this, in fact, *is* something that the minister is responsible for? Is it not?

These are legitimate liturgical concerns that need to be answered. J. B. Torrance in his Didsbury lectures was simply asking from what framework human beings were engaging in these liturgical activities. Were they engaging in worship activities to please God or because He already is pleased with the finished work of Christ? Torrance was primarily concerned with the premise that the High Priest has made effective whatever worship humanity offers. He was fond of saying that the indicatives of grace must precede the imperatives of law.[17] If the order is reversed, one ends up with a unitarian or existential framework.

T. F. Torrance had a similar concern to his brother regarding unitarian worship. In his article, "The Mind of Christ in Worship: The Problem

16. Torrance, *Atonement*, 64.
17. J. B. Torrance, "Worship and the Gospel," Regent Audio, 1984.

of Apollinarianism in the Liturgy," T. F. Torrance reviewed the liturgical concerns of St. Cyril of Alexandria, whom T. F. Torrance regarded as the most anti-Apollinarian of the church fathers.[18] While Arius, the Alexandrian Presbyter, affirmed that Christ was not truly God but a created being, Apollinarius, Bishop of Laodicea, denied the existence of a rational soul within the person of Christ. He argued that Jesus Christ had no real human mind (*nous*) and that the eternal divine *Logos* had taken its place, completing the person of Jesus Christ. In contrast, Torrance's view of atonement believed that Jesus Christ redeemed humanity through his own vicarious humanity. Atonement, for Torrance, was ontological. T. F. Torrance writes: "This redeeming worship offered by Christ within the measures of his *kenosis* Cyril spoke of as 'the worship of the economy'. That is to say, Christ is himself the true worshipper of God, who in his vicarious mediation is himself our redemption and worship, himself the altar, and as such the pattern of all our service in prayer, adoration and worship, which we offer in and through and with him to God the Father."[19]

According to James Torrance, worship that is trinitarian places the emphasis on Jesus as High Priest and mediator and on the vicarious humanity of Jesus Christ. "The church which takes her eyes off Jesus Christ, the only Mediator of worship, is on the road to becoming apostate."[20] In his humanity, Jesus offered obedience vicariously for all of humanity. Furthermore, Jesus not only offered perfect obedient worship on behalf of humanity in his incarnation and atonement, Christ also offered the perfect sacrifice that was demanded in the liturgy of the Hebrew Bible. James Torrance argues:

> When we considered the Existential Model of worship, we noticed that the God-humanward movement of grace is given to us in Christ. In virtue of it, we are summoned to respond in faith, in decision, in repentance and obedience. But the weakness here is that the only human-Godward movement is ours! In other words, it does not do full justice to the meaning of grace, for it short-circuits the vicarious humanity of Christ. . . . Grace does not only mean that in the coming of Jesus Christ, God gives himself in holy love to humanity. It also means the coming of

---

18. Torrance, "The Mind of Christ in Worship: The Problem of Apollinarianism in the Liturgy," *Theology in Reconciliation*, 139–214.

19. Torrance, *Theology in Reconciliation*, 178–79. Greek phrases omitted.

20. J. B. Torrance, *Worship, Community, and the Triune God of Grace*, 49.

God as man, to do for us as a man what we cannot do for ourselves—to present us in himself through the eternal Spirit to the Father.[21]

A Trinitarian-Incarnational Orientation

For T. F. Torrance, Jesus was both Savior and High Priest. In the worship of Israel, he argued that God appointed both a prophet and a priest. Moses functioned as the prophet, Aaron as the priest. Both offices were required: the word of the Lord *for the people* and the priestly representation *for the Lord*. Torrance was making the point that whatever response religious people think is their responsibility, Christ has fulfilled that response for them. This is a very different premise than the common perspective from within liturgical literature. Worship is typically described as our response to "the revelation" (*anhypostasia*) of Christ Jesus. Robert T. Walker writes, "*Anhypostasis* refers to the fact that the humanity of Jesus had no independent reality of its own apart from the incarnation of the Son."[22] But Torrance was arguing that "the response" (*enhypostasia*) was also provided for in the saving humanity of Jesus Christ. "*Enhypostasis* refers to the fact that the humanity of Jesus did have real personal being in the person of the Son as the result of the incarnation."[23] He argued that Christ assumed our humanity, *enhypostatically*, and thus offered the perfect human response. Elmer Colyer, emphasizing Torrance's perspective writes,

> The covenant established between God and Israel for the mediation of revelation and reconciliation was a covenant between God and an unholy people. The progressive mediation of revelation and reconciliation within Israel not only disclosed something of the nature of God, it also revealed the natural offense to God embedded in the human heart, for it was the will and way of God's grace to effect reconciliation with man at his very worst, precisely in his state of rebellion against God.[24]

21. J. B. Torrance, *Worship, Community, and the Triune God of Grace*, 43.
22. Torrance, *Atonement*, 452.
23. Torrance, *Atonement*, 452.
24. Cf. Colyer's reflection on this issue, Colyer, *How to Read T. F. Torrance*, 63. Colyer is also paraphrasing, at this point, a thought from Torrance's, *Mediation of Christ*, 28.

According to Torrance, the people of God did not just invent their own approach to worshiping the Lord, they followed the means that God had specifically prescribed. Torrance was referring to the specific liturgical instructions written down for Israel's worship. For example, the Book of Exodus is explicit in its details regarding the construction of the tabernacle and the function of the priests (Exodus 25–31). Caution and care were to be given in obeying the word of the Lord regarding the liturgical instructions communicated through Moses. This (the liturgical pattern) was foreshadowing what Christ would eventually come to do. For T. F. Torrance, it was critical not to detach Jesus Christ from Israel or the incarnation from the covenant relationship of God with Israel.[25] The Word became flesh (God-humanward) and lived among us, and we have seen his glory, the glory as of a father's only son, full of grace and truth (John 1:14). The Word dwelt among humanity and became the Lamb of God who takes away the sin of the world (John 1:29, 36).

The Torrances argued that in the same way Israel came vicariously to God through a high priest so humanity now comes vicariously through the ultimate High Priest, Jesus Christ. For the Torrances, this was foundational to their Christology, soteriology, and doxological theology. Likewise, T. F. Torrance emphasized that we live through the faithfulness of Jesus Christ (Gal 2:20). Notice Torrance's insistence on the subjective genitive (*faith of* the Son of God or *faithfulness of* the Son of God) as opposed to the objective genitive (*faith in* the Son of God). The NT scholar, Richard B. Hayes, in his book *The Faith of Jesus Christ*, later supported this insistence, as have many subsequent NT scholars.[26] In contrast, Man Kei Ho argues the following criticism of Torrance's subjective genitive interpretation:

> Torrance's unique interpretation of *pistis Christou Iesou* encountered many criticisms. Professor Moule was probably the first to criticize that Torrance was on a false trail. Moule comments that though *pistis* in the New Testament carries a meaning of faithfulness of God as that expressed in the Old Testament, however, to say that *pistis Christou Iesou* includes mainly the faithfulness of Christ is to ignore all biblical data. Moule did not agree that the grammar indicates subjective genitive instead of objective genitive, and *pistis* in some passages clearly means believer's faith instead of Christ's faith or faithfulness. Moule's

---

25. See Colyer's reflection about this in *How to Read T. F. Torrance*, 69.
26. Hayes, *The Faith of Jesus Christ*, 2002.

concern is that Torrance by his interpretation of *pistis Christou Iesou* seriously reduced the necessary reference to man's act of will in response to God's approach. What Moule means is that even though our faith is objectively endowed by God, it has to be subjectively executed by us.[27]

While Man Kei Ho's thesis is acerbic in its criticism of Torrance, it is true that some interpreters, like Moule, prefer the objective genitive. However, T. F. Torrance was certainly not alone in his preference for the subjective genitive, especially in the Galatian texts. In addition to the insistence of this interpretation by Richard B. Hayes, N. T. Wright in his translation of the New Testament chose the subjective genitive when he translated Galatians 2:20 as follows, "And the life I do still live in the flesh, I live within the faithfulness of the son of God, who loved me and gave himself for me."[28] For T. F. Torrance, the subjective genitive was not only exegetically preferable, it was consistent with his Christology. Colyer states:

> It is in Jesus Christ that the eternal Son, who is ever *homoousios* with God the Father, has penetrated the perverted personal and interpersonal reality of our fallen and estranged humanity and made it his own. In assuming our disobedient humanity in rebellion against God, Christ converted it back to a true and faithful filial relation to God in love, obedience, holiness, trust and praise throughout his vicarious human being and life for us. Torrance maintains that the Word of God incarnate in Jesus Christ not only delivered humanity from subjugation to sin and alienation but also recreates humanity's relation to God by realizing perfect humanity on the earth, offering God the true human response to God on our behalf and in our place, which we cannot make for ourselves.[29]

This idea of human-Godward movement—that Jesus Christ was engaged in active obedience in his humanity—was central to the theology of both T. F. and J. B. Torrance. This representation of a high priest, in his active obedience, on behalf of the rest of humanity was central to their soteriology. This activity is first and foremost an act of worship. For both T. F. and J. B. Torrance, the faithfulness of Jesus Christ is not just about

27. Ho, *A Critical Study on T. F. Torrance's Theology of Incarnation*, 82–84; Moule, "The Biblical Conception of Faith," 157.

28. Wright, *The Kingdom New Testament*, 384.

29. Colyer, *How to Read T. F. Torrance*, 110.

soteriology, it is about the liturgically perfect response. The Torrances argued that humanity could not come to the Father except through the saving humanity of Jesus Christ. "Thus as in the Old Testament liturgy it is always God himself who provides the sacrifice whereby he draws near to the worshiper and draws the worshiper near to himself, so in the actualized liturgy of the life, death, resurrection and ascension of Jesus Christ, it is God himself who in atoning propitiation draws near to us and draws us near to himself."[30]

James Torrance argued that the sole priesthood of the incarnate and ascended Christ as our mediator of worship was the key to having a trinitarian orientation in our liturgy. He states, "For a proper understanding of prayer we need to recover the New Testament teaching about the sole priesthood of Christ—that we have someone who stands in for us to do for us and in us what we try to do and fail to do—someone who lives forever to intercede for us (Heb. 6:20; 7:25–28; 8:1–6) and who gives us the gift of the Spirit to share in his intercession."[31] Colin Gunton employed similar language to the Torrances when he wrote, "Worship is a gift: we come to the Father through the Son and in the Spirit because they enable us to do what otherwise would be impossible for sinful human beings. To put it another way, worship is made possible and real by the fact that Jesus rose from the dead and sits at the right hand of the Father."[32] James Torrance summarized the work of Christ when he argued, "The Son of God takes our humanity, sanctifies it by his vicarious life in the Spirit, carries it to the grave to be crucified and buried in him, and in his resurrection and ascension carries it into the holy presence of God."[33]

In a trinitarian approach, according to the Torrances, the emphasis is on participation by the Spirit in the worship offered by Christ. Worship is something that is already taking place on behalf of humanity and whenever the Body of Christ engages in the work of the people (liturgy) they do it by the Spirit through the work of Christ. Drawing on one of his heroes, T. F. Torrance writes, "It was characteristic of Athanasius, that he should have equated *theologia*, in its deepest sense as the knowledge and worship of God as he is known through Jesus Christ and in the Holy Spirit and as he is eternally in himself, specifically with the doctrine of

30. Torrance, *The Mediation of Christ*, 110.

31. J. B. Torrance, *Worship, Community, and the Triune God of Grace*, 35.

32. Gunton, *The Theologian as Preacher*, 128.

33. J. B. Torrance, "Prayer and the Priesthood of Christ," in *A Passion for Christ: The Vision that Ignites Ministry*, 62.

the Holy Trinity."³⁴ As humanity participates in the Son's relationship with the Father through the power of the Spirit, true knowledge of God is being experienced according to Torrance's interpretation of Athanasius. From this perspective, theology is more than knowledge, it is union with Christ. According to J. B. Torrance, trinitarian-incarnational worship is evangelical worship. In contrast, unitarian worship is void of the gospel for it is void of Christ. James Torrance describes this trinitarian approach:

> It is the gift of participating through the Spirit in the incarnate Son's communion with the Father. It means participating, in union with Christ, in what he has done for us, once and for all, in his self-offering to the Father, in his life and death on the cross. It also means participating in what he is continuing to do for us in the presence of the Father and his mission from the Father to the world. There is only one true Priest through whom and with whom we draw near to God our Father. There is only one mediator between God and humanity. There is only one offering which is truly acceptable to God, and it is not ours. It is the offering by which he has sanctified for all time those who come to God by him (Heb. 2:11; 10:10, 14). There is only one who can lead us into the presence of the Father by his sacrifice on the cross. This is why the Reformers in their critique of certain medieval concepts of priesthood, stressed the sole priesthood of Christ, and reinterpreted the Church as a royal priesthood participating in the priesthood of Christ.³⁵

In the Torrances liturgical Christology, the key issue is the sole priesthood of Jesus Christ and the correlated implications. For J. B. Torrance, worship as participation means union with Christ, resting in what Christ has done.

J. B. Torrance's perspective can be challenged from the perspective of the biblical mandates regarding revelation and response as it applies to the priesthood of all believers. Entire chapters in the Bible seem to be dedicated to how the Body of Christ is to function as a worshiping community. A case in point would be 1 Corinthians, chapter 14. The apostle Paul delivered clear instructions for intelligible worship, that every member in the Body of Christ was to bring something to contribute (a hymn, a sermon, a prophetic word) and that worship should be understandable,

---

34. Torrance, *The Trinitarian Faith*, 303.
35. J. B. Torrance, *Worship, Community, and the Triune God of Grace*, 9.

namely that the worshiping community should conduct itself in an orderly manner for the purpose of edification.

While there are these kinds of biblical texts with clear instructions for the worshiping community, J. B. Torrance argues that what makes any of this effective in the first place is not just an orderly liturgy but a trinitarian framework where the "Who" of worship is central, not just the "how" of worship. J. B. Torrance was certainly aware of the importance of orderly worship prescribed in 1 Corinthians 14, but he argues that the saving humanity of Christ is the key to *Christian* worship. At the foundation of Christian worship is the person and work of Jesus Christ. Elmer Colyer states, "T. F. Torrance believed that the doctrine of the Trinity places the incarnation at the center of faith in God, since it establishes Jesus Christ as the one mediator between God and humanity in the movement of God's Trinitarian self—revelation from the Father through the Son and in the Holy Spirit."[36] In line with what Colyer stated, Torrance believed that we apprehend the Trinity through the incarnation of Christ.

Regarding the grace of the God-humanward movement and the human-Godward movement, James Torrance argued that grace involves both revelation and representation. Jesus Christ came as both prophet and priest. He proclaims:

> It is supremely in Jesus Christ that we see the double meaning of grace. Grace means that God gives himself to us as God, freely and unconditionally, to be worshiped and adored. But grace also means that God comes to us in Jesus Christ as man, to do for us and in us what we cannot do. He offers a life of perfect obedience and worship to the Father, that we might be drawn by the Spirit into communion with the Father, "through Jesus Christ our Lord."[37]

Jesus Christ comes from the Father to be the priest for all of humanity. He offered to the Father the worship and obedience that human beings did not offer. Likewise, Jesus' whole life of prayer and obedience and his communion with the Holy Spirit was ultimately to consecrate humanity.[38]

---

36. Colyer, *How to Read T. F. Torrance*, 290; Torrance, *The Doctrine of Jesus Christ*, 82.

37. J. B. Torrance, *Worship, Community, and the Triune God of Grace*, 55.

38. J. B. Torrance, *Worship, Community, and the Triune God of Grace*, 37–38.

At one level, it almost seems that both T. F. and J. B. Torrance downplay the role of human beings in the sanctification process. It can appear as a theology without a vibrant anthropology. Yet, T. F. and J. B. Torrance have considered this. J. B. Torrance argued that the imperatives of law *follow* the indicatives of grace.[39] Although he places the emphasis on the indicatives of grace, he does not deny the role of the imperatives. This order, for J. B. Torrance, was crucial for maintaining a trinitarian-incarnational orientation. Anything less is to slip into a humanistic variance. J. B. Torrance writes:

> Jesus comes to be the Priest of creation to do for us, men and women, what we failed to do, to offer to the Father the worship and the praise we failed to offer, to glorify God by a life of perfect love and obedience, to be the one true servant of the Lord. In him and through him we are renewed by the Spirit in the image of God and in the worship of God in a life of shared communion. Jesus comes as our brother to be our great High Priest, to carry on his loving heart the joys, the sorrows, the prayers, the conflicts of all his creatures, to reconcile all things to God, and to intercede for all nations as our eternal Mediator and advocate. He comes to stand in for us in the presence of the Father, when in our failure and bewilderment we do not know how to pray, as we ought to, or forget to pray altogether. By his Spirit he helps us in our infirmities.[40]

J. B. Torrance argued strongly for the priesthood of Christ, precisely because of humanity's failure to offer acceptable worship. Therefore, Christ the High Priest did this, by grace, on their behalf. Elmer Colyer states, "Theology can never be more than a refinement and extension of the knowledge of God that arises at the evangelical and doxological level of our living personal relationship with God through Jesus Christ in the Holy Spirit."[41] Torrance argued that the evangelical and doxological level is primarily celebrating the reality of the economy of the Trinity.[42]

Regarding God's economy, Colyer states, "In Torrance's theology, all ministry of the church, whether the corporate ministry of the priesthood of all believers or the ordained ministry of word and sacrament, is strictly participation in Christ's own high-priestly ministry, in which Christ

---

39. J. B. Torrance, *Grace, Law and the Atonement*, Regent Audio, 1995.
40. J. B. Torrance, *Worship, Community, and the Triune God of Grace*, 2.
41. Colyer, *How to Read T. F. Torrance*, 28.
42. Torrance, *The Christian Doctrine of God*, 7.

himself is present to the church through the Spirit, filling the church with his God-humanward activity and human-Godward activity in such a way that the church's obedient activity in the name of Christ is fulfilled and utilized by Christ and his ministry to build up the body of Christ and to extend Christ's kingdom."[43] Colyer's words are helpful at this point in understanding the emphasis of Torrance's theology. He emphasized that all ministry is strictly participation rather than initiation. Christ is the one who has initiated both revelation and response. What the rest of humanity does is participate in the work of Christ. They participate in the ministry of Christ the ascended high priest. They participate by the Spirit not only in the work of Christ but also in the interrelationship between the Son and the Father. It is a catching up as it were. This is the privileged role of humanity, according to Torrance, to participate in the work of Christ.

T. F. Torrance frequently told the story about teaching his daughter to walk for the purpose of making a very important theological point. The theological point was that although human beings may think that by faith we are the ones holding on to God, the reality is that he is the one holding on to us. "I can still feel her tiny fingers gripping my hand as tightly as she could. She did not rely on her feeble grasp of my hand, but upon my strong grasp of her hand, which enfolded her grasp of mine within it. That is surely how God's faithfulness actualized in Jesus Christ has laid hold of our weak and faltering faith and holds it securely in his hand."[44] Torrance's story serves to illustrate that God in Christ Jesus is the one who is doing the work on our behalf.

The Torrances believed that this trinitarian-incarnational approach focused predominately on what the Son of God has done on behalf of mankind in his own saving humanity. They argued that it was through Christ's assumption of a real humanity, not an ideal humanity, dynamically not statically, that the active obedience of Jesus Christ takes place. Gerrit Scott Dawson asked, "Does a Jesus who simply cannot sin truly have a genuine humanity? Such a Jesus would be a man in a category higher even than our first parents before their fall. Is that a person who comes as far as the curse is found?"[45] The point is that Jesus Christ assumed sinful human flesh yet was without sin. Jesus did not assume an

---

43. Colyer, *How to Read T. F. Torrance*, 273.
44. Torrance, *The Mediation of Christ*, 93.
45. Dawson, *An Introduction to Torrance Theology*, 65.

idealized humanity. And the Torrances argued that it was precisely because Jesus assumed a real humanity that he could act on the behalf of all humanity in his active obedience. "For God has done what the law, weakened by the flesh, could not do. By sending his own Son *in the likeness of sinful flesh* and for sin, he condemned sin in the flesh, in order that the righteous requirement of the law might be fulfilled in us, who walk not according to the flesh but according to the Spirit" (Romans 8:3-4). Jesus Christ, in his incarnation, offered worship through his active obedience on behalf of humanity.

Furthermore, for the Torrances, Jesus not only offered worship on behalf of humanity but specifically, on behalf of Israel. The fulfillment of Israel's worship took place through the life, death, and resurrection of Jesus Christ. T. F. Torrance asserts, "And at last in the fullness of time, the Word of God became man in Jesus, born of the Virgin Mary, within the embrace of Israel's faith and worship and expectation, himself God and man, in whom the covenanted relationship between God and Israel and through Israel with all humanity was gathered up, transformed, and fulfilled once for all."[46] Notice that T. F. Torrance emphasized that Christ came within what he calls the embrace of Israel's faith and worship. This correlated, according to the Torrances, with Christ's own words, "I have not come to abolish the law and prophets but to fulfill them." This embrace of Israel's faltering worship was then an embrace of the faltering worship of all of humanity; not only Israel but all of humanity lives vicariously through Jesus Christ and that the worship of humanity is participation in the worship of Christ. "He ministered the things of God to man and the things of man to God."[47] Torrance emphasized that in Christ both revelation and response are complete. Both initiated worship and responsive worship are satisfied in Christ. T. F. Torrance writes:

> In worship and prayer Jesus Christ acts in our place and on our behalf in both a representative and substitutionary way so that what he does in our stead is nevertheless effected as our very own, issuing freely and spontaneously out of ourselves. Through his incarnational and atoning union Jesus Christ has

---

46. Torrance, *The Mediation of Christ*, 9.

47. Torrance quotes this phrase from Athanasius in *The Mediation of Christ*, 73. Also quoted in Torrance, "Athanasius: A Study in the Foundations of Classical Theology," in *Theology in Reconciliation: Essays Towards Evangelical and Catholic Unity in East and West*, 228. Torrance cites *Contra Arianos* 1:41 ff., 50 ff; II:7 ff., 12 ff., 50 f., 65 ff., 74 ff.; III; 30 ff., 38 f.; IV: 6 ff. Note: this quote is of disputed authorship.

> united himself with us in such a reconciling and sanctifying way that he interpenetrates and gathers up all our faltering, unclean worship and prayer into himself, assimilates them to his one self-oblation to God, so that when he presents himself as the worship and prayer of all creation, our worship and prayer are presented there also. When the Father accepts us in Jesus Christ his beloved Son, who then can distinguish our worship and prayer from Jesus' worship and prayer, for they are one and the same, wholly his and wholly ours in him?[48]

Jesus Christ acts on behalf of humanity not only on behalf of God the Father. Christ is functioning on behalf of men and women providing the efficacious worship that they cannot bring. As the result, Torrance argues, Christ gathers up humanity's deficient worship and prayer and purifies it in his own self-oblation to God the Father making humanity's worship perfect. Trinitarian-incarnational worship emphasizes humanity's participation in the perfect worship of the One who provides both revelation and response on behalf of men and women.

Conclusion

J. B. Torrance asserts, "Whatever our worship is, it is the liturgical amen to the worship of Christ on our behalf."[49] Emphasizing the role of Jesus Christ in worship, not just as the object of worship but also as the one who has worshiped perfectly on behalf of humanity is critical to embracing a trinitarian-incarnational understanding of worship according to T. F. and J. B. Torrance. J. B. Torrance sums up the trinitarian worship position like this:

> Such is the wonderful love of God, that He has come to us in Jesus Christ, and in Jesus assumed our life (the life of all men), underwritten our responsibilities, offered for us a life of worship and obedience and prayer to the Father, taken to Himself our body of death, vicariously submitted for us to the verdict of 'guilty', died our death and risen again in our humanity, so that by the grace of God, His life is our life, His death is our death, His victory our victory, His resurrection our resurrection, His righteousness our righteousness and His eternal prayers and self-offerings to the Father our prayers and offering in the

---

48. Torrance, *Mediation of Christ*, 88.
49. J. B. Torrance, *Worship, Community and the Triune God of Grace*, 2.

presence of the Father. So we are accepted in the Beloved, and discover our status as sons.[50]

For both of the Torrances, there was a clear distinction between unitarian (and existential) and trinitarian-incarnational worship. This is a critical starting point for understanding their doxological theology. In the next chapter, more attention will be given to T. F. Torrance's theology of the trinitarian faith and worship.

---

50. J. B. Torrance, "The Place of Jesus Christ in Worship," *Theological Foundations for Ministry*, 352.

3

The Trinitarian Faith and Worship

Introduction

IN THIS CHAPTER, T. F. Torrance's trinitarian theology and his explicit references to the subject of worship will be compared. What is worth noting in this chapter is that Torrance believed that the trinitarian faith, *eusebia*, and worship accompany each other. According to Torrance, "Fidelity to the truth of the Gospel, belief in the Holy Spirit, and worship of the Father in and through Jesus Christ cannot be separated from one another."[1] When Torrance referred to worship, he was not referring to the logistics of the liturgy but to the faithful worship of the Triune God. Torrance's emphasis on the object of worship, namely the Triune God, as well as the faith and obedience involved in human response will be examined.

Trinitarian Worship

As for the New Testament basis for the doctrine of the Trinity, Torrance states, "While there is no formally explicit teaching about the Holy Trinity in the New Testament, belief in and worship of God the Father, the Son, and the Holy Spirit clearly belong to the essential content of the

---

1. B39 "Ecumenical Service—Kirk of the Greyfriars," 8; Eugenio, *Communion with the Triune God*, 28–29.

Gospel which the Apostles proclaimed and taught."[2] Torrance linked the proclamation of the *euangelion* with the faith and worship of the Triune God. The good message of Jesus the Messiah eventually expresses itself in the worship of the Father, Son, and Holy Spirit. Torrance writes:

> By indwelling the Scriptures of the New Testament and interiorizing their message we become drawn into the circle of God's revelation of himself through himself. Spiritually and theologically regarded, this kind of indwelling, in Christ and his Word, involves faith, devotion, mediation, prayer and worship in and through which we are given discerning access to God in his inner Communion as Father, Son, and Holy Spirit.[3]

Torrance here emphasized the role of the Scriptures in shaping and forming our doctrine of the Trinity. But he also emphasized that this indwelling of the Scriptures involved the spiritual disciplines of prayer and worship. One criticism that Colin Gunton had of Torrance was that his theology was in some ways more patristic than biblical. He said that it is remarkable how little exegesis of Scripture, as distinct from the Fathers, is to be found in Torrance's major treatments of trinitarian themes.[4] However, Torrance clearly employed to the Scriptures to discuss the Trinity:

> Within the New Testament, there were triadic formulae which entered into the central stream of the apostolic faith and message, worship and tradition, and which were spelled out in the theology of the early Church. Of special theological significance were three explicit formulae: (1) the baptismal formula, Matthew 28:19: "In the name of the Father, and of the Son and of the Holy Spirit." (2) The familiar benediction from 2 Cor. 13:14: "The grace of the Lord Jesus Christ, and the love of God and the communion of the Holy Spirit, be with you all." (3) Then the passage from 1 Cor. 12.4-6, much discussed in the early Church: "There are diversities of gifts, but the same Spirit; and there are diversities of administrations, but the same Lord; and there are diversities of operations, but it is the same God who works all in all."[5]

As the Body of Christ gathers together in the name of the Father, Son and Holy Spirit and through faith, prayer, and worship, the church's

2. Torrance, *Trinitarian Perspectives*, 128.
3. Torrance, *The Christian Doctrine of God, One Being Three Persons*, 38.
4. Colyer, *The Promise of Trinitarian Theology*, 130.
5. Torrance, *The Trinitarian Faith*, 197.

theology of the Triune God is shaped and formed. "Hence all worship and glorification by the creature is offered to God the Father through the Son and in the Spirit or to the Father with the Son and together with the Holy Spirit, that is to the one indivisible God who is Three in One and One in Three, the Holy Trinity who is blessed for ever."[6]

What is worth noting is that Torrance understood human response to be active. The creature offers worship and glorification to God the Father through or together with the Son and in the power of the Spirit. Human response is not passive as some have claimed. For example, Dick Eugenio states, "Whether this is a strength or weakness in Torrance's theology can be judged differently from various perspectives, but his Christocentric soteriology can lean towards a promotion of human passive participation, in that the only human role in the redemption drama is to share in what Christ already did for us and in us."[7] While Dick Eugenio offers considerable insight and captures this common perspective, it simply is not true that T. F. Torrance's Christocentric soteriology leaves Christian believers passive.[8] While Torrance placed extensive attention on the vicarious humanity of Jesus Christ in his writings, he also factored in the response on the part of the Body of Christ through word and sacrament, prayer and faith/obedience:

> Hence the Gospel of the reconciliation of man with God has to be understood not just in terms of God's mighty act of salvation upon our humanity, but in terms of its actualization within the depths of our human existence in the perfecting and presenting in and through Jesus of our response in faith and obedience, in love and *worship*, to God the Father. For us to share in the *worship* of the Father through, with and in Jesus Christ, belongs to the essence of our reconciliation to God, and is of the very substance of the Gospel.[9]

Worship, from Torrance's perspective, indeed was a participation in the worship offered by Christ, but this does not negate human response.

---

6. Torrance, *Trinitarian Perspectives*, 120.

7. Eugenio, *Communion with the Triune God*, 73.

8. Torrance states, "Hence in the formulation of the doctrine of the Trinity we are committed to worshipping and obeying God unreservedly, with all our heart and soul and mind in an approach which sets aside all other religious approaches and abolishes any entertainment of alternative devotions and conceptions of God as invalid." Torrance, *The Christian Doctrine of God*, 24–25.

9. Torrance, *The Trinitarian Faith*, 4.

Again, this participation in worship, according to Torrance, takes on a trinitarian shape. It is not a unitarian response without a mediator, as already examined earlier. What makes Christian worship distinctively Christian is that it is trinitarian. Torrance states, "Thereby they [Karl Barth, H. R. Mackintosh, and Karl Rahner] have shown once again that the doctrine of the Trinity belongs to the very heart of saving faith where it constitutes the inner shape of Christian worship and the dynamic grammar of Christian theology: it expresses the essential and distinctively Christian understanding of God by which we live, and which is of crucial significance for the evangelical mission of the Church as well."[10] If worship is unitarian and not trinitarian, it is most certainly sub-Christian according to Torrance. "Hence in the formulation of the doctrine of the Trinity we are committed to worshiping and obeying God unreservedly, with all our heart and soul and mind in an approach which sets aside all other religious approaches and abolishes entertainment of alternative devotions and conceptions of God as invalid."[11] Both T. F. and J. B. Torrance repeatedly made the case that the doctrine of the Trinity and Christian worship must compliment each other. T. F. Torrance writes, "It is understandable, therefore, that Didymus the Blind of Alexandria, while resolutely affirming one Being three Persons should nevertheless have said that the three divine Persons of the Holy Trinity are thus to be heard and known, worshiped and glorified 'as one Person.'"[12] Elaborating on this relationship between the Trinity and the subject of worship, Torrance argues:

> Belief in the Holy Trinity reinforces and deepens belief in the Unity, but this is due in large measure to the unifying nature of the worship that the Father, the Son and the Holy Spirit in their indivisible oneness call forth from us. Our belief in the one Being of God is not something that we think out for ourselves through reflecting on the *perichoretic* relations and properties of the three divine Persons with one another or on their common Nature. Worship is primarily the act of God upon us and arises in us as an echo of his own transcendent Nature which we offer back to the Father through the Son and in the Spirit, and takes place as in the Spirit we are given to share through Christ in the

---

10. Torrance, *The Christian Doctrine of God*, 10.
11. Torrance, *The Christian Doctrine of God*, 24–25.
12. Torrance, *The Christian Doctrine of God*, 135; Didymus, *De Trinitate.* 2.36.

inter-personal Communion of love and self-giving in the Life of God.¹³

It is worth noting again that Torrance emphasized that trinitarian worship is not only an act of God upon us but that it also arises within us as we worship the Father through the Son in the power of the Spirit. Humanity is swept up in the interpersonal communion life of God.

To make his point, T. F. Torrance quoted Athanasius: "There is one eternal Godhead in Trinity, and there is one Glory of the Holy Trinity. . . . If theological truth is now perfect in Trinity, this is the true and only divine worship, and this is its beauty and truth, it must have been always so."¹⁴ Torrance states, "These sentences of Athanasius take us into the very heart of Christian belief in God and worship of him as Triune."¹⁵ What is worth commenting on about this quotation from Athanasius is his emphasis that trinitarian worship is the only true and divine worship. Torrance agreed and argued that the doctrine of the Trinity was not only important in patristic theology for dogmatic purposes but for fidelity in worship. "The central place accorded to Jesus Christ in the faith of the Church called for a clear answer to the question as to *whether he was himself Lord and God* or only intermediary between God and man."¹⁶

The Trinitarian Faith & The Nicene-Constantinopolitan Creed.

The issue being addressed in the fourth century was whether Jesus Christ should be worshiped as *homoousios* with God the Father. Colin Gunton states, "Athanasius served Torrance as a theologian of God's being as Barth served as a theologian of his act (though the greatness of both is that they integrated the two) and it would be difficult to exaggerate the importance for him, in all aspects of his work, of the principle of the *homoousion*."¹⁷ Torrance asserts, "The *Homoousion*, pointed to eternal consubstantial relations within the Trinity and thus to the consubstantiality

---

13. Torrance, *The Christian Doctrine of God*, 134–35.
14. Athanasius, *Contra Arianos*, 1.18. Note: "Theological truth" is T. F. Torrance's translation of *theologia*. The NPNF translates *theologia*, in *Contra Arianos* 1.18, as the "doctrine of God."
15. Torrance, *Trinitarian Perspectives*, 7.
16. Torrance, *The Trinitarian Faith*, 2.
17. Colyer, *The Promise of Trinitarian Theology*, 116.

of the Trinity as a whole."[18] Again, Torrance writes, "The explicit formulation of the *homoousion* at the Council of Nicaea was an absolutely fundamental event that took place in the mind of the early Church."[19] This "fundamental event" had to take place to address Arius' denial that the Son was fully God from all eternity as the Father was God from all eternity. His doctrine was not clear, but he denied the eternal generation and assumed that "begotten" meant the same as "created." This of course had serious implications for redemption since only God could redeem humanity.

The issue at stake for the church was the question of what made Christian worship distinctively "Christian." If Jesus is not God, he should not be worshiped as God. On the other hand if the Son is of one substance with the Father, he must be worshiped as God. Torrance writes, "The same question was raised again after Nicaea in respect of the Holy Spirit. Is the Holy Spirit to be *worshiped* along with the Father and the Son as himself God, and having his being with the Son on the divine side of that absolute distinction between the Creator and the creature, or is he to be thought of in terms of the immanent forms of rationality in the created universe?"[20]

The seven ecumenical councils that took place from 325 to 787 were critical for Christian theology and liturgy.[21] Christian doctrine was undergoing a purifying process. Specifically, Christology was the central focus although other issues were addressed. Torrance argues, "From the start the theology of the Church took the form, not of a set of abstract propositions, but of embodied truth in which the knowing and worshipping of God and the daily obedience of faith and life interpenetrated each other."[22] Torrance was making a critical point here. Theology was not merely an "intellectual" pursuit. Rather, a knowing of the truth accompanied a knowing and a worshiping of God as well as of obedience and faith. Furthermore, the truth mattered for the mission of the church. Referring to the early formation of trinitarian theology, Torrance argues, "It was thus that something of immense significance for the whole life, worship and mission of the Church took place, the formation of a theological

18. Torrance, *The Trinitarian Faith*, 10.
19. Torrance, *The Christian Doctrine of God*, ix.
20. Torrance, *The Trinitarian Faith*, 3.
21. Need, *Truly Divine and Truly Human*, xiii.
22. Torrance, *The Trinitarian Faith*, 6.

paradigm of understanding which became more and more articulate as the Church sought to expound, clarify and integrate the truths of the Gospel, and defend them from damaging misinterpretation."²³

Torrance was emphasizing that the trinitarian faith of the creed formulated at Nicaea in 325 and revised at Constantinople in 381 was absolutely critical for the future of the church. This is a point that is worth appreciating. It mattered not only for the cause of truth, but also for the advancement of the worship of God. Again, Torrance argues, "Understandably, therefore, the doctrine of the Holy Trinity has been called the innermost heart of Christian faith and worship, the central dogma of classical theology, the fundamental grammar of our knowledge of God."²⁴

The Constantinopolitan-Nicene Creed also clarified the worship of the Spirit with the clause, "who with the Father and the Son together is worshiped and glorified."²⁵ The laborious work that took place at Nicaea guarded the truth and protected the essence of the Christian faith. Torrance writes, "There resulted throughout the Church a development of the distinctive doxological and theological outlook canonically upheld and regularly cultivated in its sacramental and liturgical life."²⁶

The Place of Eusebia with Theologia in Worship

Along with the emphasis of correct doctrine and worship, the concern for faith and piety or godliness was also present. Torrance emphasized

---

23. Torrance, *The Christian Doctrine of God*, ix.

24. Torrance, *The Christian Doctrine of God*, 2.

25. T. A. Noble states: "The 325 form of the creed said nothing but: 'We believe in the Holy Spirit.' That was all! Whereas by 381, Athanasius had written the Letters to Serapion to combat the Pneumatomachi, the Cappadocians had argued against the Macedonians who were dubious about the deity of the Spirit. So that in 381 the Council of Constantinople developed a much, much fuller article on the Holy Spirit, and this was the key sentence. Basil had not wanted to say outright, 'The Holy Spirit is God, *homoousion* with the Father' because he wanted to persuade those conservatives who were doubtful about that. Nazianzen was much more forthright. But the Council followed Basil's line (his younger brother Gregory of Nyssa was present) rather than Nazianzen's and made this more guarded declaration on the deity of the Spirit, not using *homousion*, nor saying outright, 'The Holy Spirit is God,' but stating their belief in the deity of the Spirit in this more guarded way: the Spirit is 'worshipped and glorified.'" T.A. Noble email correspondence on 29/03/2018. The point of this is that there was a dogmatic declaration to the church's worship.

26. Torrance, *The Christian Doctrine of God*, x.

that godliness and theology, worship and faith, went together.²⁷ In making the case that one knew whether the Holy Trinity had made a mark on the church by the godliness of the people, he wrote:

> An outstanding mark of the Nicene approach was its association of faith with piety or godliness, that is with a mode of worship, behavior and thought that was devout and worthy of God the Father, the Son and the Holy Spirit. This was a distinctively Christian way of life in which the seal of the Holy Trinity was indelibly stamped upon the mind of the Church. Godliness and theology, *worship* and faith, went inseparably together with constant attention given to reverent interpretation of the Holy Scriptures, reverent use of the reason and reverent ways of argument, in which there was no intrusion into the mystery of God or irreverent teaching about him.²⁸

What is intriguing about what Torrance is emphasizing in the Nicene approach, is the synthesis of faith, piety, and the trinitarian faith. He stated that faith, piety, and godliness are modes of worship, behavior, and thought that were worthy of the Triune God. He argued that theological formation and spiritual formation were informing one another.

Faith and Godliness

Torrance made the connection that faith was an act of godliness. He writes, "Faith is itself an act of godliness in humble worship of God and adoring obedience to him, and godliness is a right relationship to God through faith which gives a distinctive slant to the mind and molds life and thought in accordance with 'the word and truth of the Gospel.'"²⁹ Dick Eugenio states, "In short, theologians should consider that in theology we are up against God himself in his ultimate-ness and absolute Lordly authority of his almightiness, so that in our attempt to expound our limited knowledge of his self-revelation, the ethical approach is that of worship and submission."³⁰ Here we see the connection between trinitarian theology and participation in the trinitarian faith. When human

---

27. Torrance, *The Trinitarian Faith*, 17.
28. Torrance, *The Trinitarian Faith*, 17.
29. Torrance, *The Trinitarian Faith*, 28.
30. Eugenio, *Communion with the Triune God*, 29.

beings express faith and obedience in him, this is equated with an act of godliness and worship of the Triune God according to Torrance.

The term that T. F. Torrance employed to describe this godly faith was *eusebeia*. In writing about Calvin, he asserts, "This [*pietas* or *religio*] was more or less his [Calvin's] equivalent for the New Testament and patristic *eusebeia* which he also spoke of as the 'fitting worship of God'. Coupled with this approach was his profound sense of 'God's unfathomable and spiritual Being' which wholly exceeds all human conception and imagination and is more to be worshiped than investigated."[31] Again, what is interesting is Torrance's mention of Calvin's interpretation of *eusebeia* as being fitting worship of God. This fitting worship of God is clearly related to *theologia* in Torrance's thinking. Torrance argues, "All our statements about the Trinity from beginning to end must arise out of and remain rooted in a continuity of godly life and worship, or *eusebia* and *theologia*. That must be the case with our understanding of the whole economy of salvation, while all our devotion and liturgical life must be allowed to have a trinitarian structure. This is what *theologia* really is."[32] Torrance writes, "It is hardly surprising, therefore, that Athanasius should equate *theologia*, in its deepest sense as the knowledge and worship of God as he is known both through Jesus Christ and in the Holy Spirit and as he is eternally in himself, with the doctrine of the Holy Trinity."[33] Notice Torrance's explicit statements that our theology of the Trinity needs to come out of a godly life and that our liturgical life must be connected to a trinitarian structure. *Theologia* and *eusebeia* must always accompany each other, according to Torrance. Torrance expounds the term *eusebeia* from within the context of Nicene theology in which he connected the way of belief and worship that characterized faithful followers of Jesus:

> As found in Nicene theology *eusebia* referred to the orthodox understanding of truth embodied in the tradition of faith and worship that derived from the apostles. It is to be traced back to the Pastoral Epistles in the New Testament where godliness was more or less a technical word for what had been called the Way in the Acts of the Apostles, the way of belief and worship characteristic of those who are committed to Christ and who have to suffer for it. The distinctive feature of godliness is that it is an embodiment of faith or knowledge of the truth of the

---

31. Torrance, *The Christian Doctrine of God*, 10.
32. Torrance, *Trinitarian Perspectives*, 102.
33. Torrance, *Trinitarian Perspectives*, 8.

Gospel in corresponding way of life and worship in the reverent service of God.[34]

It is worth considering further Torrance's thought about what he calls the distinctive feature of godliness that corresponds with both fidelity in theology and the way in which one lives out one's faith, worship, and service to the Lord. Of particular interest is the thought that worship is not only how we live but also how we think. Faithful theology was for Torrance, an act of worship:

> Understood in the light of overarching framework of God's self-revelation as Father, Son and Holy Spirit, this mystery of godliness or godly worship came to mean thinking of God in an essentially Trinitarian way, so that the equation theology = godliness, or eusebeia, was identified with Trinitarian thinking of simply with the worship and doctrine of the Holy Trinity, as with Origen and the great Athanasius. The worship and doctrine of the Trinity belong together, for it is godly thinking of God in unrestrained awe and adoration of this unfathomable Triune Nature that must guide a move toward formulating a doctrine of the Trinity in terms worthy him.[35]

For Torrance, *eusebia* or godliness was synonymous with the worship of the Triune God. It was also correlated with trinitarian thinking. As Torrance emphasized, worship and the doctrine of the Trinity belong together. Trinitarian thinking is not only right, it is godly.

It is not uncommon today to think of godliness as right behavior (*praxis*) in contrast to right thinking (*theologia*). But Torrance was making a very important point regarding worship: worship must never be divorced from right doctrine specifically the doctrine of the Triune God. If one worships another god besides the Triune God it could hardly be considered "godly." "Trinitarian worship and Trinitarian faith thus provided the implicit controlling ground both for a faithful restructuring of the life of the church and for a godly renewing of its understanding in the Mind of Christ."[36] Torrance further states, "It is thus that Trinitarian thinking enters into the inner fabric of all our Christian worship and knowledge of the one God, and the doctrine of the Trinity is recognized to constitute

---

34. Torrance, *The Trinitarian Faith*, 29.
35. Torrance, *The Christian Doctrine of God*, 74–75.
36. Torrance, *The Trinitarian Faith*, 46.

the fundamental grammar of Christian dogmatic theology."[37] And again, he argues, "Thus it may be said that under the control of the informal undefined mystery of the Trinity imprinted upon the New Testament Scriptures and upon the mind of the worshiping Church, the formulation of the doctrine of the Holy Trinity in explicit terms, as far as that was possible, had to be done in such a godly way as to guard the great mystery of God's self-revelation, 'God manifest in the flesh.'"[38] The Nicene faith, according to Torrance, preserved the fidelity of Christian worship. "Hence it is not surprising that an essential element in redemption was reckoned by the Nicene and post-Nicene fathers to be redemption from 'false worship.'"[39] The trinitarian faith was the grammar of Christian dogmatics but that grammar also provided language to shape the minds of worshipers. Torrance writes, "We must allow worship of God through the Son in whom the unfathomable mystery of the Father is disclosed, to govern all that we confess in faith or express in theological formulation."[40]

Torrance also argued that it was within the worshiping community that the trinitarian language of faith was developed. Right within the context of the sacraments such as baptism, the trinitarian faith was given to us not only by our Lord in Matthew 28:19 but it was also preserved by the early church. Torrance writes,

> It is particularly with Irenaeus in the middle of the second century that we find the most enlightening account of how the Trinitarian pattern in the evangelical and apostolic tradition of the Faith began to be unfolded under the guidance of "the rule of faith" (*regula fidei*) or "the canon of truth, given with the ordinance of Baptism" in the context of the Trinitarian worship of God, meditation upon the Holy Scriptures, and instruction of catechumens.[41]

Thus the trinitarian faith both informs the liturgy and the trinitarian liturgy shapes and forms the faith. Worship, according to T. F. Torrance, must never be divorced from *theologia*. And worship must celebrate the Triune God. Torrance states:

---

37. Torrance, *The Christian Doctrine of God*, 82.
38. Torrance, *The Christian Doctrine of God*, 82.
39. Torrance, *The Trinitarian Faith*, 154.
40. Torrance, *The Trinitarian Faith*, 44.
41. Torrance, *The Christian Doctrine of God*, 75.

> By his atoning sacrifice he [Jesus Christ] heals and cleanses us through his own divine power so that we worship him as well as the Father, for he and the Father are one; but because he is one with us as well as with the Father, we may pray to him as our "Mediator, High Priest and Paraclete," asking him to present our desires, petitions and intercessions that ascend from us to him, to the Father, and thus we worship the Father in union with him and through him. As Son of God incarnate and High Priest Jesus Christ has shown mankind the pure way to worship God—that is what true godliness is in which our faith and understanding are confirmed in God.[42]

Again, it is interesting to point out the interaction between our human response and Christ's response. We worship and pray but we do so through the One who purifies our response. We present petitions to him who then presents petitions on our behalf to the Father.

Access to God the Father Almighty, Maker of Heaven and Earth

The Nicene Creed begins with these words, "We believe in God the Father Almighty, Maker of heaven and earth." Regarding this opening phrase, Torrance focused on *the revelation* of God the Father Almighty, Maker of heaven and earth. Andrew Purves, commenting on the scientific epistemology of T. F. Torrance states, "Knowledge is grounded in the subject of disclosure. This is a very important point. In theology, knowledge is grounded in God, in and through Jesus Christ."[43] Furthermore, according to Torrance:

> It is only as our minds are open and adjusted to God in accordance with his revealed nature, and only as we respond to him in faith, obedience and worship, that we can think and speak of God with the kind of precision that is appropriate to his divine nature. Piety and precision, godliness and exactness belong together and condition one another, for knowledge of God arises and takes shape in our mind under the determination of his

---

42. Torrance, *The Trinitarian Faith*, 40.

43. Purves, "The Christology of Thomas F. Torrance" in Colyer (ed.), *The Promise of Trinitarian Theology*, 69.

revealed nature, and his maintained in the experience of worship, prayer, holiness, and godliness.[44]

So for Torrance, the trinitarian faith begins with receiving by faith the revelation that God is who he has claimed to be as revealed in the Scriptures. Torrance argued that our minds not only need to be open but adjusted to God, as he has revealed himself. Paul Molnar writes, "It is quite obvious from what has been said that Torrance did not think we can know God with any accuracy apart from revelation."[45] Then as we respond to him in worship and obedience and faith we are able to speak of this God with accuracy and integrity. Torrance further emphasized that not only has God the Father revealed himself and not only must this revelation be received by faith but that this faith is maintained and sustained through worship, prayer and holiness. Torrance argues, "All Nicene theology was built up in the worshiping Church through biblical interpretation and mediation."[46]

This was the starting place of the Nicene faith for Torrance: revelation of the Triune God that is received in faith by the worshiping community and is celebrated by that same community. This faith, obedience, and worship consequently nurture and sustain the trinitarian faith.

God of God, Light of Light, Incarnate Savior

Regarding the economic Trinity and the topic of worship, Torrance states, "Worshipping the goodness of the Father and amazement at the saving economy of the Son belong inseparably together."[47] Worship according to Torrance involved acknowledging the goodness of the Father and being in awe of the saving economy of the Son. When Christian believers gather together for corporate worship, there must be celebration regarding what God has done for humanity in Christ Jesus. This will be manifested through the liturgical practices and disposition of the worshiping community.

Torrance not only emphasized that what God has done for humanity in Christ Jesus should be the focus of Christian worship but that the

---

44. Torrance, *The Trinitarian Faith*, 54.
45. Molnar, *Thomas F. Torrance*, 93.
46. Torrance, *The Trinitarian Faith*, 58.
47. Torrance, *The Trinitarian Faith*, 148.

way in which Christians worship the Father must take place within the Son by the Spirit. He writes,

> They [the bishops and theologians at the Council of Nicaea] not only worshiped God through and with Christ but *in* Christ, worshiping God face to face in Christ as himself the Face of God the Father turned toward them. Jesus Christ the incarnate Son of God *is* the God whom they worshiped and loved in the ontological and soteriological mode of his personal self-communicating in the flesh, so that in their union and communion with Christ they knew themselves to be in union and communion with the eternal God.[48]

Torrance believed that worship happened in union with Christ; that as humanity has union with the Incarnate Son, they vicariously have relationship with God the Father and consequently they are worshiping this eternal God. Torrance argues, "He [Christ] is both Author of divine blessing and the Object of our worship, for in him there dwells the whole fullness of the Godhead bodily. It is indeed through such faith and worship that we are brought into the closest contact with God and experience the saving power that is common to the Son and the Father."[49] Not only is the Triune God the object of our worship, it is through worship that we are brought into close relationship with him. Torrance communicated specifically that it is through worship that we are brought into closest contact with God and experience his saving power.

Torrance also emphasized that the Nicene theologians employed liturgical language to describe the work of Christ in his redemptive action. He stated, "When we ask what the precise nature of this vicarious activity of Christ was, we find Nicene theologians regularly falling back upon familiar biblical and liturgical terms like ransom, sacrifice, propitiation, expiation, reconciliation, to describe it, but always with a deep sense of awe before the inexpressible mystery of atonement through the blood of Christ."[50]

Furthermore, Torrance pointed out key atonement concepts that influenced the Nicene theologians. While discussing the liturgical work of the priest, he stated, "Christ is at once High Priest and Sacrifice, 'the Offerer and the Offering', the expression used by Basil in his Liturgy and

---

48. Torrance, *The Christian Doctrine of God*, 93–94.
49. Torrance, *Trinitarian Perspectives*, 52.
50. Torrance, *The Trinitarian Faith*, 168.

incorporated into the Byzantine rite."[51] This is central to Christian worship. His emphasis here is similar to the Epistle to the Hebrews; that Christ is both priest and sacrifice. "The basic approach of these Church Fathers at Nicaea and Constantinople was that of the worship of redeemed sinners who rejoiced in the message of the Gospel and who, like St. Paul, believed in Christ as God and Savior."[52]

And regarding the effect of the incarnation and atonement, Torrance clearly disassociated himself from those who advocated limited or particular atonement when he argued, "It is precisely in Jesus, therefore, who was born of the Virgin Mary, crucified for us under Pontius Pilate and rose again in space and time, that we are to think of the whole human race, and indeed of the whole creation, as in a profound sense already redeemed, resurrected, and consecrated for the glory and worship of God."[53] God's grace for Torrance was always for all human beings. Christ came in his incarnation, died, and rose again that all might be saved.

The Eternal Spirit

Although, the Council of Nicaea was concerned with the soteriological implications of the Arian heresy as well as the liturgical implications for the Church, there were additional concerns. One question that remained was, "What about the Holy Spirit?" If what developed from Nicaea was the trinitarian faith, what were the theological questions regarding the Holy Spirit?

Torrance writes, "At the Council of Nicaea itself, as Basil and Epiphanius point out, there had been no controversy with regard to the Holy Spirit, for in the context of the ongoing evangelical and doxological life and faith of the Church, the Holy Spirit was inseparably associated with the Father and the Son in praise and worship as the divine Source of salvation and renewal."[54]

---

51. Torrance, *The Trinitarian Faith*, 177. For characteristic reference in the liturgical tradition to the priestly office of Christ, see Apostolic Constitutions, 2.4.25.26; 5.5.6; 6.3.11; 6.6.30; 7.1.38; 7.4.47; 8.2.12; 8.5.46.

52. Torrance, *The Trinitarian Faith*, 147.

53. Torrance, *The Trinitarian Faith*, 183. See also, the chapter, "T. F. Torrance in Relation to Reformed Theology" by Alasdair Heron in *The Promise of Trinitarian Theology*, edited by Elmer Colyer.

54. Torrance, *The Trinitarian Faith*, 196.

Torrance can sound at times as if he sees the role of the Holy Spirit exclusively in a supportive and even subordinate role to the Father and the Son, employing language from the Constantinopolitan-Nicene Creed that the Spirit proceeds from the Father. Gary W. Deddo writes, "For Torrance the disclosure of the Holy Spirit reached its fullness in Jesus Christ. Consequently, the Church came to know the Spirit through the incarnate Son. There was no independent revelation of the Spirit since the Spirit has no autonomous identity. The Spirit is the Spirit of the Father and of the Son."[55] This emphasis is critical: we only come to know the Spirit through the Father and the Son. Torrance writes, "This explains in part why formally the doctrine of the Spirit developed from the doctrine of the Son. In this context, however, what was primary was once again the evangelical faith and the doxological approach of the Church in the response of worship and prayer to the holy and saving presence of God through Christ and in the Spirit—access to the Father through Christ and in one Spirit."[56]

Torrance seemed to reference the Spirit's own personhood when he wrote, "Just as the God of the old and new covenants and the Lord Jesus Christ were worshiped as sublimely and incomparably holy, so the Spirit of God in virtue of his intrinsically holy nature drew to himself the same awe and adoration, for in the Spirit it was none other than the Lord God, almighty and all-holy, who was personally and objectively present meeting and speaking with his people."[57] The idea of the Spirit's intrinsically holy nature drawing awe and adoration is a fascinating idea. Many identify with the love of God or the work of Christ promoting a worshipful response. But the Spirit's holiness also solicits a worshipful response.

Regarding the Holy Spirit, Torrance writes, "It reinforced the teaching of the New Testament that God is Spirit and is truly known and worshiped as such, for Spirit is the specific nature of God's eternal being (*ousia*), whether as Father, Son or Holy Spirit, and therefore that Father, Son and Holy Spirit in themselves and their interrelations are to be understood and expressed only in an essentially spiritual way."[58] Torrance was referencing the following text in John's Gospel: "God is spirit, and

---

55. Deddo, "The Holy Spirit" in Colyer's, *The Promise of Trinitarian Theology*, 83.

56. Torrance, *The Trinitarian Faith*, 200.

57. Torrance, *The Trinitarian Faith*, 193. To see more of Torrance's view on the *filioque* see *The Triniatarian Faith*, 231–51.

58. Torrance, *The Trinitarian Faith*, 193–94.

those who worship him must worship in spirit and truth."⁵⁹ Paul Molnar emphasizes a similar point regarding worshiping vicariously through Christ when he states, "We worship in Spirit and in Truth only as we partake of Christ's own worship. In other words: The Spirit which Christ breathes upon us . . . becomes the Spirit of our response to him and through him to the Father."⁶⁰

Torrance wanted to emphasize that the Nicene faith was in fact truly trinitarian when he said, "He [Athanasius] maintained against the semi-Arians that it is precisely with the doctrine of the consubstantiality and Deity of the Holy Spirit that the proper understanding of the Holy Trinity is brought to its completion in the theology and worship of the Church."⁶¹ Once again, note how Torrance spoke of *theologia* and *eusebia* in the same breath. Doctrine and worship complement each other according to this emphasis. Referencing Gregory Nazianzen, Torrance wrote, "It was only after clear knowledge of the Father and of the Son had been given, as Gregory Nazianzen was later to say, that in the economy of God's self-revelation the Deity of the Holy Spirit indwelling the Church was becoming clearly known, and worship of God the Father, God the Son, and God the Holy Spirit, was clarified as that of three Persons, one Godhead."⁶² While the ecumenical councils were primarily focused on the deity and humanity of Christ, theological assertions were also needed regarding the third member of the Trinity. What is also worth noting here is that the desired outcome of the doctrinal clarity of these ecumenical councils was fidelity in worship. Regarding the deity of the Holy Spirit, Torrance states, "Gregory Nazianzen and John Calvin both apply the same arguments to establish the Deity and the consubstantiality of the Holy Spirit. If he were not one in being and agency with God the Father his renewing and sanctifying acts could not be divine or therefore saving acts and we could not believe in him or worship him with the Father and the Son as we do."⁶³ And again, "This is the understanding of the Holy Trinity which called forth from Gregory the Theologian and Calvin the Theologian alike ceaseless wonder, mediation and worship."⁶⁴

59. John 4:24

60. Molnar, *TFT Theologian of the Trinity*, 200; Torrance, "Come, Creator Spirit," *Theology in Reconstruction*, 249.

61. Torrance, *Trinitarian Perspectives*, 10.

62. Torrance, *The Trinitarian Faith*, 196. Gregory Nazianzen, *Or.*, 34:26–28

63. Torrance, *Trinitarian Perspectives*, 25.

64. Torrance, *Trinitarian Perspectives*, 40.

Torrance also referenced Gregory Nazianzen regarding the Spirit's role in the church's ministry of intercession. When the church gathers together in the Spirit, they are being led by the Holy Spirit in their intercession for the needs of one another and the world. Torrance writes:

> That [the vicarious activity of the Spirit] is what happens, St Paul claimed, when we pray, for as we engage in prayer, the prayers of the whole creation are penetrated by the intercessory, intervening activity of the Spirit. Hence with Gregory Nazianzen the office of the *Paraclete* was linked especially to prayer and worship, for through the Spirit the heavenly advocacy and intercession of Christ our great high Priest are made to echo inaudibly within us, so that our praying and worship in the Spirit are upheld and made effective by him through a relation of God to himself.[65]

For Torrance the prayers and worship of the saints and the prayers of all of creation are caught up by the intercessory activity of the Holy Spirit. T. F. Torrance once again appeals to the church fathers to reinforce his argument; in this case, his argument is that the Holy Spirit is central to the worshiping community. The Holy Spirit is fine-tuning the intercessory dissonance of the church gathered to the consonance of the intercessions of our Great High Priest, Jesus Christ.

Furthermore, Torrance communicates the connection of orthopraxy with doxological orthodoxy. How we pray influences what we believe and what we believe influences how we pray. He writes:

> The principle involved here later came to be known as *lex orandi, lex credendi*, but it had a powerful place in the thought of the apostolic and early Catholic Church as we see it reflected in the writings of Origen, Athanasius, Hilary, Cyril of Jerusalem and Cyril of Alexandria, as well as Basil and in the Eucharistic liturgy attributed to him: it is reverence, adoration and worship that shape and determine belief. However, the reverse is also true, *lex credendi, lex orandi*, for true belief informs worship—belief and worship are inextricably intertwined as in the theological use of *doxologia*, which refers both to worship and to doctrine. This is supremely evident in the early liturgies of the Church and their Trinitarian character, as in the *Gloria in excelsis*, and the *Gloria Patri*, and in the doxologies, which were appended to the Psalms during the fourth century. It is not, however, the general implications of this principle that concerns us at the

---

65. Torrance, *The Trinitarian Faith*, 250. Also see, Torrance, *Theology in Reconstruction*, 209–58.

moment, so much as the fact that our worship of the Father, the Son and the Holy Spirit, worship of the Father through the Son and in the Holy Spirit, is the worship of one Lord God. It is an adoration that will not allow us when we pray specifically to the Father, or to the Son or to the Holy Spirit, to divide our prayer between them or to direct our devotion separately to the three Persons, for in worshiping and praying to each Person we worship and pray to the whole undivided Godhead, one Being, three Persons.[66]

It is worth reflecting on this premise that how we pray influences what we believe and that what we believe influences how we pray. It is not uncommon for public prayer to be the least thought through element in non-liturgical contemporary churches. While there is certainly a place for extemporaneous prayer, well thought—through prayers inspired by the Holy Spirit are critical for a worshiping community.

Finally, to reemphasize the correlation of the place of corporate worship in communicating the trinitarian faith, Torrance wrote, "Liturgical expression was given to this doxological worship in the *Trisagion*, taken over by the Church from Isaiah of Jerusalem in the vision of the enthroned Lord God before whom the Seraphim covered their faces as they called to one another, 'Holy, Holy, Holy is the Lord of Hosts, the whole earth is filled with his glory.'"[67] The church gathered needs to be reminded of the holiness of the Triune God who has invited them to draw near to his presence. They also need to be reminded that God is Father, Son and Holy Spirit. For Torrance, this was the doxological implication of the *Trisagion*. Torrance writes:

> An early statement attributed to him [Athanasius] appears to represent his concept of the Triunity of God rather faithfully. "The Trinity praised, worshiped and adored, is one and indivisible and without degrees. He is united without confusion, just as the Monad is distinguished in thought without division." For the threefold doxology "Holy, Holy, Holy is the Lord" offered by those venerable living beings, denotes the three perfect Persons just as in the word "Lord" they indicate his One Being.[68]

Again, Torrance emphasized the trinitarian implications of the *Trisagion*. And along with this he was quick to emphasize the language

---

66. Torrance, *The Christian Doctrine of God*, 134.
67. Torrance, *The Christian Doctrine of God*, 150.
68. Torrance, *The Trinitarian Faith*, 313; Torrance, *Trinitarian Perspectives*, 18.

of three persons yet one being. Torrance states, "The Trinity praised, worshipped and adored, is one and indivisible and without degrees (*aschematistos*). He is united without confusion, just as the Monad is distinguished in thought without division."[69] Father, Son, and Holy Spirit were to be worshiped together according to the Nicene faith. This is what was meant that with the Father and the Son, the Spirit was to be worshiped and glorified.

The One Church, a Worshiping Community

Trinitarian worship was to be expressed in community. It was within the worshiping context of the Body of Christ that the Nicene faith was to be communicated through its teachings and liturgy. Torrance states, "The main focus in its own self-understanding as a believing and worshipping community centered upon the apostolic *kerygmata*, that is, upon 'the word and truth of the Gospel' handed down from the apostles, rather than upon a definite ecclesiology."[70] To employ James Torrance's reference to Bonhoeffer's Christology, the "Who" of worship was more important than the "how" of worship.[71] T. F. Torrance was communicating here that the early church was focused on the "who" of worship.

The early church documents referencing liturgy (cf. the *Didache*, Justin Martyr's *Apology*, *The Apostolic Constitutions*) in some regards, seemed more focused on the *didache* (specific instruction on the praxis of worship). Yet the *kerygmata* was never lost as Torrance emphasized. Their ecclesiastical identity was certainly one of a worshiping community focused on the proclamation of Jesus Christ. Torrance argued, "Doctrinal consensus has grown out of the historical and living experience of the Church in its worship and praise of the living God, in its continuing witness to the world, and in its concern for its evangelical mission to mankind."[72] This connection must not be missed. Historically, fidelity in dogmatics was connected to the church's worship practices and its advancement of the mission of God.

Likewise, the church's historical emphasis on baptism and the Lord's Supper points us to the preservation of the trinitarian faith. Torrance

---

69. Torrance, *The Trinitarian Faith*, 313.
70. Torrance, *The Trinitarian Faith*, 255.
71. Bonhoeffer, *Christ the Center*, 30–33.
72. Torrance, *Trinitarian Perspectives*, 114.

writes, "References to the Church, of course, were made in connection with baptism and the eucharist, and the traditional ordinances of divine worship, in which the oneness of the apostolic and catholic Church was everywhere taken for granted."[73] Torrance also argues,

> I believe, we learn far more about God as Father, Son and Holy Spirit, into whose Name we have been baptized, within the family and fellowship and living tradition of the Church than we can ever say: it becomes built into the structure of our souls and minds, and we know much more than we can ever tell. This is what happens evangelically and personally to us within the membership of the Church, the Body of Christ in the world, when through the transforming power of his Word and Spirit our minds become inwardly and intuitively adapted to know the living God.[74]

Finally, Torrance, who cared about these kinds of liturgical conversations from an ecumenical perspective, quoted Professor Nikos Nissiotis who taught at the University of Athens. Torrance states, "Even the worship of the Church is to be thought of primarily as the act of God in which the Father, answering the request of the Body of Christ Jesus his incarnate Son, sends his Holy Spirit—that is how Nikos interpreted the epiclesis of the Spirit."[75]

Conclusion

Torrance continually asserted that the Nicene faith or the trinitarian faith was preserved and communicated through the liturgical practices of the early church. Furthermore, he emphasized that the purpose of doctrinal fidelity was for the doxological and missiological life of the church. Doctrine shapes what we celebrate or more specifically, *who*. Therefore, it was critical that the early church clarify the doctrine of Trinity (theology proper, Christology, and pneumatology).

Finally, regarding the early church's worship of this Triune God, Torrance summarizes the disposition in which the work was done when

---

73. Torrance, *The Trinitarian Faith*, 255.

74. Torrance, *The Christian Doctrine of God*, 89.

75. Torrance, *Trinitarian Perspectives*, 106. Torrance states, "Nikos Nissiotis was one of the most outstanding theologians in the ecumenical world of our generation. He combined a distinctively modern mind with a profoundly informed grasp of Eastern Orthodox tradition." Torrance, *Trinitarian Perspectives*, 103.

he states, "With Gregory [Nazianzen] this had a more mystical and joyous quality bound up with liturgical worship which summoned into divine service his poetic instincts. For him worship of the Trinity was the only true and saving doctrine, in tune with the hymns and praises of God above but he could only give expression to his understanding of God with trembling in tongue and mind and thought."[76]

---

76. Torrance, *Trinitarian Perspectives*, 22-23; Gregory Nazianzen, *Oratio* 39.11; 43.30.

4

The Mediation of Christ

> Jesus Christ must be seen as the sole Prophet, Priest and King so that the entire life of the congregation must be seen as the Body of *Christ alone.*[1]

Introduction

To examine more fully the theological foundations of the Torrances' theology of worship, one must examine their Christology. It was their Christocentricism that gave the basis for their understanding of worship, particularly centered in the mediation of Christ. It is the objective of this chapter, to highlight the Torrances' understanding of worship, which was trinitarian precisely because it was Christocentric. T. F. Torrance writes:

> For theology as for worship, Jesus Christ is the *place* (τόπος) where God and man meet, where God stoops down to man and man draws near to God: the one place where we have access to the Father in the Spirit, the new and living way consecrated in the flesh of Christ. As such he is the one Mediator between God and man and man and God, the apostle from God to man and the High Priest of man before God, who in and through his divine-human constitution as the incarnate Son mediates the Word of God to man, the word of man to God, and ministers the immeasurable love of God to man and the answering love of man to God.[2]

1. Torrance, *Theology in Reconstruction*, 168.
2. Torrance, *Theology in Reconciliation*, 210.

The priesthood of Jesus Christ and his mediation were essential doctrines in the theology of T. F. Torrance. It is critical to understand his insistence that the saving humanity of Jesus Christ is at the center of the gospel. Furthermore, Torrance understood the liturgical dimension of Christ's mediation. This can be seen in this language from his lectures on the incarnation: "It was only because the influence of men like Irenaeus, Melito, Athanasius and Cyril of Jerusalem *remained on in the church, not least in the liturgy* in spite of its monophysite tendencies, that room was kept for the historical Jesus Christ *in the faith and worship of the church.*"[3] According to Torrance, patristic theology was by the church and for the church. Likewise, he made this connection between the mediation of Jesus Christ and the subject of liturgy in his exegesis of several biblical texts. For example, in *The Mediation of Christ*, Torrance states:

> Thus as in the Old Testament liturgy it is always God himself who provides the sacrifice whereby he draws near to the worshipper and draws the worshipper near to himself, so in the actualized liturgy of the life, death, resurrection and ascension of Jesus Christ, it is God himself who in atoning propitiation draws near to us and draws us near to himself.[4]

God is the provider of the sacrifice that enables the worshiper to draw near to his presence. It is the vicarious humanity of Jesus Christ that enables worshipers to draw near to God. Robert T. Walker states, "Jesus is not only the God *whom* we worship and the mediator *through whom* we worship, but the one *with whom* we worship, who as man offers perfect faith and worship and who is 'the pioneer and perfecter of our faith' and the leader of our worship."[5] Jesus Christ was not only the Savior of the world, he was the High Priest who made it possible for human beings to be in relationship with the living God.

Also to be noticed is Torrance's connection of the worship of Jesus Christ to the worship of Israel. Torrance writes, "And at the last in the fullness of time, the Word of God became man in Jesus, born of the Virgin Mary, within the embrace of Israel's faith and worship and expectation, himself God and man, in whom the covenanted relationship between God and Israel and through Israel with all humanity was gathered

---

3. Torrance and Walker (ed.), *Incarnation: The Person and Life of Christ*, 210.
4. Torrance, *The Mediation of Christ*, 110.
5. Torrance, Atonement, xliv.

up, transformed and fulfilled once for all."⁶ Torrance's inclusive emphasis, that in Christ, Israel's faith and worship and ultimately all of humanity's worship underwent a metamorphosis, being perfected in the man, Christ Jesus. Elmer Colyer states:

> The immediate focus of Torrance's theology is on Jesus Christ as Mediator (the soteriological-Christocentric center); Torrance's theology is fundamentally evangelical and Christocentric. The ultimate focus is on the Trinity, whereas the movement from the economic Trinity to the ontological Trinity provides Torrance's theology with its constitutive Trinitarian structure. Since theology and worship are intertwined throughout Torrance's work, his theology is also inherently doxological; theology is one aspect of the church's response to grace in obedience and worship.⁷

Colyer identifies the connection between Torrance's Christology, soteriology and liturgy; between Torrance's trinitarian theology (whether the economic Trinity or the ontological Trinity) and the doxological implications. The incarnation, and specifically the mediation of Christ Jesus, is ultimately a worship issue as Christ has on behalf of humanity fulfilled their response of worship and obedience.

Thrown Back upon Ourselves

T. F. Torrance argued that "the old dualism in a Neoplatonic and Ptolemaic form" was the very mind-set that hindered people from understanding worship from a christological trinitarian perspective.⁸ Torrance said that this radical dualistic structure was embedded in the Graeco-Roman world and polluted Christianity giving the church so much trouble with Gnosticism, Arianism, Monophysitism, and Nestorianism.⁹ Torrance states, "Dualism was actively brought back in a powerful theoretical form, in St. Augustine's far-reaching distinction between the *mundus intelligibilis* and the *mundus sensibilis*, reinforced by a somewhat Neo-Platonic and Ptolemaic outlook upon the universe, which came to be built into the whole fabric of western thought."¹⁰ Likewise, according to Torrance, a

6. Torrance, *The Mediation of Christ*, 9.
7. Colyer, *How to Read T. F. Torrance*, 25.
8. Torrance, *Theology in Reconciliation*, 131.
9. Torrance, *Theology in Reconciliation*, 130.
10. Torrance, *Theology in Reconciliation*, 31.

dualistic worldview has permeated the western liturgical understanding of prayer and worship.[11]

The Mediation of Christ

According to both T. F. Torrance and J. B. Torrance, it is impossible to understand the topic of worship, from a biblical or theological perspective, apart from understanding the need for mediation and the necessary role of a mediator. Torrance states, "The very repetition of the Old Testament liturgical sacrifices not only showed their essential imperfection, but was designed to produce *anamnesis* or remembrance of old sins, designed to keep the wounds of conscience open, so as to point forward to real forgiveness, final and actual atonement, and to the entering in of a better hope."[12] The Torrances argued that the worship of the triune God is not a system dependent on human invention. Rather, the worship of the living God is something that has been initiated by God himself. Robert T. Walker explains:

> Although the priest represents the people, the priest is appointed by God to represent them and not by the people themselves. The whole initiative and movement comes from God. There is no concept of man acting on God, let alone of man trying to appease God by sacrifice. It is God who forgives, who wills to forgive and who takes the initiative in forgiveness. . . . The basic concept of priesthood is represented by Moses and Aaron together and in that sense may be said to be a double priesthood, with Moses and Aaron together and in that sense may be said to be a double priesthood, with Moses as the "logos" priest, or priest of the word, and Aaron as the liturgical priest, the one who witnesses to the word of God and acts only on its basis and in obedience to it. Moses' priesthood is primary: his function is to mediate the word of God to the people, he receives the word of God and takes it to the people. In obedience to it he ordains Aaron as the liturgical priest, to act in witness to the word and at God's appointment to act in liturgical witness to God's will to forgive through the provision of sacrifice.[13]

T. F. Torrance writes, "But it seems to me that we cannot have a true understanding of worship, prayer, baptism and the Lord's Supper without

---

11. Torrance, *Atonement*, 456.
12. Torrance, *Atonement*, 80.
13. Torrance, *Atonement*, xliii.

a New Testament understanding of the priesthood of Christ."[14] Worship and the sacraments all require an understanding of the mediation of Christ. This is necessary to understanding how humans approach the living God. Furthermore, worship in essence is a response to the revelation of God. This too, has been addressed in the incarnation: God's mediation of revelation.

When discussing liturgical theology, issues of time, sacrament, symbol, and artistic expression are commonly the focal points. And while these elements are important, they are in fact important only as a secondary concern. The Torrances could have said much more about liturgical activity, as they were obviously aware of the liturgical aspects of their theology. However, they both seemed to be dealing more with the first order of things. Mediation is essential for worship to be efficacious. Human beings need vicarious representation. T. F. Torrance states:

> We can approach Jesus only as sinners who need the mediation of Christ in order to go to the Father, so that in the analogical relation set up between us and Christ, we can approach Christ only in acknowledging his uniqueness and sinlessness on the one hand, but on the other hand, only in yielding ourselves to him, in obedient conformity to his saving grace and as sinners desperately in need of him.[15]

Worship in the Old Testament required the mediation of the priests. Worship in the new covenant also requires mediation. According to Torrance, Christian worship is dependent on the vicarious humanity of Jesus Christ. Torrance argues, "As both God of God and man of man, Jesus Christ is the actual Mediator between God and man and man and God in all things, even in regard to space—time relations. He constitutes in Himself the rational and personal Medium in whom God meets man in his creaturely reality and brings man without, having to leave his creaturely reality, into communion with himself."[16] In Jesus, God comes to humanity as God and to God as man. According to the Torrances, Christ Jesus is both prophet and priest. He revealed God to humanity and represented humanity to God. Colyer states:

> Torrance emphasizes the God-humanward activity of the incarnate Son in the hypostatic union assuming, healing and atoning

14. J. B. Torrance, *Worship, Community and the Triune God of Grace*, 5.
15. Torrance, *Incarnation*, 11.
16. Torrance, *Incarnation*, 52.

for our diseased, broken, and sinful humanity in Christ's life, death and resurrection. Yet Torrance also stresses the human-Godward activity of Christ in his vicarious humanity, making the perfect human response to God in faith, conversion, worship, and obedience though not in such a way as to undermine, but rather undergird, the integrity of *our* human response in repentance, faith, worship and obedience.[17]

Again, while this emphasis on Christ's perfect response of faith, worship and obedience seems to be needed today, as mentioned in the last chapter, it really begs the question: what is the role of our human response? Both the Hebrew Bible and the New Testament are replete with imperatives for how we are to live: "In view of God's mercy, offer your bodies as a living sacrifice which is your spiritual act of worship" (Rom 12:1). The text does not say, Christ will do this for you; it says this is how you should then live. In response, both T. F. and J. B. Torrance would not say that human response is unimportant but that our human response is only possible because of the human response of the Human One. Because Christ Jesus responded perfectly, our imperfect response, vicariously, is also perfected.

First Movement of Mediation: God-Humanward

Regarding the mediation of revelation, T. F. Torrance stated: "In the Hebrew idiom revelation implies not only the uncovering of God but the uncovering of the ear and heart of man to receive revelation."[18] Employing communication theory as an illustration, Torrance was making a case that revelation was not only the encoding aspect of communication but the decoding dimension as well. Jesus Christ, in his incarnation, has provided both aspects. This is critical to understand for liturgical purposes since if worship is a response to the revelation of God, the question is whether or not human beings are capable of offering an adequate response. Torrance states, "Thus in Jesus Christ the mediation of divine Revelation and the Person of the Mediator perfectly coincide. In Jesus Christ God has given us a Revelation, which is identical with himself. Jesus Christ is the Revelation of God."[19] Jesus Christ comes to mediate

---

17. Colyer, *How to Read T. F. Torrance*, 28–29. Torrance, *Trinitarian Faith*, 4.
18. Torrance, *Mediation of Christ*, 11.
19. Torrance, *Mediation of Christ*, 23.

revelation to us. He shows us the Father. Jesus is the exact representation of the Father. He and the Father are one. Jesus said, "Do not believe me unless I do the works of my Father. But if I do them, even though you do not believe me, believe the works, that you may know and understand that the Father is in me, and I in the Father" (John 10:37–38). Jesus reveals the Father. Torrance proclaims, "We worship and adore Christ as very God of very God, for he is God, God incarnate. The relationship we have with Jesus is therefore identical to our relationship with God."[20] Torrance was explicitly stating that the relationship humanity has with Christ is the same as their relationship with God the Father. Robert T. Walker, in his editor's introduction to *Incarnation*, writes, "Torrance used to quote as one of the most important verses in the Bible, 'No one knows the Father except the Son and any one to whom the Son makes him known'. Only God can know God and only through God can God be known."[21] Torrance's theological epistemology is therefore centered in Christ. Although we cannot comprehend God, we can apprehend him and we have this knowledge of God precisely because of the incarnation. The man Jesus Christ reveals the Father to us. What could be more central to the subject of worship than knowing the One whom we worship?

Second Movement of Mediation: Human-Godward

Furthermore, our worship is a participation in the worship of Christ, the one who not only reveals the Father *to us* but also responds to the Father *for us*. In the book, *Theology in Reconstruction*, T. F. Torrance argued, "Jesus Christ is not only Word of God to man, but Believer. In his obedient life he yielded the perfect response of man to the divine revelation, which is that revelation in human form. Here the doctrine of *anhypostasia* and *enhypostasia* applied to the incarnation applies equally to our understanding of revelation."[22]

These two terms, *anhypostasia* and *enhypostasia* must be employed together. Regarding the term, *anhypostasia*, T. F. Torrance said, "Because of the assumption of humanity by the Son, Christ's human nature has its

---

20. Torrance, *Incarnation*, 187.

21. Torrance, *Incarnation*, xxxi. Note: Matthew 11:27 states, "All things have been handed over to me by my Father, and no one knows the Son except the Father, and no one knows the Father except the Son and anyone to whom the Son chooses to reveal him."

22. Torrance, *Theology in Reconstruction*, 131.

existence only in union with God, in God's Existence or personal mode of being (*hypostasis*). It does *not* possess it in and for itself—hence *anhypostasis* ('not person', i.e. no separate person)."[23] And regarding the term, *enhypostasia*, he stated, "Because of the assumption of humanity by the Son, the human nature of Christ is given existence in the existence of God, and co-exists in the divine existence or mode of being (*hypostasis*)—hence *en-hypostasia* ("person in," that is, real human person in the person of the Son)."[24] Cyril of Alexandria, in the fifth century, employed the term *anhypostasia* while Leontius of Jerusalem, in the sixth century addressed the implications of *enhypostasia*.[25]

Torrance repeatedly described how in the incarnation, Christ had met the requirements of the law by bending back the will of rebellious humanity and accomplishing what they could never do in their own strength:

> In Jesus Christ the Son of God entered into our rebellious humanity, laid hold of the human nature which we had alienated from the Father in disobedience and sin, and by living out from within it the life of the perfectly obedient Son he bent our human nature in himself back into obedience to the Father. Standing in our place, in life and in death, not only to be questioned but to give a faithful and true answer, he answered for us to God; even in his terrible descent into our God-forsakenness in which he plumbed the deepest depths of our estrangement and antagonism, he reconstructed and altered the existence of man, by yielding himself in perfect love and trust to the Father.[26]

Torrance argued that Jesus Christ, in his incarnation, not only revealed God to humanity but in the assumption of that humanity, took on flesh and acted in perfect obedience to the Father on behalf of the human race. Torrance argued that Jesus, in his active obedience, was converting human nature back to God. According to Torrance, Christ sanctified our sinful human nature from conception and birth and that humanity now

---

23. Torrance, *Incarnation*, 84.

24. Torrance, *Incarnation*, 84.

25. Although the term *enhypostasia* has been attributed to Leontius of Byzantium, Aaron Riches now argues that it should be attributed to Leontius of Jerusalem. Riches argues that although Cyril does not use the word, *enhypostasia* represents his doctrine, and traces the appearance of the word itself in John the Grammarian (early sixth century), Leontius of Jerusalem, Anastasias of Antioch and John of Damascus. See Riches. *Ecce Homo*, 107–18.

26. Torrance, *Theology in Reconstruction*, 126.

lives vicariously through the One who offered perfect obedience to the requirements of the law. Continuing on in his argument, Torrance writes:

> In revelation, therefore, we are not concerned simply with the *anhypostatic* revelation and with human response, but with *anhypostatic* revelation and true human response *enhypostatic* in the Word of revelation. We are not concerned simply with a divine revelation which demands from us all a human response, but with a divine revelation which already includes a true and appropriate and fully human response as part of its achievement for us and to us and in us.[27]

The issue that brings Christ's active obedience to the forefront is that in his humanity, Christ was responding to the will of the Father (bending back a rebellious human volition) vicariously on behalf of all of humanity. Therefore, we live vicariously through his sanctified humanity and his active obedience.

Christ in prayer and worship means that Christ is the one who offered prayer and worship in his humanity, *enhypostatically*, perfectly for all of humanity. His response was the true and appropriate response for them and in them. James Torrance emphasized that Christ as Mediator transformed our inadequate prayers into prayers that are offered to the Father and accepted in the name of Jesus Christ. James Torrance maintains:

> The first real step on the road to prayer is to recognize that none of us knows how to pray as we ought to. But as we bring our desires to God, we find that we have someone who is praying for us, with us, and in us. Thereby he teaches us to pray and motivates us to pray, and to pray in peace to the Lord. Jesus takes our prayers—our feeble, selfish, inarticulate prayers—he cleanses them, makes them his prayers, and in a "wonderful exchange" (*Mirifica commutatio—commercium admirabilis*) he makes his prayers our prayers and presents us to the Father as his dear children, crying: "Abba Father."[28]

This type of emphasis on the vicarious humanity of Jesus Christ is very different from merely referring to Christ in liturgical actions. Referencing Jesus as the object of worship in the liturgy, is still primarily focused on what *human beings* do, not what Christ has done. In contrast, T. F. Torrance argues that worship is primarily about what Jesus Christ

---

27. Torrance, *Theology in Reconstruction*, 126.
28. J. B. Torrance, *Worship, Community, and the Triune God of Grace*, 34–35.

has done and about being invited into Christ's relationship with the Father by the Spirit of God: "When we say that Christ is the object of our faith and worship, we do not simply say that we believe through Christ, as we might believe through a prophet. We do believe through him, and only through him, but through him as mediator who is himself God as well as man, and so we believe through him, and directly in him, as God himself."[29] Colyer states:

> It is in Jesus Christ that the eternal Son, who is ever *homoousios* with God the Father, has penetrated the perverted personal and interpersonal reality of our fallen and estranged humanity and made it his own. In assuming our disobedient humanity in rebellion against God, Christ converted it back to a true and faithful filial relation to God in love, obedience, holiness, trust and praise throughout his vicarious human being and life for us. Torrance maintains that the Word of God incarnate in Jesus Christ not only delivered humanity from subjugation to sin and alienation but also recreates humanity's relation to God by realizing perfect humanity on the earth, offering God the true human response to God on our behalf and in our place, which we cannot make for ourselves.[30]

Notice the emphasis in Colyer (and his reference to Torrance) that Christ assumed a fallen and estranged humanity and transformed it through both his incarnation and in his obedience. It was Jesus Christ who offered the worship that the rest of humanity failed to offer. James Torrance asserts, "For a proper understanding of prayer we need to recover the New Testament teaching about the sole priesthood of Christ—that we have someone who stands in for us to do for us and in us what we try to do and fail to do—someone who lives forever to intercede for us (Heb. 6:20; 7:25–28; 8:1:1–6) and who gives us the gift of the Spirit to share in his intercessions."[31]

Prayer and worship take place in the context of union with Christ and therefore, with the prayer and worship of Christ. Torrance argued that praying by the Spirit *through* and *with* the Son to the Father makes the prayers of the Body of Christ efficacious by means of having this *parakletos* come alongside (thus the emphasis of the preposition *with*). In 1 John 2:1, Jesus is the *parakletos*: "If anyone does sin, we have an

---

29. Torrance, *Incarnation*, 187.
30. Colyer, *How to Read T. F. Torrance*, 110.
31. J. B. Torrance, *Worship, Community, and the Triune God of Grace*, 35.

advocate with the Father, Jesus Christ the righteous." When humanity prays and worships, they are joining the Holy Spirit and the Son of God in prayer and worship. And as the result of participating in the prayer and worship of Jesus Christ, their prayer and worship is lifted up or adjusted to his offering. T. F. Torrance states, "It is as our Brother, wearing our humanity, that He has ascended, presenting Himself eternally before the face of the Father, and presenting us in Himself. As such He is not only our word to God but God's Word to us. Toward God He is our Advocate and High Priest, but toward man He is the acceptance of us in Himself."[32]

Christ's prayers represented perfect submission and obedience to the will of the Father. Torrance referred to this as his active obedience or perfect human response by means of his incarnation. His active obedience is active because Christ chose to obey the requirements of the law. One could ask, does all of this emphasis on the active obedience detract from the emphasis of Christ's passive obedience? Does an overemphasis on the incarnation unnecessarily dominate the emphasis of the cross of Christ? It appears that the Torrances would emphatically say, no; that to place a balanced emphasis on both the incarnation and the cross, on Christ's active obedience as well as his passive obedience, is in fact what is so desperately needed to protect us from interjecting a humanistic unitarian view into our theology of worship. David Torrance states:

> Emphasis upon the vicarious humanity of Christ and the fact that we are saved through his life as well as his death, has troubled many evangelicals. They mistakenly believe that speaking of Christ's vicarious humanity detracts from what took place on the cross. The very reverse is the case. By speaking of Jesus' vicarious humanity we actually are magnifying what Christ did in reconciling us to God. Christ's birth, life, death, resurrection and ascension belong intimately and inextricably together in the unity of his person and work. Christ's reconciling and atoning work began at Bethlehem in his becoming man for us, continued through his life and was brought to its great climax on the cross and in his resurrection and ascension.[33]

The Torrances believed that the atoning work of Christ began with the incarnation. "For God has done what the law, weakened by the flesh, could not do: by sending his own Son *in the likeness of sinful flesh*, and to deal with sin, he condemned sin in the flesh, so that the just requirement

---

32. Torrance, *Royal Priesthood*, 14–15.
33. Dawson, *An Introduction to Torrance Theology*, 5.

of the law might be fulfilled in us, who walk not according to the flesh but according to the Spirit (Rom 8:3–4; Heb 2:14–18)." The Torrances argued that Jesus assumed a real humanity (in the likeness of sinful flesh) and yet because of Christ's sanctified humanity in conception and birth and because of his faithful obedience, he was without sin.

> It is supremely in Jesus Christ that we see the double meaning of grace. Grace means that God gives himself to us as God, freely and unconditionally, to be worshipped and adored. But grace also means that God comes to us in Jesus Christ as man, to do for us and in us what we cannot do. He offered a life of perfect obedience and worship and prayer to the Father, that we might be drawn by the Spirit into communion with the Father, "through Jesus Christ our Lord."[34]

In contrast, E. Jerome Van Kuiken traces the defense of the unfallenness view among modern theologians such as Marcus Dods, A. B. Bruce, H. R. Mackintosh, Philip E. Hughes, and Donald Macleod.[35] Others such as Oliver Crisp also rejected the idea of Christ assuming a fallen humanity.[36] Van Kuiken states, "Torrance's pronominal choices are significant: it is always 'our' sin, guilt, and corruption which Christ bears, never 'his.' To Christ's own humanity Torrance attributes the fallen state's physical effects (e.g. mortality) and moral temptations, but never inward sin."[37] Torrance argued that although Christ was without sin, texts such as Romans 8:3–4 appear to teach that in his incarnation, Christ assumed a real humanity not an idealized humanity that merely provided an ethical example for humanity. The Torrances repeatedly made the case that Christ in assuming sinful flesh was bending back this estranged humanity in perfect obedience so that the just requirements of the law could be fulfilled in us. Torrance affirms, "The Word of God comes to us in the midst of our sin and darkness at once revealing and reconciling, but it comes with strong crying and tears, pressing its way through the speech of our fallen flesh, graciously assuming it in spite of all its inadequacy and faultiness and imperfection and giving it a holy perfection in the Word of

---

34. J. B. Torrance, *Worship, Community, and the Triune God of Grace*, 55.

35. Van Kuiken, *Christ's Humanity in Current and Ancient Controversy*, 59–90. Van Kuiken's book, based on his PhD thesis, is the fullest account of the Calvinist tradition, which opposed T. F. Torrance because they associated him with Edward Irving.

36. Crisp, "Did Christ have a Fallen Human Nature?"

37. Van Kuiken, *Christ's Humanity in Current and Ancient Controversy*, 35.

God."[38] This language of metamorphosis is emphasized in T. F. Torrance's Christology anchored in patristic theology. It was Gregory of Nazianzus who said, "What Christ has not assumed has not been healed but that which is united to his Godhead is saved."[39] The contribution for liturgical theology is that it is the worship *by* Christ, not only the worship *of* Christ that the Torrances are bringing to the forefront of the discussion.

In addition to his active obedience, his passive obedience (which was still critical) was the acceptable offering for worship on our behalf. "If anyone does sin, we have an advocate with the Father, Jesus Christ the righteous. He is the propitiation for our sins, and not for ours only but also for the sins of the whole world" (1 John 2:1–2). According to Torrance, the word *hilasmos* used here in 1 John 2:2 and in 1 John 4:10 refers not only to expiation but also propitiation. Torrance asserts, "Expiation refers to the atoning act through which reconciliation is effected, while propitiation refers to the personal healing and personal reconciliation effected. Propitiation in the Bible is initiated and carried through by God, both from the side of God toward man and from the side of man toward God."[40] Torrance's usage of propitiation focused on reconciliation, restoration, and renewal. This correlates with his overall doxological emphasis namely, that we live and worship vicariously through the faithfulness of Christ. T. F. Torrance states, "It is not too much to say, then, that the proper understanding of God as Father, Son and Holy Spirit takes place only within the movement of atoning propitiation whereby God draws near to us and draws us near to himself in believing response and brings us into union with himself through the gift of his Spirit, for it is only within that two-way movement of reconciling love that God's self-revelation to mankind attains its end."[41] Theologians such as Geoffrey W. Grogan have argued that avoidance of the subject of wrath, when speaking of propitiation, is out of line with how this term has been historically employed. The term "propitiation" from Grogan's perspective is related to penal substitutionary atonement.[42] Torrance, in contrast, understood propitiation in a relational sense not merely from a substitutionary atonement point of reference.

38. Torrance, *Theology in Reconstruction*, 139.

39. Gregory of Nazianzus—Epistle 101 in *Nicene and Post-Nicene Fathers*, Vol. 7, 440.

40. Torrance, *Atonement*, 460.

41. Torrance, *Mediation*, 110.

42. Grogan, *The Faith Once Entrusted to the Saints*, 83–128.

"Christ's atoning sacrifice must not be understood in purely legal or juridical categories as though Christ's death on the cross was to be interpreted purely in terms of Christ's suffering the penalty prescribed by the law of God."[43] While Torrance positively affirmed substitutionary atonement, he clearly was not an advocate of a narrow penal substitutionary theory, which focuses exclusively on the legal and judicial aspects of atonement. Torrance states,

> Satisfaction is not the divine satisfaction in death, as compensation for violated law, nor the divine satisfaction in the fulfillment of divine righteousness, but the satisfaction of the Father in the Son who has fulfilled the Father's good pleasure in making righteous atonement. Thus in the resurrection the Father owns Christ as his Son and acknowledges his deed in life and death as his own deed.[44]

Theological concepts such as expiation and propitiation have their historical-cultural context within a liturgical framework. "Propitiation is wholly from beginning to end the movement of God's forgiving and expiating love whereby in the initiative and freedom of his own divine being he acts both from the side of God and God toward man and from the side of man as man toward God."[45] Biblically, this is how the concept of worship was understood. Worship was not primarily concerned about praise music (as some contemporary popular writers seem to think) but was rather understood in the context of sacrifice and priestly duties. "Therefore, my friends, since we have confidence to enter the sanctuary by the blood of Jesus, by the new and living way that he opened for us through the curtain (that is, through his flesh), and since we have a great priest over the house of God, let us approach with a true heart in full assurance of faith, with our hearts sprinkled clean from an evil conscience and our bodies washed with pure water" (Hebrews 10:19–22). According to Torrance:

> Under the Old Testament liturgy there is a remembrance (*anamnesis*) of sin in ever repeated act of sacrifice, but here in the new covenant there is no remembrance of sin at all, and so the conscience is purged of its guilty conscience by the sprinkling of the blood of Christ upon it, as it is liturgically expressed.

---

43. Dawson, *An Introduction to Torrance Theology*, 6.
44. Torrance, *Atonement*, 215.
45. Torrance, *Mediation*, 110.

> Conscience is strictly our con-science, our *syn-eidesis* or knowing-with God, and when guilt is judged and removed and we are reconciled to God, our conscience with him is altered from enmity to peace. But this purging of a guilty conscience means also the sanctification of the believer; that is to say, the believer is put in relation of holiness to God, and so is dedicated or consecrated to God as a worshipper. By taking away guilt from their conscience Christ sets the believer free in a relation of rightness to holy God and before him so that they may worship him properly and freely.[46]

Furthermore, in his ascension, in addition to his incarnation, we understand our Lord to be functioning as mediator and High Priest. "Integral to Christ's efficacious priesthood is Christ as 'an everlasting intercessor' who, through his pleading obtains for us divine favor."[47] Jesus Christ lives to make intercession on our behalf. "Consequently he is able for all time to save those who approach God through him, since he always lives to make intercession for them" (Hebrews 7:25). This means that Jesus Christ is interceding on our behalf and offering for us the perfect sacrifice of prayer to the Father. In his lecture entitled, "The Mystery of Christ," T. F. Torrance argues:

> *Prothesis*, has another meaning as "setting forth," *pro-thesis* where it appears primarily to have a liturgical significance. Thus in the familiar passage in Romans, Paul speaks of our justification freely by grace through the redemption that is in Christ Jesus, "whom God set forth (*proetheto*) to be a propitiation (*hilasterion*) through faith in his blood to declare his righteousness . . . ." The language of Paul recalls the language of the Old Testament in Exodus and Leviticus, and the thought that it is at the mercy-seat, *hilasterion,* where the blood of the covenant is set forth in atonement, that God communes with his covenant people.[48]

Torrance is emphasizing that the mystery of Christ is the *prothesis*, which is the election of Christ. He explicitly states that the *prothesis* is the pre-destination or the eternal election moving into time in Christ the elect or beloved one, and reaching out to fulfillment and consummation

---

46. Torrance, *Atonement*, 92.
47. Ngien, *Gifted Response*, 152.
48. Torrance, *Incarnation*, 169. See Rom 3.24–25; Exod 25.17–22; 37.13–16; Lev 16.2, 13–16.

in the church as Christ's body, "the fullness of him who fills all in all."[49] Torrance sees the liturgical significance of this particular word. At the heart of God's relationship with Israel is one of unity, worship, and prayer. This in fact is the context, as well as the outcome, of the mediation of Christ according to T. F. Torrance and James Torrance.

Mediation of Reconciliation

According to T. F. Torrance, another aspect of mediation is the mediation of reconciliation. Human beings are incapable of reconciliation in view of their estrangement from the living God. "For if, while we were God's enemies, we were reconciled to him through the death of his Son, how much more, having been reconciled, shall we be saved through his life!" (Rom 5:10). Paul asserts that humanity's reconciliation was established by what the Son has done, not what it had done. This is the way Torrance interpreted Paul:

> Perhaps the most fundamental truth which we have to learn in the Christian Church, or rather relearn since we have suppressed it, is that the Incarnation was the coming of God to save us in the heart of our fallen and depraved humanity, where humanity is at its wickedest in its enmity and violence against the reconciling love of God. That is to say, the Incarnation is to be understood as the coming of God to take upon himself our fallen human nature, our actual human existence laden with sin and guilt, our humanity diseased in mind and soul in its estrangement or alienation from the Creator. This is a doctrine found everywhere in the early Church in the first five centuries, expressed again and again in the terms that the whole man had to be assumed by Christ in the whole man was to be saved, that the unassumed is unhealed, or that what God has not taken up in Christ is not saved. The sharp point of those formulations of this truth lay in the fact that it is the alienated mind of man that God had laid hold of in Jesus Christ in order to redeem it and effect reconciliation deep within the rational center of human being.[50]

As previously mentioned, one of Torrance's theological characteristics is his emphasis on the active obedience of Jesus Christ. While Torrance most certainly did not dismiss the importance of the cross, the

---

49. Torrance, *Incarnation*, 168–69.
50. Torrance, *Mediation*, 39.

emphasis in his writings was that it was in the incarnation that God came into the midst of our depravity to save us. He further asserted that *in the incarnation* God takes upon himself humanity's fallen human nature, with its diseased mind and soul. It is at this very point that Torrance frequently appeals to the church fathers such as Athanasius and Gregory of Nazianzus. The statements "the assumed is unhealed" and "He ministered the things of God to man and the things of man to God"[51] are critical to Torrance's understanding of what kind of humanity Jesus assumed. Torrance argues in a lecture on the incarnation:

> One thing should be abundantly clear, that if Jesus Christ did not assume our fallen flesh, our fallen humanity, then our fallen humanity is untouched by his work—for "the unassumed is the unredeemed," as Gregory Nazianzen put it. Patristic theology, especially as we see it expounded in the great Athanasius, makes a great deal of the fact that he who knew no sin became sin for us, exchanging his riches for our poverty, his perfection for our imperfection, his incorruption for our corruption, his eternal life for our mortality. Thus Christ took from Mary a corruptible and mortal body in order that he might take our sin, judge and condemn it in the flesh, and so assume our human nature as we have it in the fallen world that he might heal, sanctify and redeem it.[52]

The point that Torrance is making is that unless a fallen, broken and estranged humanity was assumed, there is no reconciliation in the incarnation. On the other hand, if Jesus Christ did in fact assume fallen humanity within the incarnation, dynamically not statically, this is the humanity that he was bending back in obedience to the will of God. Reconciliation was effected deep within the depths of humanity. It is important to capture Torrance's emphasis on estrangement and alienation. Before the incarnation, humanity was not only sinful and fallen but also alienated from God according to the Torrance:

> If the Incarnation is not held to mean that the Son of God penetrated into and appropriated our alienated, fallen, sinful human nature, then atoning and sanctifying reconciliation can be understood only in terms of external relations between Jesus Christ and sinners. That is why in western Christianity the

---

51. Torrance, *Mediation*, 73. Gregory of Nazianzus, Epistle 101 (Nicene and Post-Nicene Fathers, Vol. 7), 440. Athanasius, *Contra Arianus*, 3.39f; 4.7f.

52. Torrance, *Incarnation*, 62.

atonement tends to be interpreted almost exclusively in terms of external forensic relations as a judicial transaction in the transference of the penalty for sin from the sinner to the sin-bearer. In the biblical and early patristic tradition, however, as we have seen, the Incarnation and the atonement are internally linked, for atoning expiation and propitiation are worked out in the ontological depths of human being, and existence into which the Son of God penetrated as the Son of Mary. The genealogy of Jesus recorded in the Gospel according to St. Matthew showed that Jesus was incorporated into a long line of sinners the wickedness of which the Bible does not cover up, but, as we have seen, he made the generation of humanity his very own, summing up in himself our sinful stock, precisely in order to forgive, heal and sanctify it in himself.[53]

Torrance's soteriological concern is the union of the incarnation and the atonement. When one separates the incarnation from the atonement, according to T. F. Torrance, atonement is seen in exclusively forensic terms. According to this view, the sin of humanity was transferred to the Righteous One while the righteousness of Christ was transferred to the ungodly (and within the doctrine of limited atonement within Federal Calvinism, this righteousness was imputed exclusively to the elect). While Torrance would not dismiss that such a transaction did take place, he was adamantly opposed to the idea of limited atonement. Furthermore, according to Torrance, to avoid the idea of atonement being thought of in legal terms exclusively, the atonement had to take place in the incarnation if *mediation of reconciliation* was to be more than a legal requirement met. When atonement is emphasized without reference to the incarnation, James Torrance would say that it is still up to human beings to choose to respond if the payment is to be efficacious; the work is put back on our shoulders.[54] It really is about *our* response, *our* prayer, and *our* faith. According to Torrance, this is not good news at all, for at best, humanity's response is weak, inefficient and ineffective. T. F. Torrance writes:

> Liberal theology tends to reject the concept of substitution with contempt, and concentrates upon the historical Jesus, but, as we noted earlier, it regularly tends to lose the humanity of Jesus for what is important for it is not Jesus himself but what

---

53. Torrance, *Mediation*, 40–41.
54. J. B. Torrance, *Worship, Community, and the Triune God of Grace*, 18.

he symbolizes. Fundamentalist theology, on the other hand, readily accepts the idea of substitution, and concentrates upon the saving work of God in Jesus Christ, and again tends to lose the humanity of Jesus for the Incarnation is regarded as merely instrumental and not internally related in atonement. Both Liberals and Fundamentalists, however, react with a kind of shock when the humanity of Jesus and substitution are linked together for they have not a little difficulty with the idea that it is *as man* that Jesus Christ takes our place, acts on our behalf and in our stead, and that it is precisely *as man* that God himself comes to us in the Incarnation. It is at this very point that the Gospel seems to hurt most, for it cuts like a two-edged sword into our preconceived ideas.[55]

Now, in this reference, it is unclear who the liberals are that Torrance is referring to, whether it is Schleiermacher, Adolf Von Harnack, Rudolf Bultmann, or someone else. What is clear is what he is concerned about. Torrance would not support the idea that Jesus the Messiah was a myth. It is not clear which "fundamentalists" Torrance is referring to or whether he may be referring to "conservative evangelicals" such as Martyn Lloyd-Jones, John Stott, and J. I. Packer. But it is worth noting that his friend Billy Graham was numbered with the conservative evangelicals. However, what is clear is that he is concerned about the separation of the atonement from the incarnation. This is precisely the point that T. F. Torrance made: the person of Christ cannot and should not be separated from the work of Christ. What both T. F. and J. B. Torrance repeatedly emphasized was that a response was made for humanity in the incarnation. Jesus assumed a real fallen humanity, yet without sinning himself, and in that assumption of humanity, he transformed it from within offering back to God the perfect obedience that humans have failed to offer. This is mediation of reconciliation: active obedience along with passive obedience; incarnation and atonement.

Torrance's emphasis on the mediation of reconciliation includes a comprehensive understanding of God's inclusion of Israel. This is a very important point from a liturgical perspective for Torrance argues that Christ assumes all of Israel's faltering worship and perfects it in his incarnation and atonement. "Even if Israel persists in adulterating its relationship with God, he will not divorce Israel, for the bonds of God's steadfast love retain their hold upon Israel and lock it into a relationship with God

---

55. Torrance, *Mediation*, 81.

which will finally triumph over all estrangement and bring about reconciliation and peace."[56] This means that it is critical to understand God's heart for Israel and his work of engrafting the gentiles into a work that he is already doing with Israel.

> Thus as in the Old Testament liturgy it is always God himself who provides the service whereby he draws near to the worshipper and draws the worshipper near to himself, so in the actualized liturgy of the life, death, resurrection and ascension of Jesus Christ, it is God himself who in atoning propitiation draws near to us and draws us near to himself. God does not love us, Calvin once wrote, because he has reconciled us to himself; it is because he loved us that he has reconciled us to himself.[57]

Here, T. F. Torrance made the explicit connection between the liturgy of the Old Testament (which was specifically about the relationship of God and his people) and the liturgy of the Christ events, which happened in space and time for the purpose of drawing humanity into a relationship with the living God. This is all about the connection of the liturgical acts of Christ Jesus and his reconciliation of the world to himself. If God is reconciling the world to himself in the liturgical acts of Christ Jesus, what do we do with the many passages that require women and men to believe in Christ Jesus? While Torrance's view is worth appreciation, there are many texts in the New Testament such as John 1:12 that place an emphasis not on the vicarious humanity of Christ but on the response of the believer. In a desire to respond to this concern, James Torrance states:

> Because of what he had done and is doing for us in our name, we worship the Father in Christ as well as through Christ, *en christo* as well as *dia christon*. As Calvin said also of justification, we are righteous in Christ, as well as justified by faith through the work of Christ. Jesus is the Mediator of the new covenant, the one in whom God draws near to humanity in covenant love and the one in whom we draw near to God through the Spirit. In worship we offer ourselves to the Father "in the name of Christ" because he has already in our name made the one true offering to the Father, the offering by which he has sanctified for all time those who come to God by him (Heb. 10:10,14), and because he

---

56. Torrance, *Mediation*, 27.

57. Torrance, *Mediation*, 110; J. B. Torrance, *Worship, Community, and the Triune God of Grace*, 35–40.

ever lives to intercede for us in our name. The covenant between God and humanity is concentrated in his person.[58]

J. B. Torrance is saying that we *do* offer ourselves in worship to the Father in the name of Jesus, but only because he has offered himself on our behalf. T. F. Torrance is saying in another way that we only love because He first loved us. But as it pertains to worship, the argument is that we as human beings do in fact offer ourselves to the Father through Christ, but only because the mediation of Christ is in place. Without the offering and mediation of Christ, the Torrances are stating that our offering would be "ineffective". T. F. Torrance states:

> He came, rather, to penetrate into the innermost existence of Israel in such a way as to gather up its religious and historical dialogue with God into himself, to make its partnership and its conflict with God his own, precisely as they moved to their climax with the Incarnation, and thus in and through Israel to strike at the very root of evil in the enmity of the human heart to God. He came to grapple with evil, therefore, at the very point where under the unrelenting pressure of the self-giving presence and love of God to mankind it was forced to uncover itself in the crucifixion of the incarnate Son of God, and then to deal with it decisively in atoning sacrifice. Thus it is through the weakness of the man on the Cross and on the ground of reconciliation wrought out there that God meets, suffers, and triumphs over the enmity entrenched in human existence and history and over its distortion of the socio-political patterns of human life.[59]

What is worth pointing out at this point is his connection to the religious dialogue of Israel and how Christ came into this aspect of Israel's relationship with God. Israel's liturgical life is critical to understanding the history of Israel. Altars, tabernacles, and temples, in addition to being the places where sacrifices occurred, were for the purpose of meeting with God. Liturgy was part and partial to the religious life of Israel. Israel's feasts were centered on the rhythm of the year so that Israel would not forget what God had done for them. In time, Jesus the Messiah arrived to offer the perfect response of worship on behalf of mankind, thus reconciling the estranged, both Jew and gentile, with the living God. Torrance asserts:

---

58. J. B. Torrance, *Worship, Community, and the Triune God of Grace*, 40.
59. Torrance, *Mediation*, 31.

Christ is priest and oblation in one. Atonement is Christ's self-offering. That unity of person and work, of priest and sacrifice in him, means the final end of all ritual sacrificing. The self-offering of Christ is through the eternal Spirit and is therefore eternal. It is once and for all (*hapax* and *aphapax*)—that is, once for all both in the historical sense and in the eternal sense, but it is in the combination of the two senses that the finality of atonement is really consummated.[60]

Torrance viewed the ancient liturgy of Israel for the Day of Atonement (Yom Kippur) as pointing forward to Christ. In that liturgy one goat is sacrificed within the Holy Place, whereas a second goat is driven away alive into the wilderness carrying the iniquities of Israel confessed over it by the high priest. Torrance argued that we have to keep both sacrifices in mind if we are to understand what God has done for us in Jesus Christ.

Jesus Christ was vicariously baptized at the Jordan River and consecrated as Lamb of God to bear the sin of the world. He was immediately driven by the Spirit into the desert like the scapegoat under the burden of our sin and tempted by the forces of darkness to abandon his mission as the suffering servant. Throughout his ministry Jesus was oppressed and afflicted, despised and rejected, reckoned with sinners and cut off from the land of the living. Yet he was pierced for our transgressions, crushed for our iniquities, for the Lord laid on him the sin and guilt of us all (Isaiah 53). Colyer argues that Torrance finds both sacrifices from the ancient liturgy combined and fulfilled in the passion of Christ.[61] Christ was worshiping on behalf of humanity through these acts of faithfulness during his public ministry.

The Person of the Mediator

A further consideration that must be examined at this point is the person of the Mediator. There is what the mediator does and there is who the mediator is. In the theology of the Torrances, we must never separate the person of Christ from the work of Christ. Atonement is not just about what Christ did at Calvary. It is also about what he did through his incarnation. It is absolutely critical that there is an understanding of what

---

60. Torrance, *Atonement*, 81.
61. Colyer, *How to Read T. F. Torrance*, 69.

Christ came to do, mediate (both revelation and reconciliation), as well as an understanding *who* Christ was (one with the Father). Torrance wrote:

> First, knowledge of God the Father and knowledge of Jesus Christ the incarnate Son of the Father arise in us together, not one without the other. We do not know the Father apart from the Son, for there is no Father but the Father of the Son. Nor do we know any Son of God apart from the Father, for there is no Son of God but the Son of the Father. That is why the Creed speaks of one Lord Jesus Christ, the only begotten Son of God, begotten of the Father before all ages, begotten not made, by whom all things were made.[62]

If it is true that theology should result in doxology and that doxology informs theology, Torrance argued that it is imperative that there is an understanding that the revelation of Jesus Christ is the revelation of God. Jesus and the Father are one. In trinitarian language, when one speaks of the Father, one can only know God as Father because of God the Son. Torrance said,

> It is this identity between Mediation and Mediator in Jesus Christ who is God and man in his one indivisible Person that is so supremely important for us to grasp and hold on to, for the very essence of the Gospel is bound up with it. If we let go of that inner constitutive identity between Jesus Christ and God, or between the Person and either the word or Work of Christ, then our understanding of the gospel begins to disintegrate and finally collapses altogether.[63]

Torrance argued against the view that the gospel is solely about the work of Christ. He argued that when there is an understanding of the gospel exclusively as the work of Christ, one is primarily left with a forensic understanding of the gospel. However, when one keeps the person and the work of Christ together, a more comprehensive understanding of the gospel of Jesus Christ is put on display. Torrance asserts:

> If Jesus Christ really is the Son of God incarnate, if he is one with the very Being of God, then his word of forgiveness on earth is the very Word of God Almighty, a word with ultimate validity, backed up by the Power and Being of God himself, which accomplishes what it promises. Then forgiveness really is forgiveness.

---

62. Torrance, *Mediation*, 55.
63. Torrance, *Mediation*, 57.

But cut the bond of being between Jesus Christ and God, and the bottom falls out of the Gospel of forgiveness.[64]

Torrance is clear to state that if one separates the work of Christ from the person of Christ, then one will at best end up with a Jesus that is simply a good moral example. For example, the Son was incarnate, therefore the local church should be incarnational (a popular theme within missiology). Jesus came to liberate the marginalized; the church should work for liberation (Liberation Theology). Jesus loved and sacrificed for people; the church should love and sacrifice for people. Torrance states,

> If Jesus Christ is only morally related to God himself, then the best he can be is a kind of moral leader who through his own example in love and righteousness points us to a better moral relationship with the heavenly Father, while the atoning sacrifice made by Jesus Christ on the Cross can be understood only in terms of an external moral relationship, as a demonstration of the love of God or as some kind of judicial transaction between God and Jesus For the sake of mankind.[65]

It might be asked whether it is wrong to look to Jesus as a good moral example. Followers of Jesus Christ seek to imitate the life of Christ. The essence of discipleship is becoming like Christ in character and priority. When we look at the life of Christ and how he treated sinners, we also tend to ask ourselves whether or not we should follow his example. In Luke 10:25–37, Jesus told the parable of the Good Samaritan. He concluded his message with, "Go and do likewise." This seems to make a strong case for clear ethical behavior on the part of the disciples.

In response, the Torrances do not seem to be making a case for non-responsiveness of human beings to follow Jesus. They do not seem to say that because we live vicariously through the faithfulness of Jesus Christ that we can be inactive, non-responsive or worse, licentious. They seem to be saying that to view Jesus the Messiah as merely a moral example puts him into any other category of moral examples that would eventually solicit an ethical response from humanity. They are saying that the mission of Christ was more than an ethical mission. It was a rescue mission to do for humanity what humanity could not do for itself. Should this then solicit a response from humanity? The Torrances would argue:

---

64. Torrance, *Mediation*, 58.
65. Torrance, *Mediation*, 61.

of course it should, if one realizes the implication of what Christ has done for them.

The Mediation of Christ in our Human Response

T. F. Torrance states, "With its actual fulfillment in the incarnate life and self-offering of the Son of God, Jesus Christ embodied in himself in a vicarious form the response of human beings to God, so that all their worship and prayer to God henceforth became grounded and centered in him. In short, Jesus Christ in his own self-oblation to the Father *is* our worship and prayer in an acutely personalized form, so that it is only through him and with him and in him that we may draw near to God."[66] This is quite a claim that T. F. Torrance is making: that Jesus Christ in his own self-oblation to the Father provides the only means by which we can draw near to God the Father.

Torrance argued that Jesus in his incarnation was not only assuming humanity and purifying it but offering the perfect sacrifice of worship in his saving humanity on behalf of all mankind. He takes humanity's impure sacrifices and faltering worship and cleanses, offering the worship needed to draw near to the Father on behalf of all people.

Conclusion

In conclusion, the idea that Christ gathers all of humanity's faltering worship into himself and in his perfect obedience cleanses that which is unclean, and perfects that which is imperfect, permeates the Christology of both T. F. and J. B. Torrance. It is this particular emphasis that raises a new set of questions for liturgical theology: Is worship *for* Christ *by* the church? Or, is worship *by* Christ *for* the church? The Torrances argued, most emphatically, that it is the worship by Christ *for* humanity that makes the worship of Christ *by* humanity possible.

---

66. Torrance, *Mediation*, 87.

5

The Place of Jesus Christ in Liturgical Prayer and Worship

Introduction

IN THIS CHAPTER, WE will turn our attention the place of Jesus Christ in liturgical prayer and worship. What is new in this chapter is that we will examine how the early church prior to the fourth century recognized the mediation of Christ in prayer but how this was changed due to the Arian controversy. The mediated doxology was replaced with the coordinated doxology for the purpose of defending the deity of Christ. In time however, this led to a de-emphasis on the humanity of Christ and thus on the mediation of Christ. This was replaced with the veneration of saints, Mariology, and with ministers being referred to as priests for the first time in church history.

Anthropocentrism, Christocentrism, and the Liturgy

In a recent publication, Reformed theologian, Bryan Chapell emphasized the language of "Christ-Centered Worship." Chapell compared the following historic liturgies in a variety of charts throughout his book: Rome (The Roman Catholic Liturgy), Luther, Calvin, Westminster (The Westminster Assembly), and Robert G. Rayburn who sought a well-ordered evangelical service expressed in his book, *O Come, Let Us Worship*.[1]

---

1. Chapell, *Christ-Centered Worship*, 23–25.

According to Chapell, the worship service was "gospel-centred" if the liturgical structure had elements in the service that pointed to Christ.[2] While one can appreciate what Chapell attempted to do, for J. B. or T. F. Torrance, Chapell would not have gone far enough in getting to "gospel-centered worship." In practice, Chapell's emphasis was primarily about what we do: *our* prayers, *our* songs, *our* sermons, *our* structures. In the end, it is still anthropocentric. Another deficiency with Chapell's approach, while well-intentioned, is that he started with the liturgical structure of the Roman Catholic Liturgy and later with his unique selection of liturgical histories. Contrasting Luther with the Roman Mass, as a starting place for a discussion on Christian worship, misses hundreds of years of church history especially factoring in that Chapell's critique of the Roman Liturgy demonstrates very little research on the Roman Liturgy in and of itself. There was no reference to the early church's liturgies. Chapell does not mention earlier documents such as Justin Martyr's *Apology*, *The Apostolic Constitutions* or even the christological debates of the fourth and fifth centuries. He starts with the Council of Trent and for whatever reason, associates Justin Martyr and Constantinople with Roman Catholic liturgy.[3] Another criticism of Chapell's approach is not only does he start late in church history but when he does address the liturgy in the Reformation, he emphasized liturgical structure rather than Jesus Christ as the Ascended High Priest of all creation and the place of Jesus Christ leading the liturgy.

In contrast, J. B. Torrance, regarding the liturgies of the Reformation, focused on the subject of mediation and Jesus Christ, the Priest of all creation. He stated:

> It was the concern of the Reformers to recover this New Testament and early Christian view of worship. The medieval Church had tended to substitute the priesthood, the sacrifice, the merits, the intercession of the Church—the vicarious humanity of the ecclesia (Mary and the saints)—for the vicarious humanity of Christ in a way which obscured the gospel of grace, the good news of what God has done for us in Christ. The Reformers saw clearly the significance of the Pauline teaching about

---

2. Chapell, *Christ-Centered Worship*, 15–25.

3. Chapell states, "Before Trent, there were various strands of Catholic liturgy (associated with Justin Martyr, Augustine, Constantinople, etc.) too numerous to represent here in detail." Chapell, *Christ-Centered Worship*, 26.

justification—that we are freely accepted by God in Christ, not because of our "good works," but by God's grace received in faith.[4]

James Torrance pointed out a very significant issue regarding priesthood. When the priesthood of Christ was not central in the church, something else replaced this void. Historically, veneration of saints, Mariology, or the clergy became the mediators when the centrality of the Priesthood of Christ was absent. James Torrance continued to discuss why the centrality of the priesthood of Christ was important to the Reformers for the liturgy:

> They also saw clearly that in understanding worship, this meant that God does not accept us because we have offered worthy worship. In his love, he accepts us freely in the person of his beloved Son. It is he who in our name and on our behalf, in our humanity, has made the one offering to the Father which alone is acceptable to God for all humanity, for all nations, for all times. It is he who unites us with himself in the one Body, in his communion with the Father, and in his continuing intercessions. The real agent in worship, in a New Testament understanding, is Jesus Christ who leads us in our praises and prayers, "the one true minister of the sanctuary," the *leitourgos tōn hagiōn* (Heb. 8:1,2). He is the High Priest who by his one offering for himself for us on the cross, now leads us into the Holy of Holies, the holy presence of the Father, in Holy Communion.[5]

J. B. and T. F. Torrance addressed this more central issue of Christian liturgy: what is the role of Jesus Christ himself, as High Priest, in Christian worship?

Robert T. Walker states, "As high priest, Jesus Christ presents before the Father his once and for all offering of himself on our behalf and 'ever lives to make intercession' for his people. As the eternal leader of our intercession and himself our one true prayer, Jesus is the leader and mediator of the church's worship and prayer, a point central to Torrance's understanding of Christian liturgy and worship."[6] J. B. Torrance argued that worship is mediated through Jesus Christ, the High Priest of all creation:

---

4. J. B. Torrance, *Worship, Community, and the Triune God of Grace*, 10.
5. J. B. Torrance, *Worship, Community, and the Triune God of Grace*, 10.
6. Torrance, *Atonement*, liii.

> Jesus comes, as our Brother Man, to be our great High Priest that he might carry on his loving heart the joys, the sorrows, the prayers, the conflicts of all his creatures, that he might reconcile all things to God, that he might intercede for all nations as our eternal Mediator and Advocate, that he might stand in for us in the presence of his Father, when in our failure and bewilderment we don't know how to pray as we ought, and forget to pray.[7]

Torrance argued for the vicarious humanity of Jesus Christ; that in his faithfulness, he acts on our behalf; that as our great High Priest that he prays for us when we falter at prayer. James Torrance states:

> Calvin and Knox both constantly interpreted worship in terms of our Lord's High Priestly ministry over against mediaeval conception of the priesthood and Pelagian conceptions of grace. The sole Priesthood of Christ in the Church was their constant theme. So they spoke about justification in Christ, justification by the blood of Christ, for the content of grace is Jesus Christ, given to us by God to do for us what we can never worthily do, and they spelt this out in terms of worship and prayer. So they interpreted our Lord's high Priestly prayer in John 17, seeing behind it the liturgical symbolism of the Day of Atonement in Old Israel.[8]

Joseph Jungmann and The Place of Jesus Christ in Liturgical Prayer

J. B. Torrance's article, with its emphasis on the priesthood of Christ, probably borrowed the language for the title, from an influential book for both of the Torrances, *The Place of Jesus Christ in Liturgical Prayer* by Joseph Jungmann.[9] T. F. Torrance referenced this work in his essays about the importance of the mediation of Jesus Christ in worship.[10] For example, he referenced Jungmann fourteen times in the essays in his book *Theology in Reconciliation*.

---

7. J. B. Torrance, "The Place of Jesus Christ in Worship," in Anderson, *Theological Foundations for Ministry*, 348–49.

8. J. B. Torrance, "The Place of Jesus Christ in Worship," in Anderson, *Theological Foundations for Ministry*, 353.

9. Jungmann, *The Place of Jesus Christ in Liturgical Prayer*.

10. Torrance, "The Mind of Christ in Worship," in *Theology in Reconciliation*, 1975.

Torrance appealed to Jungmann when he discussed liturgical concerns within the ecumenical dialogues of the Roman Catholic with the Orthodox Church. In his essay entitled, "Ecumenism: A Reappraisal of its Significance, Past, Present and Future" Torrance writes:

> One further characteristic of the new Roman outlook must be mentioned, which applies even more to the Constitution on the Sacred Liturgy than the Constitution on the Church: The recovery of the sole mediatorship of Jesus Christ in every area of man's relations with the heavenly Father, but above all in the sacramental and liturgical life of the Church. Behind that lay the discovery, made by patristic and liturgical scholars (notably J. A. Jungmann) of the progressively diminishing place given to the human priesthood of Jesus in the development of the classical liturgies in East and West.[11]

Torrance proceeded to remind his readers of the historical context of Jungmann's concern. In the fourth century, there was a reaction from the church to the spread of Arianism in its negation of the full deity of Christ and its emphasis and attribution of Christ being nothing more than a mediator between the Creator and humanity.[12] Torrance's concern was at the heart of Jungmann's thesis: the sole mediatorship of Christ Jesus in every area pertaining to humanity's relationship to God the Father. This was the central concern of Joseph Jungmann's thesis: how this emphasis on the sole mediatorship was eclipsed due to a needed response to Arianism.

T. F. Torrance in his desire to emphasize the sole priesthood of Christ frequently instanced Jungmann as one who studied prayer and liturgy in the first centuries. Torrance stated, "Jungmann has shown that while from Apostolic times private prayers addressed to Christ were customary, and while the great tradition of trinitarian formulae in public prayer make it clear that Christ was worshiped and adored equally with the Father and the Holy Spirit, the Church with great unanimity kept to the rule of turning to God the Father, in liturgical prayer, through Christ the High Priest."[13] Torrance wanted the priesthood of Christ Jesus to be front and center of liturgical conversation. He found Jungmann to be a good historical source for his argument.

---

11. Torrance, *Theology in Reconciliation*, 62.
12. Torrance, *Theology in Reconciliation*, 62.
13. Torrance, *Theology in Reconciliation*, 114–15.

As T. F. Torrance moved through history into the Middle Ages, his concern was how the exclusive emphasis on the divinity of Christ and the under emphasis on the priesthood of Christ promoted an Apollinarianism in the liturgy. Once again, Torrance looks to Jungmann to undergird his concern when he said, "In the subsequent developments, right on into the Middle Ages and beyond, as Jungmann reveals, liturgical prayers addressed directly to Christ as God have the effect of thrusting him up into the awful mystery of Godhead, with the result that the humanity and mediatorship of Christ recede more and more into the background, and the poor creature at worship is confronted immediately with the overwhelming majesty of almighty God."[14] This theme of the co-ordinated doxology replacing the mediated doxology in reaction and response to Arianism will be more fully addressed below.

Torrance summed up the research of Jungmann and its influence on his theology when he stated,

> The general position has been well summed up by Jungmann. "Looking back over the first centuries of the Christian era we may come to this conclusion: to judge from all that survives in documents and accounts of the Church's life in this period, liturgical prayer, in regard to its form of address, keeps with considerable unanimity to the rule of turning to God (described repeatedly as the Father of Jesus Christ) through Christ the high priest, but in such a away that the scheme that came down from the Apostles was organically developed."[15]

Jungmann's liturgical theology is seen throughout the Torrances' liturgical theology. T. F. Torrance frequently turns to Jungmann to support his own emphasis on the need for the sole priesthood of Christ. In the same way that Torrance frequently cites Athanasius to support his theology of the *homoousion*, he likewise appeals to Jungmann as the scholar to pay attention to regarding liturgical theology in the early centuries.

The Place of Jesus Christ in Liturgical Prayer by Joseph Jungmann contains a historical account of how the Church employed the language of corporate prayer. It looks at the subject of liturgical prayer in the earliest documents such as *The Didache*, Justin Martyr's *Apology*, *The Canons of Hippolytus*, and *The Apostolic Constitutions*. Furthermore, it examines the subject of prayer from early Egyptian liturgies including the St. Mark

---

14. Torrance, *Theology in Reconciliation*, 116.
15. Torrance, *Theology in Reconciliation*, 188.

Liturgy, the Coptic Liturgy, the Ethiopian Liturgy as well as Syrian, Byzantine, Gallic, and Roman Liturgies.

In Part Two of his book, Jungmann focused on the history of the christological theme in liturgical prayer. He began his study in the New Testament, by asking the question, "Did Jesus himself have anything to say as to how we should pray?" His response was that Jesus taught his disciples to address God as Father in the Lord's Prayer (Matthew 6:9–13), and that he spoke of worshiping in spirit and truth when responding to the Samaritan woman (John 4:23f.). Jungmann attempted to clarify what spirit and truth meant from his perspective with a variety of texts: "If you abide in me, and my words abide in you, ask whatever you will, and it shall be done for you" (John 15:7) and "If you ask me anything in my name, I will do it" (John 14:14).[16] It must be noted, as a point of critique, that Jungmann does not offer extensive exposition of these isolated texts. He simply responded to the question of whether or not Jesus had something to say about how we should pray. If Jungmann's conclusions are not secure, Torrance's conclusions need to be questioned as well. Torrance does not appear to critique Jungmann on his exegesis but holds his theological conclusions as valid and correct.

Continuing on through the New Testament, Jungmann, reminded his readers of the prayer of St. Stephen: "Lord Jesus, receive my spirit; Lord, do not hold this sin against them" (Acts 7:59). Jungmann stated, "What was, indeed, more natural than that the first martyr should call on him for whose teaching he is about to give his life?"[17]

> Also Paul mentions that he turns at times to Christ in prayer. 1 Tim 1:12: "I thank him who has give me strength for this, Christ Jesus our Lord, because he judged me faithful by appointing me to his service." Since the "Lord" in Paul, outside quotations from the Septuagint, is always Christ, 2 Cor. 12:8 is also pertinent: "Three times I besought the Lord about this, that it (the messenger of Satan) should leave me"; probable also Acts 22:16, where the newly-converted is urged by Ananias "to call on his name."[18]

---

16. Jungmann, *The Place of Jesus Christ in Liturgical Prayer*, 128.
17. Jungmann, *The Place of Jesus Christ in Liturgical Prayer*, 130–31.
18. Jungmann, *The Place of Jesus Christ in Liturgical Prayer*, 131.

Jungmann then cited various mediation passages in the Epistle to the Hebrews pointing out that Jesus Christ is the great high priest by whom we draw near to God. This he applies to prayer.

After Jungmann reflected on the prayers in the New Testament, he dedicated an entire chapter to dealing with the development of the liturgy up until the fourth century. He pointed out that prayer was addressed to the Lord God "through Jesus Christ." Jungmann references the memorials of the period that were from the liturgical notes from pre-Nicene writings. Christ is referenced as the Mediator between God and man. Graham Redding, exposing Jungmann's influence on other theologians states, "Catherine LaCugna confirms, virtually all extant texts of the pre-Nicene Church, including the *Didache* and *the Church Order of Hippolytus*, are characterized by a mediatory pattern of prayer, especially in the *anaphoras* and doxologies."[19] LaCugna seemed to embrace Jungmann's perspective on the mediatorial doxology when she stated, "In general, the thanksgiving of the Eucharistic prayer was offered to God because of what God has done through Christ, and the praise giving of the doxological prayer is offered up to God through Christ."[20] Jungmann states, "The priesthood of Christ, which governs our actions and prayers, is mentioned quite frequently, especially in the writings of the earlier period, with a naturalness one would hardly expect—an indication that the idea was generally familiar."[21] As an example, "Bishop Polycarp of Smyrna ends his admonitions to the Philippians with the prayer: 'May the God and Father of our Lord Jesus Christ and he himself, the eternal high priest, the son of God, Jesus Christ, build you up in the faith.'"[22]

A criticism of Jungmann's argument regarding the sole priesthood of Christ being considered in the early prayers is that Hippolytus does mention the phrase "in the holy church" as an element in the doxology. The specific text is as follows, "Through thy Servant Jesus Christ our Lord, through whom be to Thee glory, might, honor, with the Holy Spirit *in the holy church* both now and always and world without end."[23] This puts an emphasis on ecclesiology not just Christology and liturgy. Hippolytus clearly mentions the role of the church in the effectiveness of prayer. Jungmann, however, is fully aware of this reference as well as a

---

19. Redding, *Prayer and the Priesthood of Christ*, 14.
20. LaCugna, *God for Us*, 114. Redding, *Prayer and the Priesthood of Christ*, 14.
21. Jungmann, *The Place of Jesus Christ in Liturgical Prayer*, 146.
22. Jungmann, *The Place of Jesus Christ in Liturgical Prayer*, 147.
23. Hippolytus, *The Apostolic Tradition of Hippolytus*, 35.

few other similar references such as the end of the first pseudo-Cyprianic prayer and the ending of the Latin martyrium of St. Ignatius.[24] Jungmann states, "The history of the *kerygmatic* summaries of the faith, which is bound up with the history of the creed, throws a remarkable light on this manner of developing the prayer-scheme by naming the Holy Spirit, or the Church, along with Christ the Mediator."[25] While this is a minor critique of Jungmann, this does not influence the usage of Jungmann in the liturgical theology of T. F. Torrance.

The Shift from the Mediated Doxology to the Co-Ordinated Doxology

Jungmann ultimately is intent on addressing the shift of the doxological language in the fourth century in the light of the Arian struggles. In order to combat the Arian heresy and to argue for the unity of the Trinity, the mediatorial doxology was replaced by the co-ordinated doxology. Sandra Fach states:

> In the early church, the Trinitarian nature of this praise was expressed in a doxology that reflected the mediatorial role of Christ: "Glory to the Father *through* the Son and in the Spirit." In his influential work, *The Place of Jesus Christ in Liturgical Prayer*, Josef Jungmann showed how, due to doctrinal controversy, the mediatorial expression of the church's worship faded into the background. To make a rather long and complex story short, the mediatorial structure of the church's prayer, expressed by the word "through," gave way to prayer simply "to" the Father, Son and Spirit. This was expressed in the so-called co-ordinated doxology: "Glory to the Father *with* the Son, together *with* the Holy Spirit."[26]

What is historically worth noting is that the mediatorial doxology was employed to emphasize the mediation of Christ; that humanity comes to the Father through Christ in the power of the Spirit. However, it was the Arian agenda to employ the mediatorial doxology to reinforce their cause of arguing for the subordination of Jesus Christ. This is why

---

24. Jungmann, *The Place of Jesus Christ in Liturgical Prayer*, 152.

25. Jungmann, *The Place of Jesus Christ in Liturgical Prayer*, 153.

26. Fach, "Worship as Thanksgiving," *Theology in Scotland* XVI—Special Edition, 42. Redding, *Prayer and the Priesthood of Christ*, 19; Jungmann, *The Place of Jesus Christ in Liturgical Prayer*, 194–95.

the co-ordinated doxology became the preferred doxology. There was the need in the fourth century to argue for the deity of Christ. Therefore we pray to the Father and the Son and the Holy Spirit. Graham Redding states:

> Of the anti-Arian doxology employed by the Church in the East, Jungmann has identified three different forms. The first form, which became dominant in the region of Antioch, offered glory "to the Father with Christ together with the Holy Spirit." The second form, which sought to combine the old and the new and which prevailed in Alexandria, gave glory to "our Lord Jesus Christ, through whom and with whom be to Thee glory together with the Holy Spirit." The third form, which arose in the Orient and was in wide usage around Byzantium, was modeled after the words of baptism derived from Matthew 28:19, in which glory is offered "to the Father and to the Son and to the Holy Spirit." Jungmann notes that this third formula, which became connected with the psalmody, was employed by the Western Church, where it still prevails: *Gloria Patri et Filio et Spiritui Sancto*.[27]

In her essay entitled, "Worship as Thanksgiving," Sandra Fach gives the context for the doctrinal controversy that is raised above. In the fourth century, the church was responding to Arianism and consequently, was defending the full divinity of Christ. What Jungmann does is analyze how the doxologies were developing before and after the fourth century. Fach states, "For the Arians, 'through Christ' was interpreted according to their understanding of Christ as a third thing, a *tertium quid*, between humanity and God. In reaction, Athanasius and others argued for the unity of God's action, affirming that there is one divine activity in which all three persons share."[28] Regarding this specific situation, Jungmann stated, "To an Arian it was the same in the end whether one said: 'We praise God through Christ', or 'we praise the Father through the Son'. In either case it could only be the Son, the Logos as such, who was here subordinated to the Father."[29] For the Arians, the focus was not on the mediation of Christ but on the subordination of Christ. Employing the preposition "through" was a means of emphasizing subordination for the Arians. The earlier

---

27. Redding, *Prayer and the Priesthood of Christ*, 19; Jungmann. *The Early Liturgy*, 194–95.

28. Fach, "Worship as Thanksgiving," 42.

29. Jungmann, *The Place of Jesus Christ in Liturgical Prayer*, 162.

connotation of the preposition *through* (the emphasis of mediation and the priesthood of Christ) was eclipsed. T. F. Torrance states:

> When earlier in the fourth century Arians had argued for the creatureliness of the Son on the ground of his poverty and weakness, and his need to offer obedience and prayer to the Father, Athanasius had shown that this belongs to the heart of his saving economy which the incarnate Son undertook for our sake, including obedient sonship in the flesh and human prayer and worship offered to the Father. When Arians had stressed the mediatorial position and role of Christ, arguing that the Son or Logos was only an intermediary, not ultimately divine but the first of God's creatures appointed to exercise a mediating function between the majesty of God and the rest of the creation, Athanasius showed that while the Son or Logos was internal to the Being of God, and therefore co-eternal and co-essential with him, his mediatorial life and work in Jesus Christ results from his condescension to be our High Priest, Advocate and Mediator, and must be understood thereof in terms of what he came to undertake for our sake, on our behalf, and in our place, in effecting atoning reconciliation with God.[30]

What of course is revealing is how the Arians re-interpreted the mediated doxology and employed it for their own purposes, namely that Christ was only an intermediary and not deity. This is what Athanasius contended with in the fourth century. The issue that was central was the deity of Christ. That was the primary concern. T. F. Torrance writes:

> According to Arianism, "there was a time when the Son was not," for as the Logos—Son he was only the first albeit the highest of God's creatures, through whom God made all else. Hence the regular practice of the ancient Catholic Church, reinforced by several Councils in the West, of directing all public liturgical prayer to the Father through the Son (who was nevertheless equally adorable with the Father and the Spirit in the Holy Trinity) began to be played down. At the same time liturgical prayer began to be directed more and more immediately to the Son as God, that is only receiver and not also as mediator of prayer, so that there developed a kind of "liturgical monophysitism"—the human priesthood of Jesus became obscured by the majesty of his Deity, so that inevitably some third factor tended to be interposed between the suppliant and his Savior, which affected the Roman Church's understanding both of its own priesthood and

---

30. Torrance, *Theology in Reconciliation*, 115.

of the Eucharistic Sacrifice at the very points where the Reformation had called for reform in the sixteenth century.³¹

For those who could not affirm the unity of God's action, the mediatorial doxology was preferable. If they employed the mediatorial doxology, they would implicitly be making a case against the unity of God's action. In contrast, if they employed the co-ordinated doxology they would be agreeing with Athanasius that there was one divine activity shared by all three persons. Fach points out that St. Basil the Great employed both doxologies and in so doing so was accused of confusion and heresy.³² Eventually, because of the pressure of heresy, the mediatorial doxology all but disappeared. The emphasis on the full divinity was what was most important.³³ Graham Redding (citing Jungmann at the end) states: As the mediatorship and humanity of Christ faded into the background and Christ was thrust up into the majesty and grandeur of the Godhead, a gap emerged and came to yawn large in the Christian thinking between the eternal God and sinful humanity. The worshiper was confronted immediately with the overwhelming majesty of the triune God. "Stress was now placed not on what unites us to God (Christ as one of us in his human nature, Christ as our brother), but on what separates us from God (God's infinite majesty)."³⁴

Redding accurately summarized Jungmann's concern about the mediatorial aspect of the doxology being removed. When the people of God ceased praying to the Father *through* and *with* the Son, the issue of mediated worship became a void that needed to be addressed. Praying *through* the Son became praying *to* the Son or Glory to the Father *with* the Son, together *with* the Holy Spirit. Catherine Mowry LaCugna also captures and summarizes the changes taking place in the doxology, referencing Jungmann:

> The liturgical development might be charted in this way. Initially praise was given to God through Christ. Then, as the Arian controversies took hold, praise was directed to God (or Father) through Christ in the Holy Spirit (with the church); to

---

31. Torrance, *Theology in Reconciliation*, 62–63.
32. Fach, "Worship as Thanksgiving," 42.
33. This is the context in which to read Torrance's essay, "The Mind of Christ in Worship: The Problem of Apollinarianism in the Liturgy."
34. Redding, *Prayer and the Priesthood of Christ in the Reformed Tradition*, 20; Fach, "Worship as Thanksgiving," 43; Jungmann, *The Place of Jesus Christ in Liturgical Prayer*, 251.

the Father through the Son in the Holy Spirit; to the Father and Son together with the Holy Spirit; to the Father, through Christ and in Christ, in the Holy Spirit; to the Father and the Son and the Holy Spirit.[35]

The co-ordinated doxology in time eclipsed the mediated doxology. And with the change came the de-emphasis of Christ being mediator. LaCugna further argues:

> Christ's human mediation has become divine intervention; the adopted Son has come incarnate God. The praise of God through the only-begotten Son has become the praise of God the Son. Likewise, the Spirit who makes possible the praise of God becomes an object of praise, worshipped and glorified together with the Father and the Son.[36]

While advocating the full divinity of Jesus Christ was essential in the fourth century, one could say that fighting one heresy inadvertently led to producing another. Torrance writes:

> The application of the *homoousia* to Christ and the Holy Spirit arose out of and implied their equal adorability with the Father. But in the prolonged struggles against Arianism, with its notion of the Logos or Son as a semi-divine intermediary between God and the creation, there steadily grew up in reaction the practice of public prayer deliberately directed to Christ became so pushed into the sheer majesty of God that worshipers lost sight of his humanity in its vicarious and priestly role in human worship of the Father. According to Jungmann this is particularly evident in the medieval liturgies, in which there grew up a one-sided emphasis upon awe and fear in the presence of Christ, so that something had to be interposed between him and the sinner. The mass itself and the officiating priest tended to take the place of Christ, a development which as adversely affected the subsequently understanding of public prayer and worship.[37]

Lack of Mediated Doxology Produced a Spirit of Fear

Removing the mediatorial doxology was problematic in that it produced a spirit of fear. When one removes Christ as mediator in liturgical prayer,

35. LaCugna, *God for Us*, 127.
36. LaCugna, *God for Us*, 127.
37. Torrance, *Theology in Reconciliation*, 287.

mediation must still happen for humanity to approach God Almighty. Without a mediator there is a subversive spirit of fear in the human heart as the result of encountering the majesty of God. Graham Redding states:

> Jungmann detects a subtle but significant change in liturgical language around this time, calculated to inspire awe and fear in the recipient. A chapter in Basil's Shorter Rule, for example, is captioned, "With what fear . . . we ought to receive the Body and Blood of Christ." And John Chrysostom speaks about "the terrible sacrifice," about the "shuddering hour" when the mysteries are accomplished, and about the "terrible and awful table."[38]

This issue of worshiping in fear was unfortunate in that Christ's mediation was to make a way for humanity to come into the presence of God without fear. One is reminded of the text from the Epistle to the Hebrews where the author states, "Let us then approach God's throne of grace with confidence, so that we may receive mercy and find grace to help us in our time of need" (Hebrews 4:16). However, if there is no mediator, this task is indeed impossible. Torrance states:

> There took place a decided shift in the worship and theology of the Church in which Christ was identified with the majesty and power of Almighty God in such a way that the conception of his vicarious human priesthood tended to fade out of the worship and theology of the Church, with the result that the poor creature was confronted immediately with the overwhelming majesty of God inducing fear in the human heart.[39]

Graham Redding writes, "The impact of this injection of fear into the eucharistic liturgy is to be seen in the sharp drop in the reception of communion during the fourth century."[40] While confession of sin and the pronouncement of the forgiveness, often precedes the Lord's Supper, without the awareness of the priesthood of Christ, there remained a subversive fear within the heart of the worshiper. Torrance states:

> As the mediatorship and humanity of Christ recede into the background, the poor creature is confronted immediately with the overwhelming majesty of God. In the West, however especially in the mediaeval liturgies, this took on a somewhat

---

38. Redding, 20; Basil, *Reg. Brev. Tract.*172 (PG 31, 1195), cited in Jungmann. *The Early Liturgy*, 196–97.

39. Torrance, *The Royal Priesthood*, xi–xii

40. Redding, *Prayer and the Priesthood of Christ*, 20.

different aspect, for the fear and trembling, indeed the agitation and horror of the soul at presence of the divine Victim on the altar, the real presence of God in the Body and Blood of Christ in the Mass, was not relieved as in the East by an exultant doxology in the risen Christ running through the whole celebration, or by an understanding of the Eucharist Sacrifice as absorbed in the once and for all ascension and self-presentation of Christ to the Father.[41]

This fear of the majesty of God could only be addressed by understanding the role of Christ as High Priest and Mediator. Torrance, employing Jungmann's thesis, argues that this change of language was devastating for the liturgy. Historically, when the church attempts to address doctrinal error, there tends to be a pendulum dynamic where the response and reaction is so great that an anti-thetical error develops. An emphasis on the deity of Christ was necessary to address Arianism in the fourth century. However, as Torrance was pointing out, the response to emphasize the deity of Christ was so great that the humanity of Christ was then jeopardized. Every christological error is the result of not believing that Jesus Christ is fully God and fully man. Torrance reminds us:

> J. A. Jungmann directed attention to the fact that whereas in the early liturgies of the Church eucharistic prayer was regularly directed to the Father through Christ as the one Mediator between man and God, many centuries later, especially from the time of the Middle Ages, eucharistic prayers were directed mostly to Christ himself. Behind that transition lay a shift in theological emphasis which Jungmann traced back to the Church of the fourth century when in reaction to Arianism it sought to incorporate into the liturgies formal prayer addressed to Christ as God. The effect of the throughout the centuries was to thrust Christ up into the majesty and grandeur of the Godhead in such as way that it seriously diminished, and sometimes almost entirely eliminated, the ancient Biblical and Patristic stress upon the High Priesthood of Christ and his human mediation of prayer of the Father.[42]

---

41. Torrance, *Theology in Reconciliation*, 200.
42. Torrance, *Theology in Reconciliation*, 142.

Apollinarianism in the Liturgy

Apollinarianism in the liturgy was a problem for Torrance for several reasons. First of all, there was the theological displacement of Christ as High Priest and the significance of the subject of worship without the role of Christ as High Priest. When Christ is no longer a high priest, mediation is still required. This is fundamental to the subject of liturgy. Torrance argues:

> It is a curious fact that such a result could be reached from opposite roads, by Arianism and Apollinarianism: The one arguing for the creaturely status and servant nature of Christ, the other arguing against any degradation or contamination of the divine nature through the humiliation of the Son in assuming the form of a servant. That implies, however, that the reaction to Arianism of which Jungmann has written, precisely through stress upon the divine majesty of Christ, could easily provide orthodox cover for a similar error to creep in from Apollinarian presuppositions, namely, the transmutation of the human priesthood of Christ in the form of a servant into a divine priesthood in which Christ fulfills his mediatorship only as God.[43]

While Arianism threatened Christian liturgy with a Christology that denied the deity of Christ, Apollinarianism threatened Christian liturgy by denying the fully human mind of Christ. When the saving humanity of Christ was compromised, the doctrine of Christ being mediator was also denied. Torrance asserts:

> Jungmann's general conclusion as to what came over liturgical prayer in the East, Syrian as well as Greek, is convincing. However, suppression, weakening or abandonment of those text elements which make Christ appear as Mediator, especially as Mediator of the prayer, is common to the whole East. Instead, the majesty of the triune God, of the Father and the Son and the Holy Spirit, to whom in every prayer praise is offered, gains and new prominence as object of worship. Granted that the Arian assault has not changed the faith of the ancient Church, yet it has profoundly influenced, at first throughout the East, the use made in different facts of the faith in the religious and liturgical life. Hence it also became a remote cause of the particular

---

43. Torrance, *Theology in Reconciliation*, 196.

religious outlook that marks not only liturgical prayer but also the ecclesiastical art and culture of the Christian East.[44]

Torrance points out that Jungmann's concern was the history of liturgy not dogmatics per se. Jungmann was concerned with how doxological language was shifting in the early centuries by examining various liturgies. While he notes the Arian controversy in the fourth century, Torrance points out that Jungmann did not seem to realize the full impact of Apollinarianism in the next century. Torrance's primary theological concern with Apollinarianism can be detected in a statement such as this:

> As I have indicated, the rational culture of the ancient classical world found this [the need for healing in the ontological depths of our human mind and being] very difficult to accept, so that inevitably difficult problems arose whenever the gospel began to take root and find expression in Greek life and thought. Thus we find cropping up fairly early within the church an insidious heresy that came to be known as "Apollinarianism." It took its name from Apollinaris, a very clever theologian, who refused to believe that in his incarnation, the Son of God took upon himself our alienated twisted mind because it was in that mind that sin had become rooted and entrenched. If Jesus had taken our alienated mind upon himself, so argued Apollinaris, he must have been a sinner, in fact an original sinner. And so he held that the Son of God became incarnate in our human existence in such a way that in Jesus, the human mind was displaced by the divine mind. It was therefore some sort of neutral humanity that the Son of God assumed, and not the actual humanity in which we sinners all share.[45]

The previous section highlights Torrance's deep concern about Apollinarianism not just in the fifth century but also in the twentieth century by de-emphasizing the saving humanity of Jesus Christ; namely that Christ assumed the likeness of sinful flesh (Romans 8:3) *yet was without sin*. Torrance further argued his theological concern when he stated:

> The reaction to Arianism of which Jungmann has written, precisely through stress upon the divine majesty of Christ, could easily provide orthodox cover for a similar error to creep in from Apollinarian presuppositions, namely the transmutation of the human priesthood of Christ in the form of a servant into a

---

44. Torrance, *Theology in Reconciliation*, 196–97.
45. Torrance, *Atonement*, 439.

divine priesthood in which Christ fulfills his mediatorship only as God. From the perspective of such a development, one cannot but admire the shrewd theological discernment of Cyril in safeguarding the fact that Christ prays and worships the Father as one of us, with us and on our behalf, for it is there in the worship and prayer of the incarnate Son that we have the gateway into his whole ministry in the form of a servant, through which the saving economy in the flesh would finally be meaningless.[46]

Torrance's concerns regarding the impact of Apollinarianism on the liturgy is noted above. For both T. F. and J. B. Torrance, the doctrine of the humanity of Christ is fundamental to understanding their theological program and in the case of this thesis, their liturgical and doxological vision. For T. F. Torrance, this was also an issue of deep personal devotion:

> It was in order to conserve this biblical teaching that great patristic theologians in the early church enunciated as a fundamental principle, "*The unassumed is the unhealed*" (Gregory of Nazianzus), or "*What Christ has not assumed has not been saved*" (Cyril of Alexandria). They reckoned that the church would be soteriologically and evangelically deficient if it refused to take seriously that Christ took our fallen mind upon himself in order to redeem and save it. That is a truth which I first learned from my beloved Edinburgh teacher, H. R. Mackintosh, who had himself been profoundly influenced by the Christology of these Greek fathers. But it was only when I studied Karl Barth's account of this doctrine that its truth broke in upon my mind in a quite unforgettable way. I refer to that section in the *Church Dogmatics* 1.2 where Barth expounded the mystery of the virgin birth. Overwhelmed by the immense significance of what our Lord had done all for our sakes and in our place, I fell to the ground on my knees trembling in awe and wonder at the sheer miracle of God's grace in the birth, life, and passion of Jesus—the miracle that foul, wicked, depraved humanity twisted in upon itself, had been appropriated from us by the Son of God, and been cleansed, changed, redeemed, and sanctified in him.[47]

Without the saving humanity of Jesus Christ, we are left in a conundrum as to how to discuss the mediation of Christ and thus the role of Christ as our High Priest leading us in worship. Torrance, employing one of his heroes of the faith, Cyril of Alexandria, writes:

46. Torrance, *Theology in Reconciliation*, 196–97.
47. Torrance, *Atonement*, 441–42.

> Cyril thus brought together *proskynesis* and *latreia,* worship of God, in the strongest sense of worship, with *douleia,* to expound the servant ministry of Christ in our nature. In becoming man for our sake, Christ worshipped as man, in a voluntary obedience and lowliness, as an essential part of his saving economy. This worship, fulfilled in the flesh throughout Christ's life on earth and fulfilled in its heavenly mode in his heavenly priesthood, is always worship in spirit and in truth. Cyril goes out of his way to stress the noetic or mental, the spiritual and intellectual nature of this worship, in contrast to the legal and physical modes of worship found under the old covenant—a theme to which he devoted a whole book, *peri tes en pneumatic kai aletheia proskyneseos kai latreias.*[48]

The second reason Apollinarianism in the liturgy was problematic was the shift from the vicarious humanity of Jesus Christ to the responsibility for mediation being put on the shoulder of humanity itself set in motion a trajectory of mediation being the responsibility of the parish priest and institution of the church. Torrance said, "This was reflected in the change of language from *pontifex* to *sacerdos,* that is, away from Christ regarded as a bridge in his vicarious humanity between men and women and God to Christ as an omnipotent mediator of divine gifts from God to them." [49]

Mediation: From Christ to Clergy

When the responsibility for mediation was shifted from Christ to the rest of humanity, this created the need to place this responsibility upon local ministers of local parishes. Torrance writes:

> There arose a demand for other functionaries exercising a mediatorial ministry, to make up for the human priesthood of Christ, a priesthood which could stand in for Christ, mediate between the sinner and Christ, and which was endowed with power from Christ to act on his behalf and in his place and as *sacerdos* to dispense the gifts of divine grace and blessing entrusted to the institutional Church. Along with this change came a grave misunderstanding of the saving mission of Christ and the evangelical mission of the Church, and therefore of the way in which ministry or priesthood in the Church is exercised,

---

48. Torrance, *Theology in Reconciliation*, 113.
49. Torrance, *Theology in Reconciliation*, 113.

for a strong Pelagian element entered into the Roman conception of the eucharistic sacrifice and of the sacrificing activity of priesthood, as is very evident in the Tridentine doctrine of the sacrifice of the Roman mass.[50]

Torrance, referencing Jungmann, is arguing that the theology of the priesthood associated with the local parish and the Roman Mass had its inception at the very point that the human priesthood of Christ was removed from the liturgy. He says the institutional church created the priesthood (*sacerdos*) to mediate between humanity and Christ. Torrance then points out that both the saving mission of Jesus and the mission of the Church were misunderstood. Doctrinal decisions made at the Council of Trent (1545–63), especially at the twenty-fifth and last session, further demonstrate the loss of celebrating the sole priesthood of Christ such as the invocation of the saints and the veneration of relics being re-affirmed. Torrance states that the development of his kind of theology was already a problem long before the Council of Trent. Jungmann indeed does point out that up to the second century the overseers of the Christian communities preferred being known as overseers not as priests.[51] Jungmann writes:

> The functions of a ἱερεύς as commonly accepted by the Jews and pagans of the time were simply not met with by the Christians in their presbyters. The Jewish priest, in virtue of the divine commission, prayed, sacrificed and expounded the Law, and was truly a mediator between God and Israel. The priest of the Hellenistic pagans who served a particular shrine, where he had to ascertain the will of the deity and foretell the future, was likewise an independent middleman between the deity and the people. Both were regarded as mediators on account of their personal position and dignity. It was their special talent with which they tried to win God's benevolence. In Christianity, on the other hand, there was no human person exercising an independent mediation between heaven and earth. Here, only Christ could be called ἱερεύς and ἀρχιερεύς, and he was eminently worthy of the title, since he alone has a sacrifice to offer worthy of God. What the Christian presbyters do, they do only as his instruments and in his name. He is the priest, on whose behalf they perform the sacred act of the Eucharist; it is he who

---

50. Torrance, *Theology in Reconciliation*, 113.
51. Jungmann, *The Place of Jesus Christ in Liturgical Prayer*, 148.

is ever standing at the throne of God; it is through his hands that all offerings and prayers make their way to God.[52]

From Christ to Veneration of the Saints and Mariology

This vacuum for mediation in the fourth and fifth centuries not only brought about new pressures upon the ministers but also promoted veneration to the saints with the belief that they provided mediatorial powers between humanity and the living God. This also coincided with the rise of Mariology. Graham Redding states that according to Jungmann, the rise of the veneration of the saints along with Mariology was largely attributable to the church's struggle against Nestorianism in the fifth century.[53] This, however, was preceded in the fourth century with the fight against Arianism.

Criticisms

It must be noted that there are criticisms of Jungmann's work, primarily from Albert Gerhard's 1982 article, *Zu Wem Beten*?[54] Gerhard claimed that while Jungmann does adequately describe the Western church, he over-generalizes the Eastern church. Gerhard also criticizes Jungmann for drawing conclusions primarily from the *Church Order of Hippolytus* in that there were other liturgies from that period. It is probable that Jungmann would have taken issue with this criticism, for as one can see in the references above, he examined a variety of liturgies from that period.

Graham Redding, working with Albert Gerhard's material, also offers some criticism of Jungmann's thesis. Redding states, "While Jungmann's thesis is generally correct in relation to prayers made at the altar by the priest, it is not true in relation to prayers made elsewhere in the liturgy, including the hymns, where Christ was often regarded as the one to whom prayer should be directed."[55] While Redding has a good point, namely that there is more prayer taking place in any worship service than just at the altar, he does not cite specific examples of other aspects of the

---

52. Jungmann, *The Place of Jesus Christ in Liturgical Prayer*, 148.
53. Redding, *Prayer and the Priesthood of Christ*, 21.
54. Gerhards, "*Zu Wem Beten?*" ("*To Whom Do We Pray?*") *Liturgisches Jahrbuch* 32 (1982), 219–30, quoted by Redding, *Prayer and the Priesthood of Christ*, 22–23.
55. Redding, *Prayer and the Priesthood of Christ*, 23.

liturgy or specific hymns in his argument. Another criticism of Jungmann by Redding (again referencing material from Albert Gerhard) states that, "Arianism did not provide the impetus for a wholly new liturgical development, namely making Christ the object of prayer. Rather, it provided the impetus for giving great weight to one existing liturgical tradition over another."[56] What is challenging about Redding's comment is that the evidence that Jungmann puts forth, seems to outweigh this criticism. It is helpful to note that Redding states, "Gerhard does not reject Jungmann's thesis. Rather, he calls for it to be modified,"[57] But it seems that Gerhard's critique is at best ambiguous, void of offering specific recommendations.

Implications of Jungmann's Influence on Torrance

In light of Jungmann's influence on T. F. Torrance, what was Torrance's primary concern? Torrance was not just concerned with the theological implications of removing the mediatorial role of Jesus Christ in liturgical prayer. He was also concerned about the importance of placing Jesus Christ, as the leader of our worship, back in the center of liturgical consciousness. Torrance states:

> Prayer through the mediation of Jesus Christ the High Priest in the full sense, gives place to prayer on the basis of the high priestly work of Christ.... The reason for this, however, is to be found not only, as Jungmann implies, in the Cappadocian reaction to Arianism, but in a comparatively underdeveloped understanding of the vicarious role of the incarnate Son along the line that runs from Athanasius to Cyril, together with a further development of the doctrine of the Trinity as three *hypostaseis* in one *ousia* in respect of the co-equality of the Son and the spirit with the Father, which resulted in an overshadowing of the mediatorial aspect of prayer by the doxological.[58]

For Torrance, Jesus Christ must not only be the reference point of our worship activities but *the leader* of our worship as High Priest.

---

56. Redding, *Prayer and the Priesthood of Christ*, 24.

57. Redding, *Prayer and the Priesthood of Christ*, 24.

58. Torrance, "The Mind of Christ in Worship: The Problem of Apollinarianism in the Liturgy," in *Theology in Reconciliation: Essays Towards Evangelical and Catholic Unity in East and West*, 189–90. Sandra Fach states, "Torrance is dependent on Jungmann's work, though he argues that a subtle Apollinarianism is also at the root of the loss of the mediatorial aspect in the liturgy." Fach, "Worship as Thanksgiving," 57.

Christian worship, according to Torrance, should be more than Christians mentioning Jesus Christ, it should be their actual participation in the worship of Christ, the High Priest of all creation. J. B. Torrance states, "We lose sight of the fact that the Good News of the Gospel is that God has not only spoken a Word to us in Christ, but in Jesus of Nazareth given us one who from the human side has made the one true response to that Word, and submitted for us to the Judgments of that Word, and received for us the grace of that Word."[59] Sandra Fach states, "What Torrance wants is a continuing priesthood that sees Christ alongside us, a fellow worshiper, even now in the midst of the congregation praying alongside us. This qualifies the notion of Christ offering prayer on our behalf."[60] This is why Torrance's perspective offers an important contribution to liturgical dialogue. The idea of Christ being a fellow worshiper, praying alongside of us in the congregation is a foreign concept to many contemporary worshiping communities.[61] Again, to emphasize our concern, worship service planning tends to be anthropocentric instead of Christocentric. Torrance stated, "Christ himself has been thrust up into the majesty of the Godhead in such a way that he is regarded as too exalted to be associated with the prayers of the liturgy, which are 'couched in language befitting servants.'"[62] Torrance's statement is worth noting in that the mediated doxology has been eclipsed, not just in the fourth century, but in contemporary worship settings. He further states:

> There can be little doubt, therefore, that the recovery of the human priesthood of Jesus Christ, the one Mediator between God and man, in the sacramental and liturgical life of the Church, together with the deeper understanding of the humanity of Christ as the sacrament *par excellence* which clearly pervades the renewed doctrine of the Church in the *Lumen Gentium*, is likely to bear considerable fruit in healing the rift between the Roman Catholic Church and the Churches of the Reformation, particularly if the former can think out the implications of the vicarious priesthood of Christ for the hierarchy of the Church as deeply as it has done for the liturgy, and if the latter will allow themselves to rethink their "evangelical" conception of the

---

59. J. B. Torrance, "The Place of Jesus Christ in Worship," 367.

60. Fach, "Worship as Thanksgiving," 44.

61. Most of the liturgical literature, whether from a Catholic, Reformed, or Methodist context focuses on the liturgical *ordo* and the meaning and purpose of the liturgical elements.

62. Torrance, *Theology in Reconciliation*, 195.

ministry in terms of consociation with the one priesthood of Jesus Christ.[63]

This issue of neglect of the priesthood of Christ, for Torrance, must be corrected. Jesus Christ must be seen as the one with whom we worship with in the liturgy. And this must be emphasized in the present tense not just the past tense, according to Torrance. He argues that when we employ the preposition *through* without the preposition *with*, mediation is seen as something that is exclusively past tense and not present tense. Sandra Fach states:

> Torrance is wary of an expression of praise that does not understand Christ to be a fellow worshipper, one in our midst. He argues that the mediatorial language of "through" does not emphasize Christ's continuing mediatorial role. Specifically, Torrance is wary of a mediatorial doxology that only includes a mediatorial "through" and not also a mediatorial "with." So far, we have only seen the word "with" in the context of the co-ordinated doxology. "With," in this context, affirms the full divinity of Christ. What, then, is meant by a mediatorial "with"? According to Torrance, to use only the word "through" affirms Christ's past role but it does not necessarily affirm his continuing role. To use also the word "with" ensures that he is believed still to be amidst the congregation, offering up prayer with his brothers and sisters.[64]

We serve a living Christ who has ascended to the right hand of God the Father. In his ascension, the church does not experience the absence of Christ (he ascended therefore he left the church) but rather the presence of Christ (he ascended and therefore is *Immanuel* with his people). When the church gathers together to worship, they not only worship the living Christ, they worship *through* and *with* the living Christ. This is what Torrance was communicating, emphasizing Christ's continuing mediation role. Torrance argued that Jesus Christ is today the High Priest of all creation and therefore when the church worships, they are not only worshiping *through* what Christ has done but *with* the living Christ. Sandra Fach says that Torrance argues that our worship is a participation in heavenly worship. By the Spirit, we were joined to Christ who, as the writer of Hebrews insists, continues to be our *Leitourgos*—the leader of

---

63. Torrance, *Theology in Reconciliation*, 63.
64. Fach, "Worship as Thanksgiving," 44–45.

our worship.⁶⁵ The worship that Torrance is referring to is something that is done *with* the Ascended Christ. Our worship takes place *with* Christ in the heavenly realms and we do this by the power of the Spirit. As James Torrance said, "He calls us that we might be identified with him by the Spirit, not only in his communion with the Father, but also in his great priestly work and ministry of intercession, that our prayers on earth might be the echo of his prayers in heaven."⁶⁶ This indeed is what both T. F. and J. B. Torrance are referring to when they talk about the place of Jesus Christ in worship:

> Thus Jesus Christ is himself our prayer and worship. We worship God and pray to him as Father only through the mediation of Christ our High Priest, but since he is both Priest and Sacrifice, Offerer and Offering, made on our behalf, we worship and pray to the Father in such a way that it is Christ himself who is the real content of our worship and prayer: we offer Christ to the Father through our prayer, for in the Spirit the prayer that ascends from us to the Father is a form of the self-offering of Christ himself. We worship God, therefore, with nothing of our own, but with Christ as our worship who alone has offered himself to the Father in sacrifice for us and all mankind. Inasmuch as Christ associates us with himself in his worshipping and praying as those whom he has made his own and for whom he acts before the Face of the Father, we pray, as it were, through the mouth of Christ, *comme par sa bouche,* as Calvin used to say. Really to pray to God, therefore, is to pray with Christ who prays with us and for us, and to pray with him is to pray his prayer, the prayer of his life which he offered in our place and on our behalf, and in which through union with Christ in the one Spirit we are made continually participant.⁶⁷

Torrance is clear that the worship that humanity brings is through the mediation of Christ our High Priest. Furthermore, our worship is secondary. The worship of Christ is primary. Our worship is only effective because of the worship of the High Priest of all creation. Our prayers are joined to the prayers of Christ. Our prayers are integrated into the

65. Fach, "Worship as Thanksgiving," 44.
66. J. B. Torrance, *Worship, Community and the Triune God of Grace,* 2. For more on the subject of ascension and worship, see the following: Dawson, *Jesus Ascended*; Fach, Answering the Upwards Call; Canlis, *Calvin's Ladder*; Kelly, *Systematic Theology* Volume Two, 501–22; Barth, *Church Dogmatics,* I/2: 413, 421–25, 692–95; Milligan, *The Ascension of Christ.*
67. Torrance, *Theology in Reconciliation,* 209.

perfected intercession of Jesus Christ, our High Priest. This is what Torrance communicated and in essence what makes his liturgical theology unique. Torrance concluded his thoughts on the priesthood of Christ when he said:

> It is in the complete integrity of his humanity that he acts, as man for us men, in all that we as men are called to do by way of response to the creative and redemptive love of God, in obeying and believing, in repenting and surrendering, in asking and receiving, in serving and praising, in longing and adoring God the Father Almighty as his true and faithful Son—all of which Christ does not for his own sake but for our sake in redeeming, converting and re-creating our humanity in himself, thus restoring it to its truth and freedom and perfection in filial relation to the Father. It is because the unimpaired human nature of Christ is inseparably united in him to the Creator Son and Word of God, making his humanity quickening and creative, indeed humanizing humanity, that is through union with him in the Spirit we share in his humanity we on our part are so profoundly humanized that our obedience and faith, our repentance and surrender, our service and praise, our love and adoration may be the spontaneously free and glad self offering of the sons of God to their heavenly Father.[68]

Conclusion

The place of Jesus Christ in liturgical prayer, according to Jungmann and Torrance, points to Jesus, not just as a reference point in the liturgy, but as the centerpiece of worship as the High Priest of all of humanity. Christian liturgy is made possible because of the One who intercedes on behalf of men and women. According to Torrance, we live, pray and worship by the Spirit *through* and *with* the Son as we come to the Father. For Torrance, there is no other way of coming into the presence of God but through the vicarious humanity of Jesus Christ. This is antithetical to the anthropocentric approaches, which focus primarily on what we must do to enter into the presence of God (a theological impossibility without a High Priest) as well as the approaches that attempt to have a more theological framework but that do not go far enough as they do not place this emphasis on the priesthood of Jesus Christ. This is what T. F. and J. B. Torrance contribute to the subject of worship.

---

68. Torrance, *Theology in Reconciliation*, 209–10.

6

T. F. Torrance and Preaching

Introduction

IN THIS CHAPTER, WE will explore whether or not T. F. Torrance's theology of preaching was ever connected to his theology of worship. It does appear that T. F. Torrance's theology of preaching reflects the major themes of his theology: theological science, epistemology, dualism, and his emphasis on both the *homoousion* and the hypostatic union. But did he ever explicitly connect preaching to the context of the worshiping community? This is what is new and what we will explore in this chapter. T. F. Torrance was a parish minister in the 1940s and while there are boxes of unpublished sermons at Princeton Theological Seminary, as well as two collections of published sermons, Torrance does not initially seem to have an explicit theology of preaching.[1] On the other hand, it seems that for T. F. Torrance, what he believed were the critical theological issues that needed to be considered were precisely the same issues that needed to be factored into a theology of preaching. This will become apparent as we work our way through this chapter.

Robert T. Walker states, "The importance of the word and of faithfulness to the word appears through all his writings and his whole writing is actually a kind of preaching, a proclaiming of the truth of Christ, and so throughout he has made abundantly clear what the content of preaching should be. . . . The Torrance brothers did not say much about

---

1. Torrance, *When Christ Comes and Comes Again*; Torrance, *The Apocalypse Today*.

the structure or minutiae of corporate worship as they were much more concerned to emphasize the place of Christ as the leader of our worship, the one priest, victim and sacrifice, who continues to be the real leader of all our worship."[2] In light of these comments, we shall examine what Torrance does address regarding the subject of preaching, which contributes to an understanding of his doxological theology.

The Heart of the Gospel and the Preacher

T. F. Torrance begins his work entitled, *Preaching Christ Today: The Gospel and Scientific Thinking*, with a tribute to Billy Graham in gratitude for his proclamation of the gospel in Scotland.[3] That may be surprising, as Torrance's emphasis on "Christ's response" seems to be at odds with Billy Graham's emphasis on "our response." However, T. F. Torrance clearly appreciated the preaching and ministry of Billy Graham. Regarding T. F. Torrance's friendship with Graham, David Torrance reminds us:

> He initiated and was the prime mover of an invitation extended by the Church of Scotland to Dr. Billy Graham, the well-known evangelist, to visit Scotland in 1990. After the crusade, Tom helped to set up a follow-up school in evangelism. He was a friend of Billy Graham's, and Billy Graham kindly sent a telegram of sympathy following Tom's death, which was read at Tom's funeral service. Tom always wished to be known not primarily as an academic theologian but as a preacher of the gospel. That is the way that he described himself.[4]

In the preface to his booklet, T. F. Torrance referred to his beloved professor at New College, Edinburgh, Hugh Ross Mackintosh, as a model preacher. Torrance refers to a publication entitled "The Heart of the Gospel and the Preacher."[5] Mackintosh promoted doctrinal preaching of the gospel that was centered on the atonement. According to Torrance, he "recalled how the greatest preachers of the past were also great teachers of doctrine, and he pointed out that it was in the combination of preaching

---

2. Email correspondence with Robert T. Walker on the 29th of September 2017.
3. Torrance, *Preaching Christ Today*, vi.
4. David Torrance, *Participatio,* Supplement Vol. 1 (2011), 25.
5. Torrance, *Preaching Christ Today*, vii.

and doctrine that the very heart of the gospel was brought to bear with power upon people in English-speaking lands."[6]

Torrance stated that it was the preaching of Mackintosh himself that influenced the founding of the Scottish Church Theology Society dedicated to the renewal of theology in the teaching and preaching of the church in Scotland. Torrance mentioned that preaching was the end to which his own life had been dedicated.[7] Torrance states:

> What I have been trying to do is to show how the gospel can be taught and preached in ways that are faithful to the apostolic faith as it was brought to authoritative expression in the Nicene Creed, and at the same time may be taught and preached today in ways that can be expressed and appreciated within the scientific understanding of the created universe upon which God has impressed his Word and which under God we have been able to develop in modern times. Far from being hostile to one another, Christian theology and natural science are complementary to one another. I believe that science owes much more to the Christian faith than is usually recognized, and that science may be harnessed in the service of the gospel which humankind so desperately needs today.[8]

In both addresses, "Preaching Christ Today" and "Incarnation and Atonement,"[9] Torrance addressed ministers of the Gospel and theological students who were preparing for the ministry of the Gospel. The first address was given on the Jubilee of the Scottish Church Theology Society that recalled its formal inauguration at the General Assembly of the Church of Scotland in 1943. That address was a plea for Christ-centered preaching and teaching and for a return to theological evangelism. The second address was given at the Theological Student's Forum at Princeton Theological Seminary. In that address, Torrance examined the interrelations between science and theology and for the preaching of the gospel, grounded in the incarnation and atonement.

---

6. Torrance, *Preaching Christ Today*, vii.
7. Torrance, *Preaching Christ Today*, vii
8. Torrance, *Preaching Christ Today*, vii–viii.
9. Torrance, *Preaching Christ Today*, 1–71.

Preaching: An Evangelical and Theological Activity

For T. F. Torrance, preaching Christ was both an evangelical and theological task engaged in proclaiming and teaching of Christ as he was revealed in the Scriptures. Torrance was fond of quoting James Denney who said, "Our theologians should be evangelists and our evangelists theologians."[10] Torrance also referenced his former colleague at New College, James S. Stewart. Torrance described Stewart as a New Testament scholar who was faithful in his lectures, to teach in a *kerygmatic* and *didactic* mode. Torrance stated, "He interpreted the text of the Gospels and expounded the gospel in the Gospels in such a way that his students heard the living and dynamic Word of God for themselves. Not surprisingly many of them were converted in his classroom."[11]

Torrance argued that we need *didactic* preaching and *kerygmatic* theology, that the only Christ there was and is, as John Calvin said, is not a *nudus Christus* but "Christ clothed with his gospel."[12] Torrance contrasted that perspective with those who promoted the so-called quest for the historical Jesus such as Rudolph Bultmann of Marburg. Bultmann was known for his attempt to "demythologize" Jesus or to strip away from the New Testament account of Jesus, the theological aspect from which Christ was presented by the apostles. Torrance told a humorous story to communicate his concern:

> I recall how one of the professors in my old university in Basel, Fritz Buri, attempted to do just that, and set himself to strip away from Jesus not only the *didactic* material in the Gospels but the *kerygma* as well, and so to detach the historical event of Jesus completely from his evangelical message. He decided to give three public lectures on *Entkerugmatisierung*, or the *de-kerygmatizing* of the gospel, thereby going beyond Bultmann's demythologizing program in seeking to strip Jesus naked of his gospel. Karl Barth decided to go along and listen to these lectures. Later when he met Fritz Buri in the street he said to him with his customary humor: "Now at last, brother Buri, I know the difference between you and Bultmann. When Bultmann goes in for a swim he at least has a pair of bathing trunks on!"[13]

---

10. Torrance, *Preaching Christ Today*, 1.
11. Torrance, *Preaching Christ Today*, 1.
12. Torrance, *Preaching Christ Today*, 2.
13. Torrance, *Preaching Christ Today*, 2.

Although the story above is humorous, the issue of separating Christ from his gospel was devastating in Torrance's thinking. Torrance argued that when one separates the historical from the theological, everything goes wrong. Torrance asserts, "The real Jesus of history is the Christ who cannot be separated from his saving acts, for his person and his work are one, Christ clothed with his gospel of saving grace. The so-called Jesus of history shorn of theological truth is an abstraction invented by a pseudo-scientific method."[14] Torrance emphatically argued that the divorce of the empirical from the theoretical which involved the divorce of the *Geschichte* from *Historie* disrupted and damaged the biblical presentation of Jesus Christ in such a way that people found it difficult to preach.[15] He stated, "I believe this to be terribly important, for to interpret Jesus Christ under the guidance of the kind of rationalist historical scientific method long discarded by science actually destroys a proper understanding of the humanity of Jesus and of the *kerymatic* and *didactic* way in which he confronts us in the Gospels."[16] Gerrit Dawson writes:

> For years now, our mainstream seminaries and colleges have been graduating ministers who have no confidence in the texts of Scripture they are to preach. Our historical-critical methods have deconstructed the texts but we have failed to put them, and our students, back together again. These new pastors leave seminary unsure of what Jesus said and did, and suspicious of the epistles which reflect on the theological meaning of the Jesus presented in the Gospels. They have been saturated with trendy re-interpretations but parched for an in-depth knowledge of our heritage.[17]

Gerrit Dawson believed that the Torrances had an important response to the problem. He stated, "We have to recover a theology that will invigorate us to preach the truth about who Jesus is."[18] Dawson believed that the Torrances helped with such a cause. He writes, "This is what the

14. Torrance, *Preaching Christ Today*, 9.
15. Torrance, *Preaching Christ Today*, 10.
16. Torrance, *Preaching Christ Today*, 11.
17. Thomas F. Torrance, James B. Torrance, and David W. Torrance, *A Passion for Christ*, 2. Also see Torrance's scathing words when he said, "How frequently the sermon is not an exposition of the Word of God but an exposition of the minister's own views on this or that subject! And how frequently the whole life of the congregation is so built up on the personality of the minister that when he goes the congregation all but collapses or dwindles away!" Torrance, *Theology in Reconstruction*, 168.
18. Torrance, *A Passion for Christ*, 3.

Torrance brothers have given the Church. They speak a daring, vital word that springs first from Scripture, then rises through the great patristic writers, the creeds, the Reformers, and the evangelical theologians who have followed. Like many great theologians, the Torrances have spoken not only to their generation, but also to the one coming up."[19]

Preaching and the Hypostatic Union

T. F. Torrance argues, "The Jesus of whom we read in the Gospels and whom we proclaim as Christ is both man of Israel and the Lord God, for in him God himself has come to be with us, really to be with us as one of us and as God for us, who has taken our human nature upon himself, our sin and guilt, our misery and death, in order to save and heal us, and as such really to be our God."[20] Dick Eugenio states, "It is not clear whether the saving presence of God is similar to what he calls elsewhere God's *convicting presence* that leads to justification, although this seems to be the case."[21] Eugenio then quotes T. F. Torrance who said, "The nearer a man gets to God, the more he feels himself a sinner. You can only be conscious of sin in the presence of God.... It is the presence of God that discovers a man's sin to that man, but just because there is awakened the consciousness of sin, we implore Him for pardon and reconciliation, that He may come near us in mercy and not in wrath."[22] Torrance believed that everything in the gospel depended on holding these two truths together:

> His human and divine natures are united inseparably in one Person. The miracle of the Incarnation is not simply that God has come in Jesus, but that in Jesus God has come as Man, and that the human life and action of Jesus are unique in their oneness with the life and action of God. Thus His power to act is not other than the power of His Person, the power by which He lives His own personal Life. His Action and His personal Being are inseparably one, for His power is personal in itself for in His action the hypostasis of Jesus is fully present. Thus He

---

19. Torrance, *A Passion for Christ*, 4.
20. Torrance, *Preaching Christ Today*, 11.
21. Eugenio, *Communion with the Triune God*, 195.
22. Eugenio, *Communion with the Triune God*, 195; Torrance, B44 "The Pharisee and the Publican at Prayer," 6; and B43 "O Man greatly beloved," 1–5; and B47 "The Condemning Heart," 5–6.

is not known apart from His acts, nor His acts apart from His Person.[23]

While certainly Torrance places an emphasis on the divinity of Christ, as already mentioned, it was the humanity of Christ that Torrance expounded on. Regarding the humanity of Christ, Torrance argues:

> What overwhelms me is the sheer humanness of Jesus, Jesus as the baby at Bethlehem, Jesus sitting tired and thirsty at the well outside Samaria, Jesus exhausted by the crowds, Jesus recuperating his strength through sleep at the back of a ship on the Sea of Galilee, Jesus hungry for figs on the way up to Jerusalem, Jesus weeping at the grave of Lazarus, Jesus thirsting for water on the Cross—for that precisely is God with us and one of us, God as "the wailing infant" in Bethlehem, as Hilary wrote, God sharing our weakness and exhaustion, God sharing our hunger, thirst, tears, pain and death. Far from overwhelming us, God with us and one of us does the very opposite, for in sharing with us all that we are in our littleness and weakness he does not override our humanity but completes, perfects, and establishes it.[24]

Torrance furthermore seemed in awe of the idea that Jesus Christ, the Maker of heaven and earth and of all things visible and invisible, stooped down to be in union with us, so much so, that he would speak in our own human language. Torrance states, "We don't know what language God speaks in the communion of the Holy Trinity or to the angels and the blessed departed, but we do learn in Jesus that God actually speaks to us in our creaturely language on earth. In Jesus, the Word by whom all things in heaven and earth were created became human and communicates with us and addresses us in this frail creaturely form."[25] Torrance reminded us that Jesus is Immanuel, God with us. This has immense implications for preaching. Torrance puts it this way, "I wish to

---

23. Torrance, *Theological Science*, 156. Torrance also states, "It is here then in the inner life and being of Jesus Christ, in the hypostatic union, that we discern the interior logic of theological thinking, the logic of Christ, the logic that is in Christ before it is in our knowledge of Him, the logic that inheres ontologically and personally in Him but which is reflected noetically and sacramentally in us in the conformity of our life and thought to Him and in the direction of them through Him to God the Father." Torrance, *Theological Science*, 217.

24. Torrance, *Preaching Christ Today*, 13.

25. Torrance, *Preaching Christ Today*, 13.

stress in preaching Christ as *Jeshua* and *Immanuel*: there is an unbroken relation in being and act between Jesus and God."[26]

Torrance repeatedly reminded his students that dualist philosophy and science of the Graeco-Roman world, hindered if not prevented people from imagining a God interacting with the world much less of incarnating himself into that world. Torrance argued that the Western world had to repeatedly contend with dichotomous ways of thinking in Western philosophy and science. This approach to thinking was given formalization through Newtonian mechanics, which created deistic ideas of God. That kind of deity cannot interact with the world of space and time in any real way. Torrance states,

> By giving conceptual expression to oneness between the Son of God become man in our world of space and time and God the Creator of heaven and earth and of all visible and invisible reality, the early church set aside at a stroke the epistemological dualism of Greek thought, and did something that penetrated into and changed the very foundations of knowledge in the ancient world. They thereby laid the theological basis for their understanding of the unbroken relation between the sheer humanity of Jesus and God.[27]

Preaching: Encountering the Word of God

T. F. Torrance believed that when the Scriptures were taught in the worshiping context, one encounters more than the propositional truth of a particular text but rather, the encounter is with the living Christ. Torrance stated in one of his sermons:

> When we gather together for worship, sing our hymns and have our devotions, and make our offerings, all that is deeply significant and essential, but what is it that constitutes the very heart and substance of the Church? That question is answered by this saying of our Lord: "Where two or three are gathered together in my name, there am I in the midst of them." The very essence of the Church is found in that I AM of the living Lord Jesus Christ. Where He is actually present and worshipped, there you

---

26. Torrance, *Preaching Christ Today*, 14.
27. Torrance, *Preaching Christ Today*, 16.

have the Christian Church. Where He is not present, you have a sham church.²⁸

Although, it seems somewhat unnecessary to emphasize the presence of Christ in the *ecclesia*, Torrance's perspective about the liturgical elements leading us to the living Christ, was different from what might appear to be the more rationalist approach of the theology and preaching of B. B. Warfield, Carl F. H. Henry, Martyn Lloyd-Jones, and J. I. Packer. These were all godly men but for whom preaching was about communicating biblical truths through means of expositional preaching, usually book-by-book.²⁹ Torrance had a similar value for the Scriptures but he might have been critical of an approach, which sometimes appeared to put more stress on the words of the Bible than the Word. In one of his sermons, Torrance stated, "It is the mission of the Church to unlock the Bible, and to let the voice of Christ loose upon the world."³⁰ He refers to this as dialogical theology where a two-fold conversation takes place not just between humanity and a text but between humanity and the Living God. Torrance affirms, "He is at once Person and Word, who communicates Himself to us as the Word addressing us, and who communicates His Word to us in the form of His own personal Being."³¹ Developing this argument, Torrance stated that "Dialogical theology is essentially the theology of the Word, which operates through the conformity of thought with its object, but an Object who is God revealing Himself in His Word, encountering us as Subject, addressing us as subjects over against Him, and drawing us into free and spontaneous communion with Him. Dialogical theology of this kind carries with it certain scientific demands for its faithful fulfillment."³² It is critical to notice the relational dialogical aspect of the Word with humanity. Preaching was not some kind of means of dispelling religious ideas for Torrance. Preaching was an issue of communion with the Living Word and his creation. Torrance explained it this way:

> In the preaching and expounding of the Word, the minister puts the Word into our ear, and we receive it through the ear and feed on it in our soul. Then we receive the Word of God through

28. Torrance, *When Christ Comes and Comes Again*, 102–3.
29. See J. I. Packer, *Fundamentalism and the Word of God*.
30. Torrance, *When Christ Comes and Comes Again*, 29.
31. Torrance, *Theological Science*, 133.
32. Torrance, *Theological Science*, 134.

the Audible Word of preaching. In the Sacraments we receive the Word of God through the Visible Words of Baptism and the Lord's Supper, but it is the same Word of God we receive in both, the Word who has come to us in the person of Jesus Christ our Savior, for the Word that He speaks to us in all His words is Himself.[33]

Torrance again emphasized the idea of worship being essentially a dialogical activity in which humanity meets and dialogues with God through his Word. Torrance states:

> Christ wraps Himself up in His words and when His words enter our ear and our heart the living Christ himself comes within, and acts creatively there. These are life-giving words creating personal communion, communicating a personal presence; they are words that germinate in the human heart and create room for Christ there, so that He takes up permanent lodging within us. It is as we allow the Word of the Gospel to saturate our minds and imaginations, to penetrate into our memories, and to master all our thinking, that Christ is borne with us, that all that He is and has done becomes, as it were, imprinted upon us within, and becomes so truly and permanently the very center of our being that we are transformed into His image and likeness, and even partake of His nature.[34]

Although worship is a natural expression of faith, the expression of faith is in its objective orientation in the saving humanity of Christ rather than in the subjective self-expression of individual worshipers. He stated:

> The Word of God encounters us in such a way that it creates for itself a sphere of human and personal conversation in which the Word is addressed to each and all, but in which each helps the other both in hearing and in speaking it. It is thus that dialogical theology has its essential place in the Church as the sphere of a two-fold conversation between God and His people and between the different members of the Church in the presence of the Word Himself. Perhaps the truest example of dialogical theology of this kind is to be found in the catechetical theology

---

33. Torrance, *When Christ Comes and Comes Again*, 84.

34. Torrance, *When Christ Comes and Comes Again*, 109–10. It is hard to imagine that John Stott or J. I. Packer would have disagreed with T. F. Torrance. He is closer to this Evangelical tradition, with an emphasis on both the "words" and the Word, than either side thought.

of the Reformation pursued within the worshipping community gathered to listen to the Word of God.[35]

As the church gathers for worship and as they hear the words of the sermon, Christ is in their midst encountering them with his presence. The hearing of the word and encounter of the Word solicits the appropriate response of faith. And humanity's response of faith is made efficacious because of the faithfulness of Christ. Karl Barth stated, "Proclamation is human speech in and by which God Himself speaks like a king through the mouth of his herald, and which is meant to be heard and accepted as speech in and by which God Himself speaks, and therefore heard and accepted in faith as divine judgment and pardon, eternal Law and eternal Gospel both together."[36] In the sacraments, complete response is made to this God who has revealed himself. And at the center of this kind of preaching of the Living Christ is the preaching of the Christ who was crucified.

Preaching the Cross of Christ

According to Torrance, the preaching of Christ crucified was at the center of the Christian gospel. Torrance states, "The Cross, as H. R. Mackintosh once wrote in a Gospel tract, is 'a window into the heart of God.'"[37] Dick Eugenio points out, "This theme is one that Torrance repeatedly preached about. In all of these sermons, Torrance claims that it is 'at the Cross that we learn that our heavenly Father loves us, and loves us more than he loves himself.'"[38] Torrance understood that to be the key to apostolic preaching. According to Torrance:

---

35. Torrance, *Theological Science*, 135.

36. Barth, *Church Dogmatics,* I/1, 52. Regarding community discernment during preaching, see Barth, *Church Dogmatics* III/4, 498f.

37. Torrance, *A Passion for Christ*, 23.

38. Eugenio, *Communion with the Triune God*, 64. See Torrance's Unpublished Sermons in The Thomas F. Torrance Manuscript Collection, Special Collections, Princeton Theological Seminary Library: B38 and B39 Untitled sermon (Beechgrove Church, Aberdeen, 2 November 1997); B38 Untitled sermon (Penicuik Midlothian, 5 September 1993); B38 Untitled sermon (Cluny Parish, Edinburgh, 17 October 1993); B38 Untitled sermon (MacDonald Memorial Church, Bellshill, 7 June 1998); B38 Untitled sermon on Romans 8:32; B39 "He that spared not his own Son"; "The Cross—a Window into the heart of the Father'; "Greater love hath no man"; and B46 "God commendeth his love toward us."

The identification of the man on the cross with God himself is, as St. Paul once wrote, offence to the Jews and foolishness to the Greeks. Be that as it may, it is the preaching of Christ crucified that lies at the very center of the Christian gospel if only because the cross, as H. R. Mackintosh once wrote in a gospel tract, is "a window into the heart of God." He was drawing attention there to the words of St. Paul in Romans 8:32: "He who spared not his own Son, but delivered him up for us all, how shall he not with him also freely give us all things." St. Paul was thinking in the back of his mind of the readiness of Abraham to sacrifice his "only son Isaac, whom he loved" (Gen. 22:2, 16), thereby demonstrating that he loved God more than he loved himself. In giving his own dear Son to die for us in atoning sacrifice for the sins of the world, God has revealed that he loves us more than he loves himself. Far from remaining detached from us in our fearful alienation and unappeasable agony, God has penetrated through the cross into the deepest depths of our wickedness and violence and taken them all upon himself in order to judge them and redeem us from their tyranny over us.[39]

This emphasis on the preaching of the cross is quite revealing regarding Torrance's own heart for evangelistic preaching. Consequently, through the incarnation, *enhypostatically*, Christ entered into the depths of the human experience and yet because of the hypostatic union, was without sin. Torrance proclaims, "It is the cross of Christ that surely lies at the heart of our faith and of the mission of the gospel. I believe that if the church is to be faithful to its calling it must concentrate, as I have said, on the uniqueness of Christ, but on Christ clothed with his gospel as the crucified and risen Lord."[40] It must also be noted that Torrance does indeed lean on substitutionary atonement language namely, that Christ took upon himself our lost and damned condition as well as our death under God's judgment; that "In the incarnation and the cross Christ has penetrated into the darkest depths of our abject human misery and perdition, where he takes our place, intercedes for us, substitutes himself for us, and makes the atoning restitution which we could not make, thereby reconciling us to God in the Holy Spirit as his dear children."[41]

39. Torrance, *Preaching Christ Today*, 28.
40. Torrance, *Preaching Christ Today*, 30.
41. Torrance, *Preaching Christ Today*, 30. T. F. Torrance disagreed with the scholastic Calvinist tradition, which made the legal model the definitive way of understanding the atonement. T. A. Noble stated, "When we say that Torrance was in the Reformed tradition therefore, we have to specify which Reformed tradition. It was T. F. Torrance's

Yet, Torrance is clear that we must be careful of linking the substitutionary act only with his death and not with his incarnate person and life. Torrance was clear that in our preaching, we must emphasize what the New Testament calls *katallage*, Christ in our place and Christ for us in every respect. It is here that worship language emerges. "Substitution understood in this radical way means that Christ takes our place in all our human life and activity before God, even in our believing, praying, and worshipping of God, for he has yoked himself to us in such a profound way that he stands in for us and upholds us at every point in our human relations before God."[42]

Along with Torrance's conviction of keeping the person and the work of Christ together, he was emphatic about the need to preach Galatians 2:20 with the emphasis on the subjective genitive instead of the objective genitive which has already been discussed. Here we are reflecting on this as it relates to preaching. For Torrance, our faith only makes sense because of the faith of the Son of God. He argues:

> Galatians 2:20 has long been for me a passage of primary importance as it was for John McLeod Campbell and Hugh Ross Mackintosh: "I am crucified with Christ, nevertheless I live, yet not I. But Christ lives in me, and the life which I now live in the flesh, I live by the faith of the Son of God, who loved me and gave himself for me." "The Faith of the Son of God" is to be understood here not just as my faith in him, but as the faith of Christ himself, for it refers primarily to Christ's unswerving faithfulness, his vicarious and substitutionary faith which embraces and undergirds us, such that when we believe we must say with St. Paul "not I but Christ," even in our act of faith. This is not in any way to denigrate the human act of faith on our part, for it is only in and through the vicarious faith of Christ that we can truly and properly believe.[43]

---

brother, James Torrance, also teaching in the Department of Christian Dogmatics at New College, who mainly carried on the debate with "scholastic federal Calvinism" and its doctrine of Limited Atonement. But the Torrances did not reject that particular version of Reformed theology because of the influence of Barth. They were consciously part of a Scottish tradition, which they traced from John Knox through Robert Bruce and John McLeod Campbell. This perspective included drawing a clear line between Calvin himself and the Scots Confession on the one hand and the so-called "Calvinism" which developed from the Synod of Dort through the Westminster Confession on the other." *Participatio* 4 (2013), 15.

42. Torrance, *Preaching Christ Today*, 30–31.
43. Torrance, *Preaching Christ Today*, 31. Also see Hays, *The Faith of Jesus Christ*.

For both T. F. and J. B. Torrance, this idea of emphasizing the faithfulness of Christ is no small matter. They both argued that if this is missing in our teaching and preaching, that we are putting a heavy burden back on the shoulders of humanity; that when we make faith primarily an issue about "our faith," that is not gospel at all. For our faith to have meaning, it must be rooted in the faith of Christ. The Torrances repeatedly made this emphasis clear—that the faithfulness of humanity has a solid footing only when it is rooted in the vicarious humanity of Christ. T. F. Torrance referred to this as the reconciling exchange. "That is what the early church and John Calvin called 'the blessed exchange' or 'the wondrous exchange,' and even the Roman Missal calls *mirabile commercium*. This is in fact the New Testament doctrine of *katallage*, for it is an *atoning* and *reconciling exchange*, in which what is ours is displaced by Christ who substituted himself in our place and yet is restored in a new way to us."[44] Preaching Christ crucified means preaching this great exchange: mercy in place of rebellion, forgiveness in place of sin, love in place of hatred. The preaching of the cross of Christ and this reconciling exchange was central for T. F. Torrance. He states, "That is the way in which the *katallage*, the wondrous exchange of the atoning and reconciling cross of Christ, operates, by making the shameful things that divided us from him into the very things that bind us to him in life and death forever. Such is the unlimited power of the cross of Christ."[45] Torrance also affirms:

> That is precisely what took place in Jesus Christ in the whole course of His obedience from His birth to His death on the Cross, for He fulfilled in Himself the Word of God tabernacling among men, the covenanted way of response to God set forth in the ancient cult, and constituted Himself our Temple, our Priest, our Offering and our Worship. It is therefore in His name only that we worship God, not in our own name, or in our own significance but surely in the significance of Christ's eternal self-oblation to the Father.[46]

Preaching and the Lord's Supper

While the next chapter will address the sacrament of the Lord's Supper in more detail, it is critical to make the connection of the Lord's Supper

---

44. Torrance, *Preaching Christ Today*, 32–33.
45. Torrance, *Preaching Christ Today*, 34.
46. Torrance, *God and Rationality*, 158.

to preaching in the theology of T. F. Torrance at this point. According to Torrance, "It is not easy to preach the truth that we are saved by the grace of Christ alone and that it is through the vicarious humanity of Jesus and it its substitutionary bearing upon faith that we can properly believe, but this is what may be proclaimed at Holy Communion as nowhere else."[47] Torrance believed that at the table he could not rely on his own faith but only upon the vicarious faith of the Lord Jesus Christ and in the complete substitution of Christ's atoning sacrifice. He proclaims, "I have found in my own ministry that it is easiest to preach the unconditional nature of grace, and the vicarious humanity and substitutionary role of Christ in faith, at the celebration of the Eucharist, where the call for repentance and faith is followed by communion in the body and blood of Christ in which we stretch our empty hands to receive the bread and wine: 'Nothing in my hands I bring, simply to thy Cross I cling.'"[48]

Robert T. Walker said that T. F. Torrance discussed the sacraments more than preaching, no doubt because he was engaged in the ecumenical movement and there was a lot more controversy about the sacraments than over preaching.[49] Furthermore, it is probable that as Torrance moved away from parish ministry and into academics, the subject of the sacraments took on a more central role. And while there indeed is more of an emphasis on the sacraments in the doxological theology of Torrance, he clearly desired the preaching of Christ for the wellbeing of the local church.

Again, Torrance was one who constantly reminded that we do not rest on our own faith but upon Christ and the cross of Christ. Torrance stated, "Faith, as John Calvin taught, is an empty vessel, so that when you approach the Table of the Lord, it is not upon your faith that you rely, but upon Christ and his Cross alone."[50] For Torrance, this was the essence of the gospel namely that salvation and justification are by the grace of Jesus. Torrance, was concerned about the subtle temptation to make preaching anthropocentric instead of Christocentric. He states:

> There is a kind of subtle Pelagianism in preaching and teaching which has the effect of throwing people back in the last resort on their own act of faith, so that in the last analysis responsibility

---

47. Torrance, *God and Rationality*, 158.
48. Torrance, *Preaching Jesus Christ*, 27–28.
49. Email correspondence, Robert T. Walker on the 29th of September 2017.
50. Torrance, *A Passion for Christ*, 28.

for their salvation rests upon themselves, rather than on Christ. In far too much preaching of Christ the ultimate responsibility for their salvation rests upon themselves, rather than on Christ. In far too much preaching of Christ the ultimate responsibility is taken off the shoulders of the Lamb of God and put upon the shoulders of the poor sinner, and he knows well in his heart that he cannot cope with it. Is that not one of the things that keeps pushing people away from the church?[51]

There is certainly a difference of emphasis here from the evangelical tradition from Wesley and Whitefield onwards. Their stress was on the necessity of response—faith and repentance—from the sinner, and that salvation was conditional upon that response. However, both T. F. and J. B. Torrance were very concerned about this approach to preaching and teaching where the parish ministers put additional burdens on the parishioners by giving them a list of all that they were responsible for instead of leading them to encounter the living Christ who calls each of us to turn to him and to rest in him. It must be noted however, that Torrance clearly mentions the implications of being united with Jesus Christ regarding Christian ethics. He stated in one of his communion sermons:

> If you want communion with Him, then you must be prepared to share with Him His board. You must be united with Him in mind and affections. You cannot sit down with him at His table without sitting in union of spirit and purpose with Him who came not to be ministered unto but to minister and give his life as ransom for many. You must be united to Him in His gentleness and purity, in His love and forgiveness. In short, it means that you must drink His cup, and be immersed with His baptism.[52]

Torrance is communicating a very critical aspect of his theology of participating by the Spirit in the Son's communion with the Father. To participate in the life of God means to be united to him in his death and resurrection. To participate in Christ means to die to self and to be raised in the power of Christ that should manifest itself in the new life. Participation in Christ is not mere intellectual ascent. It is a wholehearted participation in the life of the Son. "What Jesus was concerned to do was

---

51. Torrance, *Preaching Christ Today: The Gospel and Scientific Thinking*, 35.

52. Unpublished works, The Thomas F. Torrance Manuscript Collection, Special Collections, Princeton Theological Seminary Library, B44 Communion Sermon on Mark 10:38, 5–6.

to teach the Word of God with power, and to make people whole again in body and soul."[53] Torrance appeared to be in agreement with the evangelicalism that emphasized the need for repentance. However, the difference was that for the Torrances, repentance was evangelical in that it was a response to the faithfulness of Christ. In contrast, legal repentance emphasized the need for repentance prior to being a beneficiary of the grace of God.

Finally, it must be noted that Torrance understood that Jesus Christ himself is the ultimate sacrament. He argues:

> In the full sense Jesus Christ is Himself the Sacrament for it is in Him that the One Truth of God comes to us in creaturely form and existence, so that in the objectivity of His particular and historical humanity we encounter the eternal objectivity of God Himself. The Word made flesh is the concrete embodiment of the Truth, and is the source and basis and norm of all God's revelation of Himself, so that relation to Him constitutes the sacramental area where human knowledge of God may actually and truthfully correspond to God's revelation of Himself. It is in Jesus that God's Word has so communicated Himself to us in our humanity that human words are taken to speak for God, and therefore it is in Jesus also that our human words may rightly and properly speak of God. Thus theological knowledge and theological statement participate sacramentally in the mystery of Christ as the Truth to whom they refer and upon which they rely for their reality. They must derive from, and be grounded in, the human nature and existence of Jesus, for it is in Him that the Word has become flesh and the Truth is embodied in humanity.[54]

Preaching Unconditional Grace

Torrance believed that there was an inclination towards Pelagianism in much of the so-called "evangelical" preaching. He mentioned that there was such a desire on the part of human beings to take credit for their salvation but that they are wholly dependent upon the unconditional grace of Christ. Torrance writes:

---

53. Torrance, *When Christ Comes and Comes Again*, 63.
54. Torrance, *Theological Science*, 150.

> Martin Luther once said that when he preached justification by faith alone, people responded to it like a cow staring at a new gate, but he also said that when he preached justification by grace alone it provoked tumults. I find this kind of disturbance again and again in the reaction not only of people, outside the church but even of would-be evangelical people within the membership of the church, for their refusal to accept unconditional grace seems to be due to the fact that it cuts so deeply into the quick of their souls. This is part of what I meant a short time ago when I pointed out that there is a subtle form of Pelagianism in the way people often preach the gospel and claim that people will be saved only if they believe, or on condition that they believe. Hidden deep down beneath all that there is a failure to take the New Testament teaching about the power of the cross of Christ and his substitutionary role seriously, a reluctance to allow it to apply to the whole of their being and to all their human activity before God, even to their believing and praying and worshipping. We need to learn and learn again and again that salvation by grace alone is so radical that we have to rely upon Christ Jesus entirely in everything, and that it is only when we rely on him alone that we are really free to believe: "Not I but Christ" yet "Christ in me." Because he came as man to take our place, in and through his humanity our humanity is radically transformed, and we become truly human, really free to believe, love, and serve him. That is the wonderful message of the cross and resurrection.[55]

Torrance believed that not preaching "Christ and him crucified" put a sermon on a different trajectory, namely that of offering an exposition on a text and giving people information instead of bringing them face to face with the Living Christ. Torrance stated in 1993:

> It was one of the lovely and refreshing things about the preaching of Billy Graham in Scotland recently that in preaching Christ he directed people to Christ and to Christ alone as Lord and Savior, in such a direct and blunt way, not through brilliant preaching, that through the Holy Spirit thousands and

---

55. Torrance, *Preaching Christ Today*, 37. It is worth asking, "What if we do not rely upon Christ?" Does this not make grace conditional? This clause could sound as if another condition were being placed upon humanity. Torrance would have responded that faith is not eradicated but that the object of our faith must be Christ, in the faithfulness of Christ. He seems to be consistent with what St. Paul taught: "For by grace you have been saved through faith; and that not of yourselves. It is the gift of God" (Ephesians 2:8).

thousands of people who were not members of the church, and thousands who were under thirty years of age, were challenged by the gospel and turned in their utter helplessness to Christ Jesus, to find in him one who has wholly taken their place so that they might freely be given his place. It is in this message of the unconditional grace and vicarious humanity of the Lord Jesus Christ that people have often told me that they have found the healing and liberation which they never thought possible.[56]

For Torrance there was a clear distinction between proclamation (*kerygma*) that leads one to the Living Christ and that promotes healing, and liberation and a kind of teaching that promoted weariness and discouragement. Torrance asserts, "The gospel must be proclaimed in an evangelical way! It is the proclamation of the cross as the power of God, and teaching about faith standing in the power of God and not in the wisdom of the world, that will open wide the gates and point the way ahead for a radical renewal of the church and its mission."[57]

Epistemology and Preaching

Understanding T. F. Torrance's epistemology is critical to understanding his view of how we encounter the Living Word, Jesus Christ. As we have already made clear, for Torrance, preaching was not just the teaching of doctrine but of bringing people face to face with the Living Christ. Torrance argues that, "Our primary task, epistemologically, is to focus our attention on the area where God is actually known and seek to understand that knowledge in its concrete happening, out of its own proper ground, and in its own proper reference to objective reality."[58] Furthermore, he states:

> Unless we have a Word from God, some articulated communication from Himself to us, we are thrown back upon ourselves to authenticate His existence and to make Him talk by putting our own words into His mouth and by clothing Him with our own ideas. That kind of God is only a dumb idol which we have fashioned in our own image and into whose mouth we have projected our own soliloquies, and which we are unable to distinguish from our own processed interpretation. In other words,

---

56. Torrance, *Preaching Christ Today*, 38.
57. Torrance, *Preaching Christ Today*, 39.
58. Torrance, *Theological Science*, 27.

we have no genuine knowledge of God at all, for we are left alone with our own thoughts and self-deceptions.[59]

For Torrance, theological science begins with understanding the God who is there and who has spoken. Torrance states, "I find the presence and being of God bearing upon my experience and thought so powerfully that I cannot but be convinced of His overwhelming reality and rationality. To doubt the existence of God would be a sheer irrationality, for it would mean that my reason had become unhinged from its bond with real being."[60] Torrance believed that if there was a problem in the knowing of God, the problem was on our side not on his side; that the disorder had resulted in the mind and that it was humanity who obstructed the knowledge of God. Torrance states, "Science is nothing more, as Einstein has said, than the refinement of everyday thinking, for it respects the fundamental nature of things and seeks to understand and explain them in their own intelligibility."[61] Torrance's desire was to keep theology objective. Scottish philosopher, John MacMurray, commenting about the influence of Christianity on science stated, "It was Christianity that gave us science by its insistence on the spirit of truth. . . . Science is sustained by the love of the truth. Apart from a passionate belief in the supreme value of truth, and from the willingness to sacrifice pleasant illusions to that faith in the truth, the whole truth and nothing but the truth, science could neither begin nor continue."[62] For Torrance, this disposition of the pursuit of truth was dominant in his doxological theology. He asserts, "Scientific theology is active engagement in that cognitive relation to God in obedience to the demands of His reality and self—giving."[63] He also states elsewhere that "Theological thinking is more like listening than any other knowledge, a listening for and to a rational Word from beyond anything that we can tell to ourselves and distinct from our rational elaborations of it."[64]

---

59. Torrance, *Theological Science*, 31. James Stewart said, "Resist all temptations to dilute your Gospel. Your task is not to send people away from church saying, 'That was a lovely sermon' or 'What an eloquent appeal!' The one question is: Did they, or did they not, meet God today?" Stewart, *Heralds of God*, 31.

60. Torrance, *Theological Science*, ix.

61. Torrance, *God and Rationality*, 10.

62. Macmurray, *Freedom in the Modern World*, 33ff. Quoted by T. F. Torrance, *Theological Science*, 76.

63. Torrance, *Theological Science*, ix.

64. Torrance, *Theological Science*, 30.

A key insight for understanding T. F. Torrance's epistemology is to once again be aware of his concern with dualism. We are reflecting on this now as it pertains to preaching. He stated, "The big problem that keeps on arising is that philosophers, theologians, and biblical scholars often tend to be trapped within dualist patterns of thought which scientists on the whole have rejected."[65] Torrance argued that the scientific community for the most part had undergone an epistemological shift brought about by general relativity theory:

> Let me try to say something about this change going on in the foundations of knowledge. In general relativity theory, physics and geometry are integrated so that one does not operate with an independent conceptual system prior to one's actual physics—that dualism was comprehensively destroyed by Einstein. As a result scientists think from beginning to end in terms of the integration of empirical and theoretical factors, both in nature and in our knowledge of it. This represents an immense epistemological revolution in which ontology and epistemology are now wedded together. That is a development which biblical scholars by and large have not yet appreciated, for many of them are still stuck in old Enlightenment, pre-Einsteinian ways of thinking. This is to a certain extent due to the massive genius of Immanuel Kant, through whom the dualism built into modern classical science by Galileo and Newton, was given a metaphysical form that has had a powerful influence on modern thought.[66]

For Torrance, when theologians worked with dualists patterns of thought, they divided the world from the Creator consequently denying any interaction between the Creator and his creation.

> Theological knowledge of God is not concerned with God in the abstract, with God as He is simply in Himself, as it were, as if our knowledge of God could be cut off from the fact that it is after all knowledge of God by man on earth and in time. Theology is concerned with God as the Creator of the world, and therefore with God in His relation to the world of creaturely realities.[67]

Likewise, theologians who worked with dualist patterns of thought, functioned with a division between God and Jesus Christ. Torrance

65. Torrance, *Preaching Christ Today*, 41.
66. Torrance, *Preaching Christ Today*, 42.
67. Torrance, *Theological Science*, 56.

believed that this was both spiritually and pastorally disastrous. The interest in natural theology was a major contributor to that situation. According to Torrance:

> When with the Enlightenment there arose as a result of dualist thinking a deistic disjunction in thought between God and the universe, there took place a resurgence of natural theology which has always arisen in the great periods of dualist thought, as in the medieval and the post-Newtonian eras, when people tried to build a logical bridge between God and the world and between faith and reason. A great deal of modern apologetics from both the liberal and the fundamentalist's camps is in different ways tied in with that. However, such a logical bridge between God and the world, and indeed between being and statement, has now been comprehensively demolished, not just by the rigorous theology of Karl Barth, but by the profound revolution in logic that has taken place, in which it has been made clear that it is impossible to state in statements how statements relate to being, without resolving everything into statements. Most theologians, however, I am sorry to say, have not begun to appreciate the far-reaching significance of this revolution.[68]

It is important to note that when Torrance lectured about philosophical dualism or dualism within the sciences, his concern was always related to how this impacted theology. When Torrance spoke about *kataphysic inquiry*, a term referring to the concept of "according to nature," he eventually was making his way towards a statement about how we know God. Torrance states, "He is the Lord God before whom our human knowing undergoes a radical change, which I sometimes speak of as an *epistemological inversion* of our ordinary knowing relation. We can know God only through his self-revelation and grace, and thus only in the mode of worship, prayer, and adoration in which we respond personally, humbly, and obediently to his divine initiative in making himself known to us as our Creator and Lord."[69] Dick Eugenio states, "That Jesus is "the light" is perhaps the most preached theme in Torrance's sermons. This is evident in the numerous sermon outlines and manuscripts on this topic."[70] Torrance went as far to say that without this epistemological in-

68. Torrance, *Preaching Christ Today*, 44.
69. Torrance, *Preaching Christ Today*, 47.
70. Eugenio, *Communion with God*, 157 (footnote). See B38 Untitled sermon on 1 John 1:5; B38 "I am the light of the World"; B38 "The Real Light"; B38 Untitled sermon on John 1:34; B39 "A Faith for Hard Times: The Living Light"; B39 "Light: Its Theology

version or *metanoia* one could not really be a theological student, much less a minister of the gospel.[71] Torrance also applied Luke 9:23, "Whoever wants to be my disciple must take up their cross daily and follow me" to "The kind of repentant thinking of all unwarranted presuppositions and objective commitment to the truth which characterize rigorous scientific inquiry."[72] Torrance believed that the theologian must work with the same rigorous calling as a rigorous scientist:

> If we regard science in this rigorous way, and hold theology also to be a rigorous science (as I do), how are they to be related to one another? Think of it like this. The theologian and the scientist live and work within the same room, so to speak, within the same empirical world of space and time, which both the theologian and scientist have to take seriously. The theologian is concerned with God as he reveals himself to us within space and time through historical Israel and in the incarnation of his Word in Jesus Christ, so that we cannot divorce what God reveals to humankind from the medium of spatio-temporal structures which he uses in addressing his Word to human beings. Empirical correlates therefore have an ineradicable place in theology, as in natural science—hence theological truths and concepts may not be resolved away or "demythologized" without losing their essential content or import.[73]

Torrance argued that the theologian and the scientist both work within the context of space and time. And although the scientist is working, empirically, with what is there to be known within creation, the theologian is working within the same context but looking at God's revelation of himself in Jesus Christ within the space-time creation.

> The scientist on his part is concerned in his inquiries only with events and forces which have space-time coordinates and only with theoretical concepts, however abstruse, that are empirically correlated with space and time. Within the same sphere of space and time which both share, the scientist inquires into the nature of created realities, but the theologian inquires into the nature of

---

and Physics"; B39 "Light"; B41 "Christ the Light of the World"; B41 "The Christian Faith and the Physics of Light"; B43 Untitled Sermon on Isaiah 50:11, 1–8; and B45 Untitled Sermon on 1 John 1:1–10; 2:1–11. For a discussion of light in relation to daily Christian life, see B47 "If we walk in the light," 1–8.

71. Torrance, *Preaching Christ Today*, 48.
72. Torrance, *Preaching Christ Today*, 48.
73. Torrance, *Preaching Christ Today*, 48.

> God, the Creator of those realities. When the scientist inquires into the nature of the world, he does that not by looking at God but by looking away from him at the world, but when the theologian inquires into the nature of God as he has revealed himself he does that not by looking at the nature of the world, which God has created out of nothing, but by looking away from the world to its Creator.[74]

Although the scientist and theologian move in opposite directions, they are both concerned with the created and contingent universe. Both disciplines of science and theology are dealing with what is already there. This is in contrast to mere speculation. For Torrance, this was a proper theological understanding of the nature of the universe, created with a rational order, which reflected God's transcendent rationality. Torrance argues, "This is part of the Christian doctrine of contingence, upon the truth of which in the last analysis empirical science and its historical development rest."[75] There was also a desire from Torrance to look for the basic connections between the spatio-temporal concepts of natural science and the concepts of theological science, which contain spatio-temporal ingredients. For Torrance, it was impossible to discuss the incarnation or the atonement except as involving space-time coordinates.

Preaching, Theological Inquiry, and the Early Church

Regarding theologians dealing with dualism in the early centuries of the Christian era, Torrance wrote,

> The questions that they faced had to do to a large extent with the radical dualism that affected all classical culture, that is, Graeco-Roman culture, in which a sharp line of demarcation or separation, a χωρισμός was drawn between the intelligible realm and the sensible realm, that is, a realm of eternal ideas and a realm of empirical events, or a realm of reality and realm of appearance. Consequently for the Greeks anything that took place in the empirical or phenomenal realm was regarded as lacking in reality, an evanescent appearance, and even as evil.[76]

---

74. Torrance, *Preaching Christ Today*, 48.
75. Torrance, *Preaching Christ Today*, 49.
76. Torrance, *Preaching Christ Today*, 49–50.

Torrance argued that with that kind of worldview, with its radical disjunction between appearance and reality, temporal and eternal, earthly and heavenly, the sensible and intelligible, that the teaching of the New Testament regarding the incarnation was regarded by the Greeks as a crude mythological way of thinking.[77] When the gospel was preached within that kind of dualistic framework, it was thought to be a sort of mythology projecting this world of appearance into the real eternal forms and truth.

Torrance emphasized that it was Athanasius who addressed these false assumptions by arguing that in Jesus Christ, the Logos of God had become incarnate in our world. Torrance states, "This had the double effect of de-divinizing the rational forms of Greek thought and of affirming the reality of the empirical world of space and time, which must therefore be regarded as worthy of rational or scientific attention."[78] Torrance warned not to think of myth as something that is exclusively primitive. The theologians in the early church discovered that in order to preach the gospel, they had to figure out ways of addressing the dualist habits and patterns of thought and replace them with a worldview that factored in a Creator who created the universe and that God's redemptive purposes have all take place within that created universe. Torrance writes, "The teaching of Gnostics and Arians in different ways gave the early church a great deal of trouble, for the dualism that lay behind it threatened to undermine the gospel of God's objective revealing and saving activity in Jesus Christ and reduce it to a merely symbolical and mythological way of thinking."[79] Torrance pointed out that for the church fathers to preach effectively that Jesus Christ was Immanuel (God with us) within the context of Greek culture and philosophy and in such a way that the gospel message would be received and understood, they had to combat dualism as the foundation of knowledge; that was precisely what they did in giving formulation to the incarnation of the Word by whom all things visible and invisible were made. Torrance writes:

> Christians taught that in Jesus Christ God himself has come into our world and become man, yet without ceasing to be God. He is a creature of our world and yet the Creator by whom all things are made. He is true God of God and yet true man of man, so

---

77. Torrance, *Preaching Christ Today*, 49–50.
78. Torrance, *Preaching Christ Today*, 49–50.
79. Torrance, *Preaching Christ Today*, 52.

that when we know God in Jesus Christ our knowledge terminates on the very Being of God, and not just on the being of man. This carried with it two very fundamental principles: that Jesus Christ the incarnate Son of God is of one and the same being (ὁμοούσιος) as the Father, and that in Jesus Christ divine and human natures are united in one person (*henosis hupostatike*). It was on the basis of that teaching that the great theologians of the fourth century destroyed the epistemological and cosmological dualisms endemic in Hellenistic culture and transformed the foundations of knowledge, and incidentally laid the basis upon which our modern empirico-theoretical science rests.[80]

Torrance was interested in the evangelical significance of what happened in the fourth century. If there was no ontological connection between God and Jesus Christ, if he was merely a man speaking about God, then how can one take anything Jesus said with authority? For example of this is when Jesus said, "Son, your sins are forgiven." If Jesus was not fully God and fully man then those sins were not forgiven. According to Torrance:

> Take divine revelation: if you say that Jesus Christ is the revelation of God, while as a matter of fact he is not God, then you have no way of claiming that what he says is really of God; there is then no fidelity between what he reveals and what God really is, and so the whole structure of divine revelation falls apart. In the second century Irenaeus had formulated the basic principle at stake as God reveals himself through himself. That was taken up by Karl Barth in our day, who, with the central point of the Nicene Creed in mind, expressed it thus: the content of God's self—revelation is identical with Jesus Christ. Sever that relation between Christ and God and revelation is emptied of any ultimate truth or reality, and you are then flung back upon a merely symbolical or mythological way of thinking and speaking. That is why the fathers at Nicaea held the unbroken relation in being and act between Jesus Christ the incarnate son of God and God the Father to be absolutely central. They fought very hard for it, for in it the very gospel was at stake.[81]

Torrance was concerned about the implications of severing the ontological bond between the work of Christ and the person of Christ. The early church was combating the heretical denial of the deity of Jesus

---

80. Torrance, *Preaching Christ Today*, 53.
81. Torrance, *Preaching Christ Today*, 54.

Christ. This is why it was critical for them to insert a clause in the Nicene Creed regarding the oneness of Jesus Christ with the Father. Torrance indicated that the purpose was to secure the truth of Christ's salvific work at the cross and in his sacrifice.

For Torrance, the implications of the Nicene faith were not only theological but pastoral. He writes, "When I was a pastor I not only preached the gospel from the pulpit but I read the Scriptures and prayed with people in their homes regularly. When I had done that two or three times, they opened their hearts and talked frankly with me, which allowed me really to minister the gospel to them in a direct and personal way."[82] Torrance believed that this is what allowed him to preach to them in a personal way, which he believed helped him when he became a professor of Christian dogmatics. He believed that the decade he invested in two parishes helped him understand the depths of human nature more than any psychological textbooks or university lectures could have ever done. T. F. Torrance stated the following, which could be argued, was the center of his philosophy of preaching:

> In preaching the Word of God and ministering the gospel to people, the most important thing with which we must be concerned is to bring them face—to—face with God in Jesus Christ, for it is only God in Jesus Christ who can forgive and heal—only God in Jesus Christ who can reveal the ultimate truth to us about himself. It is Jesus Christ alone who defines God for us, and defines him in a radical way that calls in question false notions of God arising out of alienation from him which obscure the truth and hide him from us. Today we need to learn again with the early Christians how, through faith in Jesus Christ as the one Mediator between God and humankind, to face and overcome the insidious effect of dualism, not only in our theology and science, but in our practical ministry, our pastoral care, our daily prayer, and our spiritual life.[83]

For Torrance, the written word exists to proclaim the Living Word. This, once again, is what he meant when he talked about *didactic* preaching and *kerymatic* theology. "The Reformation taught us that we do not know God in His isolation from us but only in personal communion, that is, in a two-way relation between subject and object; nevertheless along with this the Reformation brought into great prominence the doctrine of

---

82. Torrance, *Preaching Christ Today*, 55.
83. Torrance, *Preaching Christ Today*, 56.

election which asserts that we do not know God or worship His through action upon Him but through being acted upon by Him."[84] Evangelical preaching must proclaim not only the work of Christ but also the person of Christ. Dualisms, separating the work and person of Christ, are devastating to Evangelical preaching according to Torrance. He argued that the person and work of Christ must always be held together. For Torrance, this was critical for preaching Christ in a scientific way. This is what he meant when he talked about the gospel and scientific thinking. Torrance stated, "In the Early Church the stress was more on the Being in the Act, i.e. on Christology; in the Reformation Church the stress was more on the Act in the Being, i.e. on Soteriology—but they were complementary attempts to inquire into and to determine the objective and right ground of the Church's existence and understanding."[85]

Conclusion

Regarding the vocation of preaching Christ, David Torrance offer words of wisdom for every pastor:

> In preaching and in pastoral ministry we dare not direct attention to ourselves, to our preaching or our oratory. If we do this, we will turn people's attention away from Christ and will hinder the work of the Gospel. Our aim must always be to direct attention to God in his Triune nature. John the Baptist said, "He must become greater; I must become less" (John 3:30). Our constant prayer must ever be that in preaching and through worship, as in pastoral care, people will become deeply aware of God's presence and will hear him speaking to them in love and saving power. We want people to meet personally with Christ Jesus. We are called in the words of Paul in Gal. 3:27 to be "clothed with Christ."[86]

David Torrance not only articulated the sentiment of the apostle Paul but also of his brother. For T. F. Torrance, preaching existed to herald the good news of Jesus Christ; the purpose of preaching was to announce good tidings and to remind people of what God has done for them in Christ Jesus; that what Christ did in his faithfulness, made it possible

---

84. Torrance, *Theological Science*, 96.
85. Torrance, *Theological Science*, 344.
86. David Torrance, *A Passion for Christ*, 79.

for the rest of humanity to believe. "This then is the given fact, the indispensable presupposition of theological knowledge, and with which Christian theology stands or falls, that God himself, the only God, has condescended to enter within our creaturely and contingent existence, to objectify himself for us there in Jesus Christ, so that Jesus Christ is the Way, the Truth, and the Life, in whom and through whom alone we go to the Father, and by reference to whom alone we have true knowledge of God."[87]

---

87. Torrance, *Theological Science*, 52.

7

The Sacraments of Incorporation and Renewal

Introduction

IN THIS CHAPTER, WE will examine T. F. Torrance's theology of the sacraments. T. F. Torrance commenting on the liturgical acts in the Old Testament stated, "We cannot emphasize enough then that the sacrificial and liturgical acts were regarded as witness and only witness to God's own action and appointment. The real agent in the Old Testament liturgy is God himself. God is not acted upon by means of liturgical sacrifice. Liturgical sacrifice rests upon God's self-revelation and answers as cultic sign to God's own word and action, which is the thing signified."[1] T. F. Torrance emphasized that God was the subject as well as the object of worship, in the Old Testament liturgy. Likewise, regarding the New Testament, worship was about what Christ offered.

T. F. and J. B. Torrance argued that the role we play is one of participating in the worship of Christ. One of the primary ways we do this is through participation in the sacraments. According to Torrance, in baptism, we are incorporated into the death and resurrection of Jesus Christ and in the Lord's Supper, we participate in our renewal in Christ. Robert T. Walker states, "In the church's ministry of word and sacrament, it is Christ himself who speaks to people through its word, who incorporates

---

1. Torrance, *Atonement*, 18–19.

them into his baptism and feeds them with himself the Word of God incarnate in our humanity, the bread of his living word and risen life."[2]

The Influence of Robert Bruce

The sermons of the sixteenth-century minister of the High Kirk of Edinburgh (St. Giles), Robert Bruce, were very influential on T. F. Torrance's theology of the sacraments. He was one of most influential ministers of the gospel that Scotland has ever known. He was the successor to James Lawson and John Knox and it was his leadership that gave stability to the Reformation in Scotland. Behind his famous sermons on the sacraments were the teachings on the person and saving work of Christ as well as the need to receive this work by faith.

These sermons on the sacraments by Robert Bruce were published in 1590 and 1591, then republished in 1614 and then republished again by William Cunningham in Edinburgh in 1843 under the title, *The Mystery of the Lord's Supper*. In the edition of 1958, edited and introduced by Thomas F. Torrance, we find these words that highlight their influence:

> From my early years the historic Sermons of Robert Bruce on the Sacrament formed an essential and unforgettable part of my theological diet. I was brought up on them at home, and when I came to New College, in the University of Edinburgh, as a divinity student, I found myself giving them fuller study on the urgent recommendation of Professor H. R. Mackintosh. His inspiration from Bruce's sermons taught me to treasure them even more highly as the very marrow of our sacramental tradition in the Church of Scotland.[3]

Since these sermons were first delivered in the great Kirk of St. Giles, Edinburgh, in 1589, their doctrine infused the very soul of the Kirk, strengthening its faith and informing the worship at the Table of the Lord according to T. F. Torrance.[4] In that the original edition of the sermons were written down as Robert Bruce was preaching and published without any editorial work, the force of Bruce's language is apparent. John Livingstone, a younger contemporary said, "Master Robert Bruce I heard several times, and, in my opinion, never man spake with greater power

---

2. Torrance, *Atonement*, liv.
3. Bruce, *The Mystery of the Lord's Supper*, iv.
4. Bruce, *The Mystery of the Lord's Supper*, iv

since the Apostles' days."⁵ T. F. Torrance wrote that Bruce "was one of the most deeply spiritual and powerful ministers of the Gospel Scotland has ever known."⁶ And to emphasize the importance of Robert Bruce's theological influence, Torrance asserts, "It is as a theologian above all that we must appreciate him today. He wrote no works of theology, but there can be no doubt from what he has left us that he was a man of commanding theological power and spiritual insight, as also a man of rare faith."⁷ It is obvious from these comments that Robert Bruce inspired T. F. Torrance. Continuing in his admiration, Torrance writes:

> The alliance of theology with preaching and worship, in the great tradition of Knox and Calvin, was a prime characteristic of Robert Bruce. Like Calvin, also, Bruce was steeped in the learning of the Fathers of the Early Church, being particularly influenced by Augustine, and Irenaeus, "that ancient writer", as Bruce called him. It was probably this combination of Biblical and Patristic theology that kept him so close to Calvin especially at a number of significant points where rationalist Calvinism lost touch with Calvin himself owing to its combination of theology with a revived Aristotelianism, and later indeed with Cartesian philosophy, both so markedly evident in the great theologians of the Netherlands who came to occupy a dominant influence over many Scottish divines.⁸

T. F. Torrance was moved by the relationship between theology, preaching, and worship. And this combination of theology and worship was present in the ministry of Robert Bruce according to Torrance. Torrance was drawn to this Reformed faith of Calvin and Robert Bruce.

Robert Bruce of Kinnaird (1554–1631)

Torrance states, "It was largely under his [Robert Bruce of Kinnaird] leadership that the Reformation in Scotland was given the stability and permanence which it had not attained even under the leadership of Knox, while the evangelical tradition in Word and Sacrament and the pastoral care of the flock of Christ was given lasting character through

---

5. Bruce, *The Mystery of the Lord's Supper*, iv.
6. Bruce, *The Mystery of the Lord's Supper*, 1.
7. Bruce, *The Mystery of the Lord's Supper*, 22.
8. Bruce, *The Mystery of the Lord's Supper*, 22–23.

his outstanding ministrations."[9] In his introduction to his sermons, Torrance wrote about Bruce's remarkable ability to make very difficult matters quite plain and was furthermore used by God to speak directly to the conscience of his parishioners. Regarding his personal pastoral countenance, he was very short in prayer but "every sentence was like a strong bolt up towards heaven."[10] In the introduction to his sermons we find these words, "The godly for his potent and moving doctrine loved him; the worldly for his parentage and position revered him; and the enemies for both reasons stood in awe of him."[11] These words demonstrate the respect that Robert Bruce had in his day. T. F. Torrance wrote:

> Few men in the history of the Kirk can stand beside Bruce in sheer godliness and absolute fidelity to conviction. The resolute uprightness, the righteous tenacity in which he lived his life from beginning to end, was in itself a supreme contribution to the nation. His example as a true minister of Word and Sacrament, and as a faithful and tender pastor with his flock at all times and in spite of every difficulty and rebuff, taught and inspired not only those who followed him immediately in the ministry, but thousands of others since who have been called into the holy office of the Gospel in Scotland. Even greater has been the impact of his teaching which Bruce applied the high doctrines of the Reformed Church directly to the personal conscience. No Scottish divine, to my knowledge, had more of Calvin's supreme sense of the Majesty and Mercy of God, but in the piety of Bruce emphasis is laid upon the *feeling* of that Majesty and Mercy in a way that it is not in Calvin.[12]

As we shall see shortly, the influence of Robert Bruce's theology was clearly seen in Torrance's view of the sacrament as one of participating in the real presence of Jesus. According to Robert Bruce, union with Christ is an experienced reality when we celebrate the Lord's Supper for it is the Living Christ drawing us unto himself, through the Spirit, when we partake of the consecrated bread and wine.

---

9. Bruce, *The Mystery of the Lord's Supper*, 1.
10. Bruce, *The Mystery of the Lord's Supper*, 20.
11. Bruce, *The Mystery of the Lord's Supper*, 8.
12. Bruce, *The Mystery of the Lord's Supper*, 17–18.

A Sample of the Sermons on the Sacraments by Robert Bruce

The Sacraments in General

For three of his sermons including his sermon entitled, *The Sacraments in General*, Bruce employed the text of 1 Corinthians 11:23 "For I have received of the Lord that which also I delivered unto you, that the Lord Jesus the night in which he was betrayed, took bread." Bruce highlighted a number of key ideas in this first sermon. First of all, he stated, "The Word leads us to Christ by the ear; the Sacraments lead us to Christ by the eye: of the two senses which God has chosen as most fitting for the purpose of instructing us and bringing us to Christ."[13] Bruce argued that when the word is preached, the gospel is heard. But when the Eucharist accompanies the word, the gospel is also visibly and tangibly experienced bringing us to the Living Christ. Bruce admonished his parishioners "whenever they come to hear the doctrine, whether it be of the Sacraments or of the simple Word, ask that God may be present by His Holy Spirit."[14]

In this sermon, where Bruce emphasized the importance of word and table and why both need each other, he stated, "Therefore the Word alone cannot be a Sacrament nor the element alone, but Word and element must together make a Sacrament."[15] Bruce argued that word and sacrament are conjointly held together; that one does not make sense without the other; that the minister gives the earthly thing (the elements) and Christ Jesus, the Mediator, gives the heavenly thing (himself); that the one is taken in a natural way (the elements) and the other in a spiritual way (by faith); that in the command "take, eat" we are required to obey and that in the promise "This is my Body," we are required to believe.[16] Bruce stated that "the Sacrament is appointed that we may get a better hold of Christ than we got in the simple Word, that we may possess Christ in our hearts and minds more fully and largely than we did before, by the simple Word."[17]

Regarding the meaning of a sign in the sacrament, Bruce states, "There must therefore be two sorts of signs: one sort, the bread and wine, which we call elemental; another sort, the rites and ceremonies, by which

---

13. Bruce, *The Mystery of the Lord's Supper*, 30.
14. Bruce, *The Mystery of the Lord's Supper*, 31.
15. Bruce, *The Mystery of the Lord's Supper*, 33.
16. Bruce, *The Mystery of the Lord's Supper*, 58.
17. Bruce, *The Mystery of the Lord's Supper*, 59.

they are distributed, broken and given, which we call ceremonial."¹⁸ This point seemed to be elaborated throughout this particular sermon. For example, Bruce states:

> I call them signs because they have the Body and Blood of Christ conjoined with them. Indeed, so truly is the Body of Christ conjoined with the bread, and the Blood of Christ conjoined with the wine, that as soon as you receive the bread in your mouth (if you are a faithful man or woman) you receive the Body of Christ in your soul, and that by faith. And as soon as you receive the wine in your mouth, you receive the Blood of Christ in your soul, and that by faith.¹⁹

Notice the emphasis on the phrase, "by faith." We receive the body of Christ into our soul *by faith* and we receive the blood of Christ into our soul *by that same faith*. We are to come to the Lord's Supper with a faithful believing heart. Bruce emphasized, "It is chiefly because the Lord has appointed the Sacraments as hands to deliver and exhibit the things signified, that they are called signs."²⁰ Furthermore, Bruce stated, "This flesh is spiritual food, ministering unto my spiritual life, therefore it is called a spiritual thing."²¹ Particularly helpful in understanding Bruce's perspective on how the elements are conjointly held together by what they represent are his words in the middle of this sermon:

> Strictly speaking, no one has power to deliver Christ but God the Father, or He Himself. No one has power to deliver the Mediator, but His own Spirit. Nevertheless, it has pleased God to use some instruments and means by which He would deliver Christ Jesus to us. The means are these: The ministry of the Word, and the ministry of the Sacraments; and because He uses these as means to deliver Christ, they are said to deliver Him. But here you have to distinguish between the principal efficient deliverer, and the instrumental efficient deliverer, which is the Word and Sacraments. If we keep this distinction, both these are true: God by His Word, and God by His Spirit, delivers Christ Jesus to you. I call them signs, then, because God has made them potent instruments to deliver the same thing that they signify.²²

18. Bruce, *The Mystery of the Lord's Supper*, 35.
19. Bruce, *The Mystery of the Lord's Supper*, 35–36.
20. Bruce, *The Mystery of the Lord's Supper*, 36.
21. Bruce, *The Mystery of the Lord's Supper*, 40.
22. Bruce, *The Mystery of the Lord's Supper*, 37.

Regarding the emphasis of Robert Bruce preaching to the conscience which Torrance emphasized in his introduction, in this sermon entitled, "The Sacraments in General," Bruce admonished his parishioners to "think of his own domestic idol, that lodges within his own heart, and strive to rid himself of it, otherwise you cannot see the face of Christ, to be a partaker of His kingdom."[23] Also, he said, "There is no other lesson in Christianity than this; this is the first and last lesson: to shake off your lust and affections more and more, and so more and more to renounce yourself that you may embrace Christ."[24] And finally, "Examine your own heart when you will: if there is anything in the world you love better than Christ, if you are not ready to leave father and mother, to leave wife and children, or whatever is most dear to you in this world for Christ's sake, you are not worthy of Him. If you are not ready to cast off whatever estranges you from Christ, you are not worthy of Him."[25] Robert Bruce certainly had the tone of a prophet, yet there is an underlying grace with his desire to point his parishioners to Christ.

The Lord's Supper in Particular 1

In another sermon entitled *The Lord's Supper in Particular 1*, Bruce expounded on the various names given to the Sacrament. For example he stated, "It is called 'The Supper of the Lord' to distinguish it from a common supper. This is the Lord's Supper, a holy Supper, not a profane or common supper, but a Supper appointed for the increase of holiness, for the food of the soul in holiness, to feed the soul for the life everlasting."[26] He further stated, "If any of you would ask when the minister in this action breaks or distributes the bread, pours out and distributes the wine: 'what kind of things are these?' The answer is: they are holy things."[27] And regarding speaking to the need to perceive Christ by faith, we find the following words:

> If Christ is not perceived, except by faith, then, we say, no wicked person can perceive Him. He who lacks faith cannot perceive Him. He who lacks faith may receive the Sacrament of the bread

23. Bruce, *The Mystery of the Lord's Supper*, 51.
24. Bruce, *The Mystery of the Lord's Supper*, 51.
25. Bruce, *The Mystery of the Lord's Supper*, 51.
26. Bruce, *The Mystery of the Lord's Supper*, 67.
27. Bruce, *The Mystery of the Lord's Supper*, 75.

and wine, and may eat of the bread and wine, but He who lacks faith may not eat of the Body and Blood of Christ, signified by the bread and wine. So this is the ground: no faithless person can receive Christ or eat the Body of Christ in the Sacrament.[28]

In light of the Robert Bruce's influence on T. F. Torrance, it is fascinating that Bruce here preaches regarding the need of the faith of the worshiper. As previously mentioned, Torrance, puts the emphasis of faith on the faithfulness of Christ and not on the faith of the worshiper. There does appear to be an incongruity between Robert Bruce and T. F. Torrance regarding this matter. In Bruce's sermon, there is a repeated admonition to examine one's heart and to turn to Christ instead of searching for moral strength in human reform alone. However, there is probably not as much of a difference in thought regarding the outcome: faith in the fidelity of Christ. Bruce seemed to advocate "evangelical repentance" rather than "legal repentance." This is specifically how James Torrance made the distinction:

> Legal repentance says: "Repent, and if you repent you will be forgiven!" as though God our Father has to be conditioned into being gracious! It makes the imperatives of obedience prior to the indicative of grace, and regards God's love and forgiveness and acceptance as conditional upon what we do—upon our meritorious acts of repentance. Calvin argued that this inverted the evangelical order of grace, and made repentance prior to forgiveness, whereas in the New Testament forgiveness is logically prior to repentance. Evangelical repentance, on the other hand, takes the form: "Christ has borne your sins on the cross, therefore repent! Receive his forgiveness in repentance!" That is, repentance is our response to grace, not a condition of grace. The goodness of God leads us to repentance.[29]

In the remainder of Bruce's sermons, there are many ideas such as remembering the passion of Christ, belief in the death of Christ, the Spirit's work in the sacrament, the connection of this seal to the covenant of grace and mercy, the importance of the sacrament being publicly administered, along with details on the preparation of the Supper (which also includes a detailed analysis of how to examine our conscience).

---

28. Bruce, *The Mystery of the Lord's Supper*, 85.
29. J. B. Torrance, *Worship, Community, and the Triune God of Grace*, 44.

Significant Implications of Robert Bruce's Sermons on the Sacraments

While it is obvious that T. F. Torrance had a high view of Robert Bruce, the important question is, "What are the significant implications of Bruce's sermons on the subject of the sacraments for T. F. Torrance?" First of all, according to Torrance, there was a synthesis of high doctrine and personal application in the preaching of Robert Bruce. In these sermons there was an emphasis placed upon "the integration between doctrinal teaching and personal application, between sacramental ministration and evangelical quickening so characteristic of the Scottish tradition."[30] Torrance states:

> It was above all at the Sacrament of the Lord's Supper that this was apparent, for the Sacrament was not only the supreme ordinance of prayer and worship and of feeding upon Christ, but emphatically an evangelical ordinance through which the Gospel was proclaimed in the most vivid and potent way and through which multitudes were brought into Christ and sealed by the Spirit. In the language of a later day, the Sacrament was also a "converting ordinance," for it was at the Sacrament, before the gracious presence of the divine Majesty, that sinners were convicted of sin and converted to godliness. This combination of sacramental and evangelical experience secured the latter from subjectivist pietism, and the former from a doctrinaire sacramentalism.[31]

The second implication of these sermons for Torrance was that, while the emphasis of the inward sense of the majesty and mercy of God promoted the temptation to doubt in Luther, it never did so with Calvin or Knox. In the introduction to his sermons, Torrance pointed out that Bruce had the "tendency to be afflicted with seasons of doubt not due to a naturally sceptical mind but rather to a serious wrestling with the problems of conscience, and it was always correlative to his evangelical

---

30. Bruce, *The Mystery of the Lord's Supper*, 18.

31. Bruce, *The Mystery of the Lord's Supper*, 18–19. It must be noted that T. F. Torrance does in fact admit that "where in this development the emphasis tended to fall upon the conscience rather than upon the Word of the Gospel, upon self-examination rather than thankfulness and praise to God, the ground was laid for that reproachful self-questioning of faith, and almost morbid fear of the Majesty of God and His requirements in the Sacrament, which are still marked characteristics of Scottish piety in parts of the Highlands."

experience. It was this that helped Bruce to understand so deeply the fearfulness of those hounded by their conscience, and helped him to preach as no other on the pacification of the conscience in the mercy of God."[32] This comment from Torrance is fascinating in that Robert Bruce seems to be more like Luther than Calvin or Knox and yet Torrance clearly is more like Calvin and Knox yet influenced by Bruce. The point that Torrance seems to be making is that Bruce's preaching was effective precisely because he wrestled with his own conscience in light of his evangelical experience.

The third implication for Torrance was that in Bruce's case, the emphasis of the divine Majesty along with an emphasis on an upright conscience, "tended to breed an unduly punctilious sense of honor."[33] Based on Torrance's comments in his introduction to the 1958 publication of Bruce's sermons, there was certainly the sense that in addition to Bruce's ecclesiological influence, he also had tremendous public influence as he was twice Moderator of the General Assembly, enjoying favor with the King and yet at times, at odds with the King. Robert Bruce in fact offered a dedication of his sermons to James the Sixth, King of Scots, with the following blessing that is found at the beginning of many of the Pauline epistles: "Grace and Peace from God the Father, and our Lord Jesus Christ."[34] Torrance respected Bruce's public influence not just his ecclesiastical influence. The gospel was always meant to have influence into society. In 1976, Torrance himself was Moderator of the General Assembly of the Church of Scotland. Like Bruce he had considerable notoriety.

The fourth implication was that the doctrine of union with Christ and of our participation in his saving and sanctifying humanity was front and center. This was a key doctrinal emphasis within Torrance's own Christology and soteriology. Regarding Robert Bruce, Torrance states, "It was because Calvin and Bruce grasped the proper place in our salvation of the obedient humanity of the crucified and risen Jesus that they gave it full place in the doctrine of Holy Communion as our sharing through

---

32. Bruce, *The Mystery of the Lord's Supper*, 19. Torrance further emphasizes that "once such a conscience is cut adrift from the evangelical message and moralized, as it tended to be through the exaggerated moralism of the Larger Catechism, it could lead only too easily into the moral and philosophic doubt that have so often characterized Scottish Universities, not always excepting their theologians." Bruce, *The Mystery of the Lord's Supper*, 19–20.

33. Bruce, *The Mystery of the Lord's Supper*, 20.

34. Bruce, *The Mystery of the Lord's Supper*, 26.

the power of the Spirit in 'the flesh of Jesus', and therefore as our quickening and nourishment with the new humanity God has provided for us in Christ."[35] Referring to Bruce's sixth sermon on Isaiah 38, published in 1591, Torrance pointed out that Bruce addressed three aspects of the work of Christ. First of all, he emphasized the passive obedience of Jesus Christ by addressing the atonement. Secondly, Bruce emphasized Christ's active obedience by addressing Christ's mediation in his incarnation. But thirdly, Robert Bruce emphasized our Lord's sanctification of our very human nature.[36] T. F. Torrance states:

> He delivered us from the disorder and rotten root from which we proceed. For, as you see, Christ Jesus was conceived in the womb of the Virgin, and that by the mighty power of His Holy Spirit, so that our nature in Him was fully sanctified by that same power. And this perfect purity of our nature in His Person covers our impurity, for He was not conceived in sin and corruption as we are, but by the power of the Holy Spirit, who perfectly sanctified our nature in Him, even in the moment of His conception. Thus in that He was thoroughly purged, His purity covers our impurity. . . . It is this "whole Christ" that we are given to participate in the Sacrament of the Lord's Supper, and therefore we are given to share not only in the benefits of His death on the Cross and in His righteous fulfillment of the Will of God, but also in His sanctified human nature so that we are sanctified in the purity of His Incarnation through union with Him in His humanity.[37]

Jesus Christ as the Primary Sacrament

Again, for T. F. Torrance, Jesus Christ is the primary sacrament. Torrance wrote, "The primary *mysterium* or *sacramentum* is Jesus Christ himself, the incarnate reality of the Son of God who has incorporated himself into our humanity and assimilated the people of God into himself as his own Body, so that the sacraments have to be understood as concerned with our *koinonia* or participation in the mystery of Christ and his Church through the *koinonia* of communion of the Holy Spirit."[38] Torrance's em-

---

35. Bruce, *The Mystery of the Lord's Supper*, 23–24.

36. Torrance argued that in the assumption and hypostatic union, humanity's sinful will was being bent back in obedience to the Father.

37. Bruce, *The Mystery of the Lord's Supper*, 25–26.

38. Torrance, *Theology in Reconciliation*, 82.

phasis is consistent: worship is about participating in the Son's communion with the Father by the Spirit. Robert T. Walker writes, "For Torrance there is a sacramental relation between Scripture and the divine-human Word of Christ in which Scripture as the secondary text partakes of but points to the basic text of the true divine-human Word of Christ."[39]

It must also be noted that Torrance framed his thinking about the sacraments in a way that affirmed both his cosmology and his non-dualistic epistemology. Torrance was constantly criticizing any form of Platonist Augustinian dualistic tendencies. By stating that Christ is the ultimate sacrament, he is saying something about God's love for creation and that the material is intrinsically good. Because of the incarnation and the redemption provided through the saving humanity of Jesus Christ, Torrance promoted a doxological theology that emphasized the real presence of Christ in the sacraments.

Torrance's Pastoral Call for Word and Sacrament

T. F. Torrance's parish ministry also influenced his desire for evangelical and sacramental liturgy. He came to believe that engaging in liturgical worship and especially participation in the Lord's Supper was vital for spiritual renewal in the local kirk. He believed that celebrating Holy Communion complemented the preaching of Christ. Torrance states:

> I was still committed to the preaching and teaching of the gospel, but with a deeper concern to overcome the tendency to damage the relation between belief in Christ and belief in God which had resulted from a resort to natural theology fostered by liberal theologians and ministers. I was haunted by the question of a mortally wounded soldier, half an hour before he died, about whether God was really like Jesus. I was all the more concerned to encourage theological change throughout the Kirk, and to help restore in it the centrality of the crucified and risen Lord Jesus Christ. This also had the effect of deepening my concern for more liturgical worship, and for more attention to the celebration of Holy Communion. In a lax or dying church it is the evangelical and sacramental liturgy that keeps alive and deepens the beliefs and spiritual life of people.[40]

---

39. Torrance, *Atonement*, lix.

40. Torrance, *Gospel, Church, and Ministry*, 60. Robert J. Stamps states, "Nothing illustrates the pragmatic orientation of Torrance's theology more vividly than the fact

Torrance linked the terms evangelical and sacramental, that it is, word and sacrament. Together, they keep the congregational life of a local parish alive and deepen the faith of the community. Robert Stamps asserts, "The Eucharist has no evangelical substance or strength for Torrance apart from its association with God's speaking his own word."[41] For Torrance, the word must accompany the sacrament. Stamps argues, "The Eucharist is thus envisaged as the principal visual correlate in the Church. Torrance never suggests, however, that the sacrament somehow says in pictures what the word cannot say otherwise. His point is that the sacrament enhances the Church's ability to hear God speak."[42] This emphasis on the hearing of the word was imperative for Torrance. This was a critical point that was essential for Torrance's liturgical worship. The sacraments clearly relate to the hearing of the word in Torrance's thinking. "Apart from the word", Torrance said, "the sacraments cannot exist. Apart from the word there is only an empty sign that is nothing but a ceremony."[43] "Just as the head without the body is useless, so the word without the sacraments is an abstraction, and the sacraments without the word are a torso."[44] For Torrance, hearing of the word was why the sacraments existed.

Torrance on the Sacraments

In Robert T. Walker's introduction to Torrance's Atonement Lectures, he provides a quick overview of T. F. Torrance's general view of the sacraments. He describes the sacrament of baptism as one of incorporation into Christ and the Lord's Supper as a sacrament of renewal and nourishment:

---

that he wrote all three of his major essays on the Eucharist in books which had ecumenical objectives. The intention he states for his Eucharistic theology as early as 1960 underlines this; he said then that his desire was to build a theological bridge for "the fullness of sacramental communion" between the Churches. Stamps, *The Sacrament of the Word Made Flesh*, xv.

41. Stamps, *The Sacrament of the Word Made Flesh*, 209.

42. Stamps, *The Sacrament of the Word Made Flesh*, 82.

43. Torrance, "Eschatology and the Eucharist" *Intercommunion*, 303–350. Quoted by Stamps, *The Sacrament of the Word Made Flesh*, 82.

44. Torrance, *Royal Priesthood*, 101; Torrance, *God and Rationality*, 160. Stamps, *The Sacrament of the Word Made Flesh*, 82.

For Torrance, the sacraments are given to us to express more fully than words ever can the mystery of the atonement and of our incorporation in Christ. In baptism, we are incorporated into Christ's baptism completed on the cross, baptized into his death and united with him in his resurrection. In holy communion, we are given the sacrament of his passion so that in its celebration we may show forth his death until he comes again and as we eat the bread and drink the cup have communion with him through his body and blood shed on the cross. As Torrance says, "That is the meaning of the atonement which the sacrament expresses better than words." The importance of the sacraments for the nourishment of faith and for the eschatological perspective embedded in them is seen in the number of times Torrance refers to them.[45]

When T. F. Torrance described the sacraments, he was usually referencing the Christ events when defining baptism or the Lord's Supper. For example, he said that baptism is our incorporation into Christ's baptism *completed on the cross*. He linked our union with Christ at baptism and Christ's finished work on the cross. For Torrance, our baptism was a real incorporation, a participation into the finished work of Christ's saving humanity. Regarding Holy Communion, Torrance believed in a real participation in the atonement made by Christ. Stamps writes, "Because God in his own reconciling humanity actively presents himself to the Church in the sacraments effectively to apply the power of his death and resurrection, Torrance can refer to them as 'converting ordinances.'"[46]

Torrance on Baptism

Torrance referred to baptism as the sacrament of incorporation. It is common in many traditions to emphasize the faith of the believer prior to baptism. Baptismal candidates are often asked to describe how they came to faith in Christ. They might be asked to share their testimony about how *they* accepted Jesus. According to Torrance's contemporary, G. R. Beasley-Murray, "Faith is needful before baptism, that Christ and his gospel may be truly confessed in it; in baptism, to receive what God

---

45. Walker in T. F. Torrance's, *Atonement*, xlii. Regarding baptism into communion, see Smail, *Once for All*, 142–62.

46. Stamps, *The Sacrament of the Word Made Flesh*, 172. Also see, Purves, *Exploring Christology & Atonement*, 183–84.

bestows; and after baptism, in order to abide in the grace so freely given and to work out by that grace what God has wrought within."[47]

In contrast, Torrance placed the emphasis on what Christ had done and not on the obedience of the catechumen. Torrance writes, "There is *one baptism* and *one Body* through the *one Spirit*. Christ and his Church participate in the one baptism in different ways—Christ actively and vicariously as Redeemer, the Church passively and receptively and the redeemed Community."[48] He elaborated on this perspective when he said:

> As an ordinance, then, baptism sets forth not what we do, nor primarily what the Church does to us, but what God has already done in Christ, and through His Spirit continues to do in and to us in the Name of the Triune God, and our part is only to receive it, for we cannot add anything to Christ's finished work. Rather does he act upon us through his Spirit in terms of his atoning and sanctifying incorporation of himself into our humanity in such a way that it takes effect in us as our ingrafting into Christ and as our adoption into the family of the heavenly Father. That is why in the New Testament the ordinance of baptism and the vicarious baptism of Christ are spoken of so indivisibly that it is impossible to separate our understanding of the ordinance from what has been done for us in the birth, life, death and resurrection of Jesus Christ. It is precisely that union or inseparable relation which is the very meaning of the sacrament in which we are baptized in Christ's baptism, and why the sacrament is spoken of, not as *baptismos,* but as *baptisma*. It is not a separate or a new baptism but a participation in the one all inclusive baptism common to Christ and his Church, wrought out vicariously in Christ alone but into which he as assimilated the Church through the baptism of the one Spirit, and which he applies to each of us through the same Spirit. It is baptism in the Name of the Triune God.[49]

Regarding where the emphasis should be for this sacrament, Torrance writes, "Baptism tells us that in our believing we do not rely on our own faith but on the vicarious faith of Christ which in sheer grace anticipates, generates, sustains, and embraces the faith granted to those

---

47. Beasley-Murray, *Baptism in the New Testament,* 274. I incorporated Beasley-Murray's quote, a contemporary of T. F. Torrance, to contrast their perspectives about the role of faith prior to baptism.

48. Torrance, *Theology in Reconciliation,* 87.

49. Torrance, *Theology in Reconciliation,* 87–88.

who are baptized."⁵⁰ He further argues, "All this helps to make it clear that while baptism is both the act of Christ and the act of the Church in his Name, it is to be understood finally not in terms of what the Church does but in terms of what God in Christ has done, does do and will do for us in his Spirit."⁵¹ Torrance believed that it was the faithfulness of Christ that gave meaning to the sacraments. He wrote:

> Baptism is thus not a sacrament of what we do but of what God has done for us in Jesus Christ, in whom he has bound himself to us and bound us to himself, before ever we could respond to him. But it is also the sacrament of what God now does in us by his Spirit, uniting us with Christ in his faithfulness and obedience to the Father and making that the ground of our faith. As an act done to us, baptism tells us that it is not upon our act of faith or on our own faithfulness that we rely, but upon Christ alone and his vicarious faithfulness; it also tells us that in the freedom of his Spirit God makes himself present to us and binds us creatively to himself in such marvelous ways that not only is faith called forth from us as our own spontaneous response to the grace of God in Christ, but it is undergirded and supported by Christ and enclosed with is own faithfulness, and thus grounded in the mutual relation between the incarnate Son and the heavenly Father.⁵²

This was a repeated emphasis from T. F. Torrance that "our faith" was a secondary issue regarding the sacrament of baptism. His perspective was that when we are baptized, we are a baptized not as a demonstration of our faith (which is an anthropocentric perspective of worship) but into the love that Christ has for us. We are baptized into the faithfulness of Christ. When we are baptized into the name of the Father, Son and Holy Spirit, we are participating *in his work* for our salvation *not our work* for our salvation. This was really central to Torrance's theology of the sacraments and baptism in particular. Torrance argues:

> Is baptism the sacrament of what Christ has done for us in the gospel, or of our faith and decision to accept him as our savior? It is surely primarily the sacrament of what Christ has done on

---

50. Torrance, *The Mediation of Christ*, 100; Vander Zee, *Christ, Baptism, and the Lord's Supper*, 114.

51. Torrance, *Theology in Reconciliation*, 84.

52. Torrance, *Theology in Reconciliation*, 103–4. For a criticism of Torrance at this point, see Man Kei Ho, *A Critical Study on T. F. Torrance's Theology of the Incarnation*, 87–88.

our behalf when he incorporated himself into our humanity and acted in our place and in our name before God. Then why do we not baptize every one for whom Christ died? If not, are we then to turn round and say, no, we baptize people only on the ground of what they do in their decision of faith, so that baptism then becomes not primarily the sacrament of the obedience of Christ, but of our obedience to him? No, we say that baptism is the sacrament of the fact that God has bound himself to us and bound us to him before ever we bind ourselves to him, and that takes place within the community of the covenant where it is established subjectively as well as objectively. Thus baptism is the sacrament of inclusion into the covenant community, and then only secondarily is it the sacrament of attestation of our faith in Christ as our substitute and savior.[53]

Torrance emphasized the importance of the incarnation as it related to the sacrament of baptism. He believed that when a person is baptized, they are not only baptized into the death and resurrection of Christ but also into the life of Christ. Torrance writes:

> While Baptism is usually spoken of only as the Sacrament of our incorporation into Christ, it is ultimately grounded upon the fact that in Jesus the Son of God incorporated Himself into our humanity. . . . That is to say, alongside the important fact that Baptism is the Sacrament of the death and resurrection of Christ they laid down the important fact that Baptism is the Sacrament of Incarnation, the Sacrament of Nativity, as it was sometimes called.[54]

Here Torrance is connecting baptism not only to the life, death, and resurrection of Christ but also to the nativity. Clearly, Torrance is repeating his emphasis of our incorporation into the totality of the life of Christ through our baptism. When we are baptized, we are united to the life of Christ not just the work of Christ. According to Torrance:

> In humbling himself to receive the baptism unto repentance Jesus identified himself with sinners in obedience to the Father's will that he should make righteousness available for "the many." It was then that God the Father openly acknowledged him as his beloved Son, the heavens were opened over him, and the Holy Spirit manifested his descent upon him. The early Church

---

53. Torrance, *Atonement*, 192.

54. Torrance, *Conflict & Agreement in the Church, Vol. 2*, 117–18; Vander Zee, *Christ, Baptism and the Lord's Supper*, 107.

regarded that, not as Jesus' adoption to be the Son of God, but as the public proclamation of his Sonship, pointing back to his birth from above of the Spirit, to be the savior of the world, and pointing forward to his death on the Cross when he was to fulfill the whole work of atoning redemption.[55]

Commenting on Torrance, Elmer Colyer says "we have to think 'stereotypically,' holding together a single yet differentiated reality and event: (1) Jesus' vicarious baptism on our behalf in water and the Spirit at the Jordan, (2) Jesus Christ's baptism in blood in his death and resurrection, and (3) the baptism of the church in Christ's Spirit at Pentecost uniting the church with Christ in his vicarious baptism in (1) and (2) on our behalf."[56] According to Vander Zee:

> T. F. Torrance beautifully weaves Christ's baptismal anointing as the Messiah with our anointing as his people. "What happened to Jesus at his baptism . . . was given its counterpart in the church when the Holy Spirit sent by the Father in the Name of the Son came down upon the Apostolic church, sealing it as the people of God redeemed through the blood of Christ, consecrating it to share in the communion of the Father, the Son, and the Holy Spirit, and sending it out into the world united with Christ as his Body to engage in the service of the Gospel."[57]

Torrance linked narratives (the baptism of Jesus and Pentecost) to emphasize that as the people of God, when incorporated into the life of Christ, they are incorporated into the totality of the person of Jesus along with the Christ events; that is what happened at the baptism of Jesus which had its counterpart event, the giving of the Spirit by the Father in the name of Jesus which was the foundation for the church's mission. T. F. Torrance asserts, "Thus whenever the church in obedience to the command of Christ baptizes specific individuals with water in the name of the Father and the Son and the Holy Spirit, it believes that Christ himself is present baptizing with this Spirit, acknowledging and blessing the actions of the Church as his own, fulfilling in the baptized what he has already done for them in the fruit of his finished work."[58] Further elaborating on

---

55. Torrance, *Theology in Reconciliation*, 85.

56. Colyer, *How to Read T. F. Torrance*, 264–65. Vander Zee, *Christ, Baptism and the Lord's Supper*, 84.

57. Vander Zee, *Christ, Baptism and the Lord's Supper*, 81, 86.

58. Torrance, *Theology in Reconciliation*, 87.

the connection between baptism, regeneration and the person and work of Christ, T. F. Torrance argues:

> Regeneration is sacramentally enacted as an image and likeness of the birth and resurrection of Christ. Our regeneration does not take place at baptism, or when we first believe. Our regeneration has already taken place in Christ. It belongs to the peculiar nature of Baptism that it promises us a redemption which has already been accomplished in Christ; and therefore in Baptism the end is given to us in the beginning.... When we look into the waters of Baptism we see our faces reflected in it, not very clearly, but very brokenly. In the Sacrament of Baptism we see the image of our regeneration only, as it were "in a glass darkly," in an enigma. It is essentially a sacramental mystery which under the veil of water directs us back to the work of our renewal which has once for all taken place in Christ, and directs us forward to the day when we shall see Jesus face to face and become like Him.[59]

Again, it is worth noting Torrance's approach of bringing various narratives together. Here he re-interprets the text in 1 Corinthians 13:12 by employing the phrase, "in a glass darkly," to connect it with the sacrament of baptism. In its original context, in 1 Corinthians, this phase referenced limitations in this age with the anticipation of the return of Christ. Torrance's usage is directed towards communicating that when we come to the baptismal waters, we are not coming as experts in the faith. We are but beginners. The true Believer is Christ Jesus. This is what Torrance wants to communicate:

> No finer teaching on baptism is to be found in the whole of the early Church than that which has come down to us from Irenaeus. It was characteristic of him that he thought of our redemption not simply as a mighty act of God on our behalf, but also as man's consent to God's Word in the humble obedience of Jesus in whom God had re-created our humanity, reversing Adam's disobedience by Christ's obedience. This meant that Jesus Christ is not only the Agent of our salvation, but its very matter and substance, for God's saving activity has been translated into his worldly reality in terms of the whole vicarious and sanctifying life of Jesus from his birth of the Virgin Mary to his resurrection from the dead. On this ground baptism is expounded as

---

59. Torrance, *Conflict and Agreement in the Church, Vol. 2*, 131–32; Vander Zee, *Christ, Baptism and the Lord's Supper*, 107.

> the sacrament of the incarnational reversal of the estate we have lost in Adam and of our participation in the new humanity of Jesus Christ. Hence the reality of our baptism is to be found in the objective reality of what has already been accomplished for us in Jesus Christ and is savingly operative in us through union and communion with Christ effected by the Spirit. The distinctive contribution of Irenaeus lies in his stress on the relation of Christian baptism to the miraculous birth of Christ as well as to his death and resurrection, for our birth of the Spirit is derived from Jesus' own birth and is dependent on it, and of course it is in infant baptism above all that that relation becomes most apparent.[60]

Although Torrance appeals to Irenaeus to reinforce his theology of participation in the vicarious humanity of Christ, the early liturgical documents, such as Justin Martyr's Apology (150–160 C.E.), had clear expectations of the catechumens with the emphasis on the faith of the one to be baptized.[61] However, participation in the baptismal waters, for Torrance, was a participation in the Christ events:

> Certainly ritual and ethical acts have their proper place in the administration of baptism, but baptism itself embodied in Jesus Christ in such a way that, when the Church baptizes in his name, it is actually Christ himself who is savingly at work, pouring out his Spirit upon us and drawing us within the power of his vicarious life, death and resurrection. Because the saving act of God is identical with Jesus Christ, and because Jesus Christ constitutes himself the content, reality and power of the baptism, it is as effectively operative in the Church as Jesus himself is risen and alive.[62]

One important point to make is that T. F. Torrance was meticulous regarding the terms he employed for baptism. He made a distinction between *baptisma* and *baptismos*. Vander Zee commenting on Torrance's distinction of baptism terms writes:

---

60. Torrance, *Theology in Reconciliation*, 94.

61. If one was persuaded to be baptized, one first needed to adhere to apostolic teaching, then pray, fast (for the remission of one's sins), and seek to be baptized. There was no mention of living vicariously through the faithfulness of Christ in the chapter on baptism. Justin Martyr, *The First Apology of Justin Martyr* (Roberts-Donaldson's English Translation), Chapter LXI, Christian Baptism.

62. Torrance, *Theology in Reconciliation*, 83.

> T. F. Torrance, whose emphasis on the "vicarious humanity of Christ" has done much to renew the emphasis of the early church fathers and Calvin in our day, lays great stress on Jesus' baptism as an essential aspect of Christ's identification with us and our new life in him. He calls attention to *baptisma* as the normal (and possibly newly minted) New Testament term for baptism as opposed to the Greek term *baptismos*, which might have been expected. *Baptisma* refers to the reality signified, pointing to what Torrance called the "depth dimension," namely our union with Christ, while *baptismos* refers to the rite itself.[63]

This emphasis allowed Torrance to speak both of the sacrament of baptism and what baptism is actually accomplishing. He is once again consistent in connecting the rite to the reality of incorporation into Christ. Of course, there are those who would disagree with Torrance's emphasis. Karl Barth for example, believed that the sacraments were less about God's movement towards us and more about our reciprocity to the Gospel of Jesus Christ. He said that the sacraments were to confirm faith as a means of assurance but not a means to the creation of faith. The role of the sacraments was to witness to what was already objectively true.[64] Barth's rejection of infant baptism, however, seems inconsistent with his Christology. The need for confirmation of faith assumes incompatibility with the belief that salvation is dependent on what Christ has done.[65] While Barth influenced Torrance, they clearly had different views on the sacraments.

One critique of Torrance is that his narrative of the vicarious humanity of Jesus Christ influenced the way in which he interpreted everything else. It has already been noted, in an earlier chapter, that Colin Gunton criticized Torrance for relying more on patristics than the Scriptures for his hermeneutic. A similar case could be made here regarding his theology of the sacraments. Torrance would be inconsistent if he were to change his hermeneutic for the sacraments. In fact, he remained quite consistent and consequently, predictable. This again is seen in the way he connected the various Christ events to the language of participation through the sacrament of baptism. For Torrance, when one is baptized,

---

63. Vander Zee, *Christ, Baptism and the Lord's Supper*, 81; See Torrance, *Theology in Reconciliation*, 82–105.

64. Barth, *The Heidelberg Catechism for Today*, 106–41.

65. McMaken addresses this issue in his book, *The Sign of the Gospel*, 151–208.

one is not only baptized in the name of the Triune God but also, one's participation is by the Spirit in the person and work of Jesus Christ.

Torrance argued, "*Baptisma* is to be understood as referring not simply to the baptizing of someone in the name of Christ but to the baptism with which Jesus Christ himself was baptized for our sakes in the whole course of his redemptive life from his birth to his resurrection, the one baptism which he continues by his Spirit to apply to us in our baptism into him, thereby making himself both its material content and its active agent."[66] He also wrote, "When we regard Christian baptism in this way, not as *baptismos* but as *baptisma*, we find it to be grounded in the whole incarnational event in which the birth of Jesus, his baptism in the Jordan, his vicarious life, as well as his death and resurrection, and the pouring out of his Spirit upon the Church at Pentecost, all have their essential place, and must be kept in focus in our understanding of it."[67] Therefore, for Torrance, the sacrament of baptism was one way in which humanity participates by the Spirit in the Son's communion with the Father.

For the remainder of the chapter, we will examine Torrance's theology of our participation in Christ through the Lord's Supper. We will also examine his theology of real presence.

Torrance on the Lord's Supper

Torrance linked the celebration of Holy Communion to the person and work of Christ in a way that argued for the real presence of Christ. According to Torrance:

> Thus instituted, the Lord's Supper or the Eucharist is both the act of Christ and the act of the Church in his name, but in the nature of the case the act of the Church is one which serves the act of Christ and directs us away from itself to Christ. The Eucharist is what it is not because of what it is in itself as act of the Church but because of what it is in its grounding beyond in what God in Christ has done, does do, and will do for us in his Spirit. Very serious problems arise when the focus of attention is shifted from that objective ground to the ritual act in the foreground, that is, from the person of the Mediator, God manifest in the flesh, to the sacramental rite as a means of saving grace,

66. Torrance, *Theology in Reconciliation*, 83–84.
67. Torrance, *Theology in Reconciliation*, 84.

for then the New Testament teaching about the paschal mystery of Christ has to be read into the ritual act as though it enshrined the mystery in itself.[68]

Robert Stamps commenting on Torrance's perspective writes, "The mystery of the Eucharist is objectively grounded in the Paschal mystery of Christ which gives it its meaning."[69] Torrance maintains consistency with his emphasis on the sacraments being a means of participating in the vicarious humanity of Christ. There is nothing new here:

> It is when St Paul comes to expound the Christian life and ministry in the witness of believers to the death of Christ that he employs the liturgical language of sacrifice. Liturgy for St. Paul is primarily the liturgy of life actualized in flesh and blood. Theology itself belongs to "rational worship, *logike latreia*." In this way the liturgy of the Lord's Supper is acted out in the life of the one body that bears about the dying of the Lord Jesus, that the life of the Lord Jesus may be made manifest in our mortal flesh. In other words, here liturgy is the eucharistic life of the new humanity which the church has in Jesus Christ.[70]

T. F. Torrance placed the emphasis of the sacrificial meaning of the Lord's Supper, on Christ's own eternal offering. One misunderstanding that should be corrected at this point is that while T. F. Torrance did in fact place most of his emphasis on the active obedience of Christ, he also had a vibrant theology of the passive obedience of Christ as demonstrated in his lectures.[71] At times, Torrance appears to be referring to both Christ's active and passive obedience. We may notice how he linked participation in the Eucharist with participation in the worship of Christ. Torrance asserts:

> The Eucharistic sacrifice means that we through the Spirit are so intimately united to Christ, by communion in his body and

---

68. Torrance, *Theology in Reconciliation*, 107.

69. Stamps, *The Sacrament of the Word Made Flesh*, 100. Robert Stamps also states, "In no one book does Torrance order his thinking on the Eucharist into a single, systematic treatment (although he has published three major essays devoted to the subject). 'Eschatology and the Eucharist' in *Intercommunion* (1952), 'Toward a Doctrine of the Lord's Supper' in *Conflict and Agreement in the Church* (1960) and 'The Paschal Mystery of Christ and the Eucharist' in *Theology in Reconciliation* (1973)." Stamps, *The Sacrament of the Word Made Flesh*, xiii.

70. Torrance, *Atonement*, 97.

71. See Torrance and Walker, *Atonement*.

blood, that we participate in his self-offering to the Father and thus appear with him and in him and through him before the majesty of God in worship, praise and adoration with no other sacrifice than the sacrifice of Jesus Christ our Mediator and High Priest.[72]

Furthermore, T. F. Torrance connected the celebration of The Lord's Supper to the nature of the resurrection and ascension. He argued, what he called "millennium time" is hidden from sight, but seen by faith and present in the Eucharist. The church is connected to the past and present but she also functions as an eschatological people. The church is currently participating in the new creation according to Torrance:

> Because the church is already participant in that new creation that is in the millennium time of the resurrection, the kingdom of the risen and ascended and advent Christ already knocks at the door of the church. That happens above all at the holy supper, where the risen Lord is present, in the *eucharistic parousia*, and we taste already the powers of the age to come and are given an antepast or foretaste of the great banquet of the kingdom that is to come. As often as we communicate in the sacrament, we participate in the new time of that kingdom. That is why the New Testament thinks of the sacraments as falling within the overlap between the two ages, this present age that passes away and the age that is to come but which in Christ has already telescoped itself into the present and catches us up into it in the communion of the Spirit. Thus as often as the church partakes of holy communion in the *real presence* or *parousia* of Christ it becomes ever anew the body of the risen Lord.[73]

Along with the idea of the sacrament of the Lord's Supper being a participation into the person and events of Jesus, "T. F. Torrance called the sacraments not just a 'confirming ordinance' but a 'converting ordinance', for in and through them the gospel strikes home to us in such a way as to draw us within the vicarious response to God which Jesus Christ constitutes in his own humanity."[74] Again, this is a departure from

---

72. Torrance, *Theology in Reconciliation*, 134; Vander Zee, *Christ, Baptism and the Lord's Supper*, 209–10.

73. Torrance, *Atonement*, 260. For a comparative on the eschatological orientation of the liturgy, see Chan, *Liturgical Theology*, 78–82.

74. Torrance, *The Mediation of Christ*, 107; Vander Zee, 234; John Wesley also referred to the sacraments as "converting ordinances." See Hammond's, *John Wesley in America*, 67, footnote 135 "Later references by Wesley to communion as a converting

traditions that see the sacraments merely as symbolic. For Torrance, there is an engagement with the person and ministry of Jesus Christ when we celebrate the sacraments. According to Stamps:

> Torrance also rejects this sign-as-symbol mentality for epistemological reasons. As far as our knowledge of the natural elements is concerned, to speak of the sacrament as an "outward and visible sign of inward and invisible grace" suggests a world depending on another reality for significance. What Torrance wants to say is that the natural element in the sacrament is truly significant in itself.[75]

This was very important for Torrance. Epistemologically, dualism was detrimental to our understanding of the sacraments. If there is nothing sacred about the material world, there is nothing sacred about bread and wine. It is all merely symbolic. But for Torrance, his doctrine of creation and his epistemology argued against this dualistic cosmology. According to Stamps, "Every aspect of Torrance's eucharistic theology has underlined his rejection of Augustinian/Neo-Platonic cosmology and dualism."[76] Therefore, there should be no separation between the spiritual and the material; between the sacred and the secular. God is working through it all. "The mystery of the Eucharist is to be understood in terms of our participation through the Spirit in what the whole Jesus Christ, the incarnate, crucified, risen and ascended Son, is in himself, in respect both of his activity from the Father towards mankind and of his activity from mankind towards the Father."[77] T. F. Torrance argues:

> Eucharistic worship of this kind takes place, as John McLeod Campbell used to say, "within the circle of the life of Christ." It is, in fact, a form of the life of Jesus Christ ascending to the Father in the life of those who are so intimately united to him through the Spirit, that when they pray, it is Christ in the incarnate Son who honors, adores and glorifies the Father in them. Expressed the other way round, in eucharistic worship there takes place through prayer, in word and act, a living presentation of Christ

---

ordinance include: Sermon "The Means of Grace", *Works*, 1:381, 393; JWJ, 19:93, 121, 158, 20:42, 101, 21:233, 244; hymn 47 in *Hymns on the Lord's Supper*. The majority Anglican position was that communion was a "confirming ordinance" rather than a "converting ordinance."

75. Stamps, *The Sacrament of the Word Made Flesh*, 63.
76. Stamps, *The Sacrament of the Word Made Flesh*, 254.
77. Torrance, *Theology in Reconciliation*, 117.

to the Father in so far as it is a participation in the same eternal Spirit through whom Christ fulfilled his life of obedient sonship within our humanity an in his self-offering without spot to the Father presented that sonship to him on behalf of all humanity as their worship of God. But by its very nature, therefore, the Eucharist, while being the worship of men on earth, is essentially a participation in the worship of the heavenly sanctuary which Jesus Christ their ascended High Priest renders to the Father in the oblation of his endless life, for it is worship in the same Spirit by whom we are made one with the Son as he is one with the Father, in whom we have access to the Father, and through whom we are taken up into the eternal communion of the Father, the Son and the Holy Spirit.[78]

Torrance here is emphasizing that the Eucharist is not some kind of isolated spiritual ordinance or sacrament that is somehow efficacious in and of itself, but that the Lord's Supper is correlated with our participation in the vicarious humanity of Jesus.[79] When the Body of Christ celebrates the Eucharist, they are participating by the Spirit in the Son's communion with the Father. Torrance emphasized *sursum corda*, that when we participate in the celebration of the Lord's Supper, we are lifting up our hearts to participate in the heavenly self-offering of Christ.[80] Torrance stated it this way, "Ascension introduced the 'distance' between the symbols of bread and wine on earth and the ascended Christ, but nevertheless a 'distance' bridged by the real presence of the risen and ascended Christ through the Spirit. Hence the place of the *sursum corda* in the heart of the Reformed Eucharistic Rite—the ascension with Christ became of primary importance again: we are made to sit with Christ in the heavenly places."[81]

For Torrance, the sacraments were not primarily for the purpose of giving a believer assurance of faith. They were the very means by which we participate in the real presence of Jesus Christ. According to Robert Stamps:

> Torrance takes all this to what he thinks is its natural, realist conclusions in eucharistic theology, something Barth will not do. Torrance criticizes Barth for this failure to shake off a

78. Torrance, *Theology in Reconciliation*, 109–10.
79. See Torrance, *The Royal Priesthood*, xvi-xvii, 10, 14, 19, 21–22.
80. See Fach, *Answering the Upwards Call*.
81. Torrance, *Scottish Theology*, 40.

lingering "dualist orientation" in his sacramental doctrine. . . . Torrance insists that the incarnation instantiates the free intercourse God may have with his Church in filling all its sacraments with his presence and power. Barth hesitates in ascribing any power to the rites of the Church, even by the adventitious power of Christ. He interprets the sacraments mainly as aids for giving the believer an assurance of faith, and as "imaging" for the Church "the objective permanence of faith," positively realized in the "once and for all self—offering of Christ on the cross and in the Ascension."[82]

Torrance's concern was that the focus is not shifted from the Living Christ to the eucharistic elements. For Torrance, that is a misplaced emphasis. The focus should not be on the eucharistic bread and wine. The focus should be on the resurrected and ascended Lord and that by partaking of the eucharistic elements, we are feeding on the presence of Jesus not because something supernatural happens to the elements but because through the participation in the Eucharist, we are participating in the presence of the living Christ. Torrance states:

> If Christ is not himself our Offering and Oblation to the Father, then the Eucharist becomes a rite which tends to substitute for that, even if it is grounded on a once and for all act of God in Christ. As such it absorbs our immediate attention which should be directed in the Eucharist to Christ and through him to the Father. In rather different ways in Roman Catholic, Anglican and Reformed Churches eucharistic celebration can easily become something having a meaning in itself as an act performed, for example as a sacred mystery embodying spiritual life in material elements, instead of as a correlate to the ascension of the crucified and risen Jesus and participation in the heavenly worship of praise and thanksgiving which surround the throne of the Father where he too has been exalted as the glorified Lamb of God . . . the relevant question for us to ask ourselves, therefore, is this: Does the Eucharist mean to us the mediation of access through Christ to the Father, or does it tend to mean something in itself?[83]

Torrance reflects here Calvin's doctrine of the Lord's Supper—agreeing neither with Luther's consubstantiation, nor with Zwingli's alleged memorialism. Torrance mentioned Calvin's concept of *historia*

---

82. Stamps, *The Sacrament of the Word Made Flesh*, 67.
83. Torrance, *Theology in Reconciliation*, 205.

redemptionis along with his attempt to recover a proper doctrine of the Spirit had far-reaching effects, all of which affected Calvin's approach to the Eucharist, which sought to interpret in terms of the saving act of God in Christ through the Spirit.[84] Torrance places the emphasis that the eucharistic elements exist to point us to Christ; that as we partake of the bread and wine, our hearts are lifted up by the Spirit to the Savior in whom we worship the Father. Having said that, a critical question that is raised when discussing the sacraments is, how does one understand the presence of Christ?

The *Manducatio Impiorum*

Throughout church history, theologians have disagreed on interpretation regarding the presence of Christ in the sacraments. This is especially the case regarding the celebration of the Lord's Supper. Stamps states, "Since medieval times the questions raised by the *manducatio impiorum*[85] have been the ultimate test in determining belief in the objective presence of the soul and body of Christ in the sacrament. . . . Torrance criticizes Luther and the Lutherans for making the *manducatio impiorum* the 'decisive test' as to the real presence."[86] This eating of the *manducatio impiorum*, that is the eating of unbelievers, distinguished eating Christ by faith and orally in bread and wine. The Lutheran perspective held that when an unbeliever eats the Lord's Supper, they in fact receive Christ's body and blood in the Supper but to their condemnation.[87] Luther believed that even unbelievers, who eat and drink the Eucharist, eat and drink the body and blood of Christ. In contrast, Calvin believed that while Christ's body is given to all communicants, it is only received by those who have faith. Stamps argues:

> Christ's presence is determined by the gospel alone. . . . For Calvin, as for Torrance, the eucharistic presence is a spiritual presence, though by this neither means a pure spiritual presence. It is a presence realized by the Spirit. Unlike Torrance, however, Calvin insists on addressing the presence of Christ in

---

84. Torrance, *Theology in Reconciliation*, 126.
85. *Manducatio Impiorum (eating by the impious)*.
86. Stamps, *The Sacrament of the Word Made Flesh*, 188–89.
87. Hale, "Eating and Drinking Damnation to Oneself: The Place of 1 Corinthians 11:27–29 in the Lord's Supper." Nebraska Lutherans for Confessional Study, February 17, 2011, 10.

the Spirit in "non substantial" terms. Torrance has no hesitancy in this regard, suggesting an intensely substantial, though non-corporeal, ontic presence which Calvin would not allow. Even if Calvin could have entertained the real presence of Christ being offered to all in the sacrament, it is doubtful that the presence he would have understood as being there—"no other . . . than that of a relationship"—would have been the kind of objectively constituted presence which unbelievers could have received without the facility of faith.[88]

Although the differences might seem nuanced, they are real nonetheless. As T. F. Torrance stated, "We believe that when the Church celebrates the Eucharist in the name of Jesus Christ, its only Priest and Mediator who has consecrated for us a new and living way into the holiest through the veil of his flesh, it is Christ himself who is really present pouring out his Spirit upon us, drawing us into the power of his vicarious life, in death and resurrection, and uniting us with his self-oblation and self-presentation before the face of the Father where he ever lives to make intercession for us."[89] Torrance writes:

> We have come now come to the point where we must consider more carefully the real presence of Christ, the eucharistic *parousia*. This is not directly, at any rate, the *parousia* of the Lord either in the historical form that was his in the days of his flesh or in the glorified form that is his now at the right hand of the Father. But it is never the less the real presence (*parousia*) of the whole Christ, not just the presence of his body and blood, nor just the presence of his Spirit or Mind, but the presence of the actual Jesus Christ, crucified, risen, ascended, glorified, in his whole, living and active reality and in his identity as Gift and Giver. How he is thus present is only explicable from the side of God, in terms of his creative activity which by its very nature transcends any kind of explanation which we can offer. That is what it meant by saying that he is really present through the Spirit, not that he is present only as Spirit, far less as some spiritual reality, but present through the same kind of inexplicable creative activity whereby he was born of the Virgin Mary and rose again from the grave. Because it really is the presence of the Lord Jesus Christ in his living, creative reality, in his personal self—giving to us, it is a presence over which we have no kind of control, ecclesiastical, liturgical or intellectual. It is the

---

88. Stamps, *The Sacrament of the Word Made Flesh*, 191.
89. Torrance, *Theology in Reconciliation*, 107.

> kind of presence that confronted the disciples on the first Easter morning at Emmaus or in the upper room at Jerusalem, and indeed it is the same presence except that now it takes another form, the eucharistic form specifically appointed by Jesus as the particular empirical form in which he has promised as the risen and glorified Christ to meet his people in the closest and most intimate way, through all history, in anticipation of his unveiled form when he will come again in great power and glory.[90]

While some would argue for transubstantiation and others for consubstantiation, both perspectives are still predominately focused on what happens to the elements after they have been prayed over (*epiclesis*). Torrance is arguing that the focus should not be on what happens to the elements at all but that through participation in the Eucharist, the church is participating by the Spirit in the Son's communion with the Father. It is a real participation with a real resurrected Christ. This is what Torrance is communicating above. Torrance also states:

> It is because the New Testament thinks of justification in this eschatological relation between "It is finished" on the cross and the "Behold I make all things new" of the *parousia*, that it speaks of it in terms of "reckoning" or as the Reformers interpreted it, "imputation" or "reputation." Imputation describes the perfected work of grace. It indicates that justification is forensic in the sense that it is grounded on the once and for all judgment of Jesus Christ on the cross, but it indicates that what happened there, while complete in its reality, is yet to be fully disclosed at the advent of Christ. The Pauline "reckon" (*logizesthe*) or the Reformer's "impute" is the concept which holds together those two moments, the forensic and the eschatological, in one, the once and for all completed work and the full disclosure of it in the *parousia*, in one. It is because justification is involved in that tension that we are given the two sacraments of baptism and the eucharist, with baptism enshrining the once and for all corporate act of total justification in Christ, and the eucharist enshrining our continual participation in Christ's new humanity until he comes again. Then the need for both sacraments will be done away and faith and hope will pass away and agape—love only will abide as the eternal being of the new humanity in righteousness and truth.[91]

---

90. Torrance, *Theology in Reconciliation*, 119–20.
91. Torrance, *Atonement*, 136.

What T. F. Torrance is communicating at this point is worth noting particularly his language of "a sacrament of renewal." He is stating that in this time "in between" the inaugurated kingdom and consummated kingdom, the church is sustained by the presence of Jesus and this is most notably realized when we participate in the Eucharist, the sacrament of renewal. Christ has promised to be with us always even to the very end of the age (Matthew 28:20). According to Torrance:

> Until he comes, then, the form instituted by Christ in the Eucharist which he takes to himself as the form of his actual and active presence among us, is the form of his humiliation, the breaking of his body and the shedding of his blood, figured and represented in the liturgical fraction of the loaf and the pouring out of the wine, that is, the form in which Jesus Christ sacrificed himself upon the Cross in atoning reconciliation for the sin of the world, for it is precisely there, at the Cross, that the risen and glorified Lord comes to meet us and gives himself to us that we, united with him through communion in his body and blood, may be lifted up with him into the holiest in the power of his resurrection and exaltation, and worship the Father with, in and through him.[92]

Criticisms

While Torrance offers a eucharistic theology worth appreciating, some of his ideas must also be critiqued. This is especially true regarding Torrance's appeal to patristic theology and the influence of the East. According to Stamps:

> A basic difference between Torrance and the East centers around the concept of the epiclesis and the role of the Spirit in the Church's sacrament. In the East, the epiclesis constitutes an appeal to the Spirit to "bring about" the presence of Christ in the sacrament as well as to unite the Church's praise with that of its Great High Priest. While the epiclesis in Torrance's eucharistic theology is a similar invocation toward similar ends, what actually transpires by the Spirit's coming is entirely different from what the East perceives. For Torrance the Spirit's presence in the sacrament itself constitutes (by virtue of the *perichoresis*) the presence of the worshiping Christ and causes the prayer

---

92. Torrance, *Theology in Reconciliation*, 120–21.

of Christ to echo in the prayer of the Church. For the East the Spirit's presence will not suffice for the presence of Christ, nor will an "echo" of Christ's prayer in the Church's liturgy pass for genuine participation of the earthly liturgy in that of heaven. Torrance, of course teaches that our "worship and prayer" have their place in heaven, but by the fact that we "freely and fully participate in the ascension of Christ." The substantive factor is the incorporation of our humanity in Christ's divine humanity, and thereby our participation in his heavenly worship, and not the Church's participation in his heavenly worship, and not the Church's participation in the Spirit. In Eastern thought the Spirit affords the Church's Eucharistic liturgy such real participation in the worship of heaven that it is even said to transpire there. A reflexive echo of the heavenly liturgy as delineated in Torrance's eucharistic theology would be hardly concrete enough for the Eastern Church.[93]

Stamps is pointing out clear differences between how Torrance thinks about what is transpiring during the Lord's Supper and what the Eastern Orthodox Church believes is happening. Stamps continues his critique, "In the light of these inadequacies as the East would reckon them, Torrance's eucharistic theology finally ought not to be judged by what it aspires to be, but by what it actually is, a Eucharist in the Reformed tradition operating from a highly developed Christology richly informed by patristic sources."[94] Stamps is in essence arguing that while Torrance appeals to the Eastern tradition, his eucharistic theology is hardly Eastern. Stamps is simply arguing that there is a real difference between Torrance's eucharistic theology and eucharistic theology of Eastern Orthodoxy. Stamps states, "Torrance's eucharistic theology offers us an opportunity to observe him seeking to identify as much as possible with the East, with their hermeneutic as well as their language. It represents an attempt on his part to distance himself as far as possible from the dualistic cosmology and the idea of an inert deity intrinsic Augustinianism."[95]

---

93. Stamps, *The Sacrament of the Word Made Flesh*, 243.
94. Stamps, *The Sacrament of the Word Made Flesh*, 244.
95. Stamps, *The Sacrament of the Word Made Flesh*, 265.

Conclusion

In conclusion, "The Eucharistic sacrifice means that we *through the Spirit* are so intimately united to Christ, by communion in his body and blood, that we participate in his self-offering to the Father and thus appear with him and in him and through him before the majesty of God in worship, praise, and adoration with no other sacrifice than the sacrifice of Jesus Christ our Mediator and High Priest."[96]

Finally, Torrance's Christology and soteriology that emphasize the incarnation and atonement along with a dominant emphasis on the saving *and sanctifying* humanity of Jesus Christ, clearly demonstrates Torrance's reliance on Robert Bruce's *Sermons on the Sacraments of 1589* entitled, *The Mystery of the Lord's Supper*. For Torrance, Robert Bruce left a legacy which in the words of the editor of the 1614 edition, is "worthy to be written in letters of gold."[97]

Torrance's theology of the sacraments highlights his Christology as well as how we participate by the Spirit in the Son's communion with the Father. For T. F. Torrance, the sacrament of baptism is how we are incorporated into the Body of Christ and the sacrament of the Lord's Supper is how we are renewed in the faith.

---

96. Torrance, *Theology in Reconciliation*, 134.
97. Torrance, *Sermons by Robert Bruce*, 27.

Conclusion

Review

THIS WORK SET OUT to argue that the doxological theology of T. F. and J. B. went further in providing a theological foundation for the subject of worship than others who have attempted something similar. It was noted that this was the first comprehensive theology of worship in the writings of the T. F. and J. B. Torrance. Many of the comparative approaches to the subject of worship are anthropocentric in nature in the sense that they focus on what we, as human beings are responsible for in the corporate worship setting. Furthermore, much of the liturgical literature is focused on praxis not on the theological foundations for worship. This anthropocentric approach was further exposed in the contemporary worship movement, which began in the late 1960s and early 1970s. This criticism has nothing to do with the term "contemporary" and everything to do with the theological foundations for its praxis.

And while some have tried to address the subject of worship from more of a biblical and theological perspective, it has been argued they simply did not go far enough. The suggested correctives to the anthropocentric approaches were to replace human-centered nomenclature, in the liturgy, for God-centered vocabulary. Others advocated re-introducing the liturgical church year into the church-programing calendar in order to celebrate the person and work of Christ annually.

However, T. F. and J. B. Torrance suggested a completely different corrective to the anthropocentric approaches. They promoted an emphasis on the vicarious humanity of Christ. They argued that Christ in his incarnation and atonement did for humankind what humans were unable to do for themselves: offer acceptable worship.

In chapter 1, it was argued that the Torrances' missionary upbringing, theological education, and pastoral ministry influenced their doxological approach to theology. Their godly parents had a love for reading the Scriptures (three chapters a day and five on Sundays), and both were people of prayer. Furthermore, these missionary parents had a passion to communicate the good news of Jesus Christ to those who had not yet heard of God's love. This evangelistic and missionary zeal stayed with the Torrance brothers throughout their life.

While educated at New College, Edinburgh University, it was common for the Torrances to experience daily prayers and the weekly celebration of the Lord's Supper. All their professors had been chosen jointly by the university and the church and were practicing Christians and men of faith. Theological education at New College was in the context of a worshiping community preparing those who were planning on serving in the Church of Scotland. During T. F. and J. B. Torrance's own tenure, their lecturing contained the spirit of preaching and they themselves carried on the tradition of offering prayers prior to their lectures.

Their pastoral and chaplaincy experiences also influenced their doxological approach to theology. While both T. F. and J. B. Torrance were brilliant theologians, they were also men of the church who were passionate about heralding the good news of Jesus Christ in the worshiping community. They wanted men and women to experience the presence of Jesus Christ.

In chapter 2, the theological background to the anthropocentric approaches was addressed. James Torrance argued that there are in essence two very different theological approaches to worship.[1] The first is a unitarian approach and the second is a trinitarian approach. The unitarian approach places the responsibility of worship on us and our liturgical actions. Furthermore, there is no mediation or mediator factored into this approach. We are our own mediators. A variation of the unitarian approach is the existential approach, which places the emphasis on human choice. This is seen in evangelistic appeals (*receive, accept, or believe on* the Lord Jesus Christ) as well as in preaching that focuses on having parishioners make a decision before the end of the service. It is common for preachers to feel that the sermon was a failure if they did not employ imperatival language "preaching for application." This emphasis on human choice is also seen in the worshiping context when the emphasis is

---

1. J. B. Torrance, *Worship, Community, and the Triune God of Grace*, 6–31.

placed on the responsibility of the minister, others leading the corporate worship service, or the parishioners themselves to mediate God's presence. An example of this is the thought that we can lead people into the presence of God through forty minutes of uninterrupted worship music. All of this is but an example of existentialism at work in the liturgy. James Torrance argued that existentialism in the liturgy was nothing more than a sub-category of unitarian worship.

A critique of James Torrance's criticism of the unitarian position is that the Scriptures indeed ask for a response from humanity. There is an emphasis on human responsibility in the Bible (e.g., Deut 30:11–19; Matt 22:37). Human beings cannot simply be passive in liturgical activity. The Bible is replete with admonitions and imperatives to praise and worship the Lord. James Torrance, however, never suggested that we are passive. Rather, he emphasized that our worship is an inclusion in the worship of Christ. Our worship is a participation by the Spirit in the Son's communion with the Father.[2] So there is a role that men and women have according to the Torrances, but that is only made possible because of the faithfulness of Christ.

As a corrective to the unitarian approach, James Torrance advocated a trinitarian-incarnational approach. The critical difference between this approach and the unitarian approach is the presence of mediation. Jesus Christ came to mediate the presence of God for men and women. This is critical for understanding the Torrance's approach to the subject of worship. This could simply be summed up as follows: no mediation, no Christian worship. While liturgy, preaching, prayers, music, the arts, and the sacraments are all important aspects of worship, they are not the *means* to our worship. They are an *expression* of our worship.[3] The *means* of our worship is *our union with Jesus Christ*. We can only come into the presence of God through Christ and because of what Christ has done for us.

In chapter 3, it was argued that the Torrances suggested the need to return to the Nicene-Constantinople Creed as a way of focusing on the trinitarian faith in corporate worship.[4] T. F. Torrance believed that the heresies addressed by the ecumenical councils, presented themselves because of an embedded dualism from the Graeco-Roman world.

2. J. B. Torrance, *Worship, Community, and the Triune God of Grace*, 8–11.

3. Best, *Unceasing Worship*, 119. *Means* of worship is not be confused with *means* of grace. "*Means* of worship" in this quote is referring to access to God's presence.

4. Torrance, *The Trinitarian Faith*.

Throughout the writings of T. F. Torrance, one of his primary concerns was with how Neo-Platonic structures continue to show up throughout church history influencing Christian dogmatics and consequently, liturgical practices. T. F. Torrance argued that a lack of awareness of the vicarious humanity of Christ produced a sort of Apollinarianism in the liturgy.[5] Since no weight is given to the human mind of Christ (even now in his heavenly intercession), then the Mediator enacts the God-humanward role, but does not or cannot enact the human-Godward role. That takes us one step beyond the healing and sanctifying of the human mind to the significance of that for Christ's role in worship.

Torrance was clearly not only concerned with doctrine but how doctrine was promoted—through the liturgy and the worshiping community. If in the incarnation, Christ assumed a human body and a human soul but not a human mind,[6] then that part of humanity was not healed and redeemed.[7] In the historical context, Apollinarianism quickly revealed the real theological problem: Greek dualism, which, he argued, was behind every heresy addressed by the ecumenical councils. It was the formulation of the *homoousion* that addressed this particular heretical perspective in the fourth century.

This led us into chapter 4, where an emphasis was placed on the mediation of Christ. The subject of mediation was central to the theology of worship for the Torrances. Mediation involves two movements for them: the God-humanward movement and the human-Godward movement. Both movements are essential for mediation. Both movements are critical in redemptive history. Both movements are critical for how we worship God. But Jesus Christ takes up both initiated worship and responsive worship. Our response is a secondary response made efficacious by the faithfulness of Jesus in his incarnation according to the Torrances.

In the God-humanward movement, Jesus Christ not only provides revelation from God but *is the revelation* of God. "In the past God spoke to our ancestors through the prophets at many times and in various ways, but in these last days he has spoken to us by his Son, whom he appointed heir of all things, and through whom also he made the universe" (Hebrews 1:1–2). Critical for the subject of Christian worship is *who* it is

---

5. Torrance, "The Mind of Christ in Worship: The Problem of Apollinarianism in the Liturgy," in *Theology in Reconciliation*, 139–214.

6. In the patristic world, the Platonic tripartite view of a human being was assumed: body, soul, and mind. See Need, *Truly Divine and Truly Human*, 71–72.

7. Attribution of the quote, "The unassumed is unhealed" is discussed in chapter 4.

that is being worshiped. That, indeed, is the theological question. Again, liturgical studies tend to be replete with recommendations for praxis. But the God-humanward movement reminds us that the most critical aspect of Christian worship is our knowledge of the God who is there and who has revealed himself in the incarnation. Indeed, in these days, God has spoken to us through the Son of God (Hebrews 1:1–2).

But not only has God in Christ Jesus revealed himself in the God-humanward movement but also in the human-Godward movement. For both T. F. and J. B. Torrance, this is an aspect of their theology that is highlighted and that brings into play the subject of mediation *and* the priesthood of Christ. It is common in worship studies to emphasize that God reveals himself and that worship is *our* response to that revelation. This is what was meant earlier, that many who have attempted to address the subject of worship from a theological perspective have not gone far enough. The Torrances argued that Christ not only provided revelation but the perfect response of worship as well. The human-Godward movement has critical implication for worship in that we are not the ones who offer the perfect response but Christ in his incarnation. From the assumption of humanity, through his public ministry, at the cross, in the resurrection, in his ascension, Christ leads those who would seek to come into the presence of the Father. This is the christological doctrine, which they proposed.

In chapter 5, the place of Jesus Christ in liturgical prayer and worship was emphasized. Joseph Jungmann, in his work, *The Place of Christ in Liturgical Prayer*,[8] highlighted how the early church referred to Christ as mediator through their doxologies. The mediated doxology, frequently employed, emphasized "*to* the Father, *through* the Son, *in* the Holy Spirit." These prepositions stated that one came *to* the Father *through* the Son and *in* or *by* the Spirit. However, in the fourth century, the Arians employed the mediated doxology to emphasize subordinationism. The response from Athanasius was to change the mediated doxology to the co-ordinated doxology, which stated, "*to* the Father *and* the Son *and* the Holy Spirit." While the co-ordinated doxology helped address the problem of subordinationism with the Arians, it inadvertently created a new problem: the lack of emphasis on the mediation of Christ. By the fifth century, to fill this void, the veneration of Mary and the saints took this place. Furthermore, for the first time in church history, ministers were

---

8. Jungmann, *The Place of Christ in Liturgical Prayer*.

referred to as priests. Prior to this, ministers were referred to as overseers and elders but never as priests.[9] T. F. Torrance appealed to the need to highlight the high priesthood of creation. Regarding the subject of worship, it is impossible to worship the living God without the High Priest, Jesus Christ. Although this theme is highlighted in the book of Hebrews in the New Testament,[10] it was T. F. Torrance who brought this to the forefront theologically in chapter 4 of the book *Theology in Reconciliation*.[11] Ironically, with the exception of a small chapter in David Peterson's work, *Engaging with God*,[12] and Margaret Barker's work, *The Great High Priest*, this emphasis on the priesthood in the book of Hebrews in liturgical literature is strangely missing.

In chapter 6, the ministry of preaching was addressed. Although both T. F. and J. B. Torrance preached when they lectured and exemplified a heart for the gospel of Jesus Christ in their theology, the subject of preaching is sparse in their writings. This is odd in that they came from a Reformed tradition with its emphasis on preaching. T. F. Torrance had two books of published sermons entitled *When Jesus Christ Comes and Comes Again* and *Apocalypse Today*. There are also boxes of unpublished sermons at the Princeton Theological Seminary Library.[13] J. B. Torrance also lectured with the disposition of a preacher. And while there are relatively little instructions on the subject of preaching, the value for preaching was certainly present with both of the Torrance brothers.

While they taught the Scriptures, their primary concern was that people come face to face with Jesus Christ. Preaching was not merely an issue of teaching propositional truth or working their way through the Bible, book by book. Rather, the Scriptures exist to point people to the Way, the Truth, and the Life: Jesus Christ. T. F. Torrance's acknowledged Barth's influence when he stated, "I cherished the Bible as the Word of God spoken to mankind. However, when I opened the pages of Karl

---

9. The common term from the NT through the first centuries was *presbyteroi*—"elders." "Priest" of course was *iereus*, and that applied to all believers (1 Peter 2:5,9). Specifically, however, ministers were not referred to as priests in the sense of providing mediation.

10. Hebrews 7–10.

11. Torrance, *Theology in Reconciliation*, 139–214. Also, Torrance's, *Royal Priesthood* and *Conflict & Agreement in the Church Vol. 1&2*.

12. Peterson, *Engaging with God*, 228–60.

13. Unpublished Sermons in The Thomas F. Torrance Manuscript Collection, Special Collections, Princeton Theological Seminary Library

Barth's books and read the Holy Scriptures in the light of the startling questions he asked about the strange new world within the Bible and the dynamic nature of the Word of God, my study of the Bible changed into a higher gear."[14] Hugh Ross Mackintosh, T. F. Torrance's other influential mentor, insisted that preachers be evangelistic by "preaching for a verdict."[15] And while this admonition from Mackintosh could seem at odds with what James Torrance referred to as unitarian worship, Mackintosh advocated for a response to the person and work of Christ, which T. F. and J. B. Torrance both endorsed.

Furthermore, they believed in the importance of preaching the cross of Christ. Specifically, they believed in the importance of preaching the wonderful exchange that Jesus Christ offered to us when he died at Calvary. He offered mercy in place of judgment, forgiveness in place of condemnation, and life in place of death. When we preach "Christ and him crucified," this is what T. F. Torrance believed should be emphasized.

Finally, this work concluded by exploring T. F. Torrance's theology of the sacrament of incorporation (baptism) and the sacrament of renewal (The Lord's Supper). It was emphasized that T. F. Torrance was influenced by the sermons of the sixteenth-century minister of the High Kirk of Edinburgh (St. Giles), Robert Bruce.[16] Robert Bruce displayed a theology rich in highlighting the work of Christ while preaching the need for faith from those who participated in the Lord's Supper. This must be emphasized because worship for the Torrances was focused on the worship by Christ *but was to be received in a spirit of humility and gratitude by the communion of saints*. This point is critical since one of one of the criticisms of the Torrances' approach to their theology of worship, is that it does not seem to leave room for *our* response. Relationship always assumes reciprocity. The theology of the Torrances does seem to be exclusively focused on what Christ has done and does not appear to leave room for *our human response*. While their theology does have this tone, they did believe that there was a place for our response. For James Torrance, the imperatives of law *follow* the indicatives of grace. For T. F. Torrance, our worship is a vicarious participation in the faithfulness of

---

14. Torrance, *Karl Barth, Biblical and Evangelical Theologian*, 83.

15. McGrath, *T. F. Torrance*, 29. It is also worth noting that T. F. Torrance, in his later years, seemed more focused on the sacraments in conjunction with his ecumenical relationships and conversations.

16. Bruce, *The Mystery of the Lord's Supper*.

Christ. Our worship, for the Torrances, is always a participation to the worship of Christ.

For example, in T. F. Torrance's theology of baptism, Torrance focused on the person and work of Christ. He connects the Christ events and the sacrament of baptism in his emphasis on the meaning of baptism. For T. F. Torrance, the baptism of Christ was not an isolated event but was central to what makes our baptism efficacious: Christ's faithfulness. Again, this is very different from the perspectives that emphasize that baptism is an ordinance that communicates *our* commitment to Jesus Christ.

Likewise, Torrance's theology of the Lord's Supper is focused on the objective reality of what Christ has done in history and not on the ordinance of what we do: remembering what Christ has done. The Torrances seem to go too far at times. The Scriptures clearly link the active engagement of our memory with what Christ did at the cross when celebrating the Lord's Supper (Mark 14:22–25; Luke 22:18–20; 1 Corinthians 11:23–25). For the Torrances however, while they did not negate the importance of the above admonitions, their writings were consistent that worship is first and foremost about what God has done for humanity in Christ Jesus and not about what we do. Our worship is only possible because of the faithfulness of Jesus Christ.

Criticisms

The first criticism of the Torrances' doxological theology is that it can have a propensity to be reactionary. T. F. Torrance was addressing dualistic tendencies within theological systems that were detrimental to the health of evangelical theology. In light of this, he tended to overstate his positions. For example, when he argued that Christ assumed a fallen humanity, it is common to interpret Torrance arguing for a Christ who assumed a sinful humanity and, consequently, with sin. Yet, he argued the antithesis. He argued that Christ assumed a fallen humanity but was *without sin*. He argued that when Christ assumed humanity from the time of the conception, he was "bending back" the will of humanity, and thus sanctifying it.

Likewise, when J. B. Torrance argued that unitarian worship was focused on what *we* do, it is easy to conclude that he did not believe that worship involved any participation from us. It would have been helpful had J. B. Torrance offered a more balanced view in his lectures and writings. He argued that worship was *a participation* by the Spirit in the Son's communion with the Father. However, J. B. Torrance, like his brother, tended to overstate his arguments for his message to be heard. The message of Jesus Christ became eclipsed because of the unitarian and existential tendencies and practices in worship. The Torrances thundered against these dualistic tendencies with a prophetic theological voice. But in doing so, they did not offer a balanced perspective. As a contrast, Donald Baillie stated, "God works in our hearts. He bestows on us the gift of faith, by winning us, gaining our confidence, not forcing it. His graciousness overcomes our mistrust, his grace creates our faith, so that when we come to Him, it is really *our* faith, and we come willingly."[17] What is appreciated about Baillie's comments is that there is still the emphasis on God's initiative and his grace towards us. However, his grace creates within us a disposition of reciprocity where we love because he first loved us (1 John 4:19). This is the kind of balance that does not seem to be developed in the theology of the Torrances.

This leads us to the critical question that was asked at the outset of this book: if Christ has worshiped perfectly on behalf of humanity, is all of humanity included in the perfect response of Christ? Will all of humanity be saved? With the Torrances' emphasis on the vicarious humanity of Christ, can they escape the charge of universalism? In a chapter entitled "Karl Barth and the Latin Heresy," T. F. Torrance wrote:

> If in Jesus Christ the Word of God, by whom all things are made and in whom they have their creaturely being, became incarnate, died on the Cross and rose again, then we must think of the *whole creation* as having been affected by what he had done. If in Jesus Christ the Creator himself became a human creature, without of course ceasing to be Creator, and if in him divine nature and human natures are not separable, as Nestorian heresy would have it, then we must think of the being of every man, whether he believe or not, as grounded in Christ and ontologically bound to his humanity. It is precisely in Jesus, as St. Paul taught, that every human being (and indeed the whole creation) consists. It was as such that he died and rose again, so that we cannot but hold that the whole creation has been redeemed and sanctified in him, including the whole human race. But at this

---

17. Baillie, *The Theology of the Sacraments*, 54.

point some evangelical theologians object and charge Barth with what they call "universal salvation."[18]

Here T. F. Torrance argued that what was going on behind these accusations of universalism is what he called the Latin heresy which he said was antithetical to salvation by grace alone. Torrance argued that behind this charge of universalism was a frame of thought that operated with a "notion of external logico-causal connections."[19] For example, "If Christ died for all men, then, it is argued, all men must be saved, whether they believe or not; but if all men are not saved, and some, as seems very evident, do go to hell, then Christ did not die for all men."[20] Torrance argued that behind these two alternatives were two mistakes: The first mistake was the Nestorian disjunction between the two natures of Christ. There was a separation between the incarnation and the atonement in this approach and consequently between the person and work of Christ. From this perspective, the humanity of Christ was not united in one person with his deity. "Hence his humanity is not regarded as having any inner ontological connection with those for whom he died, but is regarded only as an external instrument used by God as he wills, in effecting salvation for all those whom God chooses and/or for those who choose to accept Christ as their personal Savior. Thus a separation is projected between the universal power and range of the kingdom of Christ and the limited efficacy and range of his atoning sacrifice."[21]

Torrance argued that it was high mediaeval theology that promoted that the death of Christ was only efficient for the elect. Interestingly, Torrance also argued that John Calvin rejected this even though Calvinist "orthodoxy" brought it back. Torrance believed that the erroneous doctrine of limited atonement was a departure from the apostolic doctrine of the primacy and completeness of Christ.[22]

Torrance further wrote about the efficacy of atonement in terms of a logico-causal relation between the death of Christ and the forgiveness of our sins and thus, the removing the rest of the Jesus story from birth to resurrection. Torrance stated, "It is a logico-causalism of this kind, with Augustinian-Thomist, Protestant scholastic and Newtonian roots, that

---

18. Torrance, *Karl Barth, Biblical and Evangelical Theologian*, 236.
19. Torrance, *Karl Barth, Biblical and Evangelical Theologian*, 237.
20. Torrance, *Karl Barth, Biblical and Evangelical Theologian*, 237.
21. Torrance, *Karl Barth, Biblical and Evangelical Theologian*, 237.
22. Torrance, *Karl Barth, Biblical and Evangelical Theologian*, 237.

appears to supply the deterministic paradigm within which there arise the twin errors of limited atonement and universalism both of which, although in different ways, are rationalistic constructions of the saving act of God incarnate in the life, death and resurrection of the Lord Jesus Christ."[23]

So in conclusion of this particular issue, Torrance rejected both universalism and limited atonement as opposite errors. And regarding the liturgical connection, yes, Torrance argued that Jesus Christ, in both his being and action, offered perfect worship on behalf of humanity, but far from soliciting passivity, this glorious reality should promote an enthusiastic joyful hallelujah on behalf of humanity. And this grace-filled worship is not just a relief that the burden for perfect worship has been lifted off of our shoulders but that we are free in Christ to offer wholehearted worship through prayer, preaching, sacrament, symbol, song, art and so much more. This is good news indeed.

Another criticism is that the Torrances do not seem to emphasize the work of the Holy Spirit within our human response, that was just mentioned in the above paragraph. Trinitarian theology is usually connected with their high Christology. This is indicated by the connection of the terms "trinitarian" and "incarnational." Their position was clear: one cannot understand the Trinity without understanding the person and work of Christ. While they obviously had a pneumatology and referenced the Holy Spirit, a fuller account of the Holy Spirit's involvement in *our* sanctification and in *our* worship does not seem to be expressed.

T. F. Torrance does discuss the work of the Holy Spirit in relation to the Nicene-Constantinople Creed, as pointed out in chapter 3. Likewise, much of the secondary literature employs an outline from the Nicene Creed (including a section on pneumatology) to discuss the theology of the Torrances. However, if one compares the sheer volume of writing on the person and work of Jesus Christ in comparison to the writings developed on the Holy Spirit, it is easy to conclude that Torrances were more pre-occupied with Christology than with pneumatology. The role of the Holy Spirit for the Torrances was to illuminate the person and work of Christ.

J. B. Torrance believed that the Holy Spirit came to meet us in worship through the ministry of word and sacrament. He also believed that the Spirit helps us in our infirmities, lifting us up to Christ who in his

---

23. Torrance, *Karl Barth, Biblical and Evangelical Theologian*, 238.

ascended humanity is our God-given response.[24] This means that we when we worship, we should acknowledge that it is the Holy Spirit who is present in the preaching of the word and in our participation of the sacraments and who is leading us to Christ, the Living Word of God. This is what it means for James Torrance to participate by the Spirit in the Son's communion with the Father.

And yet, like his brother, the strength of J. B. Torrance's theology was not in his pneumatology but in his Christology. There was very little attention regarding the role of the Holy Spirit creating faith *in us*, which is *our* spiritual act of worship (Romans 12:1–2). Tom Smail's thoughts are helpful at this point:

> I find Torrance most helpful in explaining how our response to God is dependent upon Christ's response on our behalf. He gives Christological depth to the assertion that we cannot respond by ourselves. He expounds in contemporary terms the basic Pauline insight that being saved by grace through faith means that God has to work not just on our behalf outside us but within us as well.... I am bound to say, however, that Professor Torrance leaves me dissatisfied with his failure to take adequate account of the equally important New Testament insight, that Christ's response on my behalf has to become my own response to Christ before it can take effect in me. It is indeed true that I cannot respond *by* myself till Christ has responded for me; it is also true that I must answer *for* myself and that I have not done so until the Spirit brings Christ's vicarious "Yes" to God on my behalf, and makes it available to me on my side of the relationship. It is then that I say my own "Amen" in the Spirit to the answer he has given, and glorify him as I say it.[25]

Smail offers a different perspective than Torrance regarding the role of the Spirit creating faith *in us*. While we certainly need the vibrant Christology that the Torrances brought to theology, we also need a robust pneumatology that includes an emphasis on the work of the Spirit *in us* and *with us* if we are to have a vibrant *trinitarian* theology of worship.

Christian Kettler responds to Smail's criticism by asking, "Does Torrance really disallow the importance of one's personal response of faith? A careful reading, it seems, would answer, no. Torrance is concerned with

---

24. J. B. Torrance, "Worship in the Reformed Church: The Purpose and Principles of Public Worship," 9. Note: This document is the text of a student "handout" from J. B. Torrance at New College, Edinburgh.

25. Smail, *The Giving Gift*, 109.

the radical implications of the vicarious humanity of Christ."[26] Kettler says that liberals and evangelicals have difficulty with the idea of Christ's total substitution for us. He goes as far as saying that, "Smail's critique reflects epistemological and christological problems and that his argument seems to reflect a lack of concern for the ontological reality of salvation."[27] One can see that Kettler is quickly coming to Torrance's defense. However, a careful reading of Smail shows he too has a deep appreciation for Torrance's Christology. Yet, Smail remains consistent in his criticism that Torrance's pneumatology does not place an emphasis on the Spirit's work in *our response* to Christ's response.

Alexandra S. Radcliff engages with those who believe that the Torrances have an underdeveloped pneumatology and with those who defend the Torrances against those claims. While honoring the Torrances, she states, "A fuller discussion of the Spirit's action upon Jesus's humanity would be beneficial for a better awareness and understanding of the Spirit's action upon our own humanity today."[28] As Radcliff also points out from those who defend the Torrances' pneumatology, "The Holy Spirit is ineffable and self-effacing, pointing away from himself to Christ and the Father."[29] This indeed is the role of the Holy Spirit in the Torrances' theology. But it also reaffirms the desire from some, for a more developed pneumatology, at it pertains to *our* faith, from the Torrances.

Finally, the Torrances did not focus on a theology of music and the arts. Music is so embedded in our discussions about worship today. But there was no attention given to this matter in the theology of the Torrances.[30] Public worship was primarily focused on the ministry of the word and sacraments. Also, worship for the Torrances was about Christ's worship on behalf of men and women. The Torrances were addressing theological foundations regarding a theology of worship. Having a solid theology of the priesthood of Christ provides the basis for other matters including a theology of music and the arts.[31]

26. Kettler, *The Vicarious Humanity of Christ and the Reality of Salvation*, 139.
27. Kettler, *The Vicarious Humanity of Christ and the Reality of Salvation*, 140.
28. Radcliff, *The Claim of Humanity in Christ* 88.
29. Radcliff, *The Claim of Humanity in Christ*, 90.
30. It is worth noting however that there are those who have studied under James Torrance who are writing prolifically on the subject of worship and the arts. Jeremy Begbie and Trevor Hart come to mind.
31. Jeremy Begbie has related the theology of the Torrances to music and the arts. See the following works by Jeremy Begbie: *Beholding the Glory*; *Music, Modernity, and*

Implications

What are the implications of what T. F. and J. B. Torrance taught regarding worship? What difference does it make for the worshiping community today? Does this not reflect a liturgical theological elitism disconnected with the person in the pew? In response to these questions, it would be fair to say that one of the reasons we may be uncomfortable with the doxological theology of the Torrances is because anthropocentricism is embedded in our liturgies. For example, there is far too much pressure on preachers to employ rhetoric to convince their parishioners to believe the message and the messenger. This is a far cry from the apostle Paul who explicitly stated:

> When I came to you, brothers and sisters, I did not come proclaiming the mystery of God to you in lofty words or wisdom. For I decided to know nothing among you except Jesus Christ, and him crucified. And I came to you in weakness and in fear and in much trembling. My speech and my proclamation were not with plausible words of wisdom, but with a demonstration of the Spirit and of power, so that your faith might not rest on human wisdom but on the power of God. (1 Corinthians 2:1–5)

Likewise, musicians and artists invest a tremendous amount of time working on the "performance" of worship. Without spiritual and theological leadership, these worship performances can quickly decline into mere entertainment. Worship can become about having "the right sound" and "the right look." Meanwhile, the theological premise undergirding this kind of thinking is nothing more than unitarian worship. The focus is centred on the performers and their responsibility to mediate the presence of God by how well they execute their skill as artists. This can be true not only in the contemporary setting but also in settings with classical choral music. While I am not sure the Torrances would call this focus on performance and entertainment idolatrous, they would indeed call it unitarian, non-trinitarian, and sub-Christian. If we factor in the warning in Romans chapter 1, however, worshiping the creation is indeed idolatrous. And the stage can be an idolatrous place indeed.

Finally, how liberating would it be for preachers, musicians, and artists of all types to know that their worship is perfect not because of what they do but because of who they are in Christ. For an artist, performing

---

God; *Redeeming Transcendence in the Arts*; *Resonant Witness*; *Resounding Truth*; *Theology, Music and Time*; *Voicing Creation's Praise*.

and the evaluation of the performance can become all-consuming. Yet, if preaching and artists knew that their worship was perfect because a perfect response has already been offered, their worship could indeed become an act of praise and thanksgiving. We do not have to live a life of gratitude; we get to live a life of gratitude because a way has been made for us to participate in the worship of Christ. Because of the indicatives of grace, we can participate in the imperatives of law. Also, this is about what God is doing not just about what he has done. The activity of his grace is always ongoing. It is relational not transactional. We are therefore free to participate. This is the needed inspiration for a vibrant worshiping community. In the language of the book of Hebrews, "Since we have a great priest over the house of God, let us approach with a true heart in full assurance of faith" (Hebrews 10:21–22). This is glorious news!

While one may not agree with everything that the Torrances advocated, it would be fair to say that an acquisition of a trinitarian-incarnational approach to liturgical theology could benefit the Christian worshiping community. Replacing unitarian tendencies with trinitarian awareness could help recover the emphasis on the *who* of worship without neglecting the *what* and the *how* of worship. Considering the idea that Christ is both the object *and subject* of worship could promote renewal in evangelical worship. Andrew Purves said, "Theology is to the end of the deeper faithfulness of the church in faith, worship and ministry. Whatever else theology must do, it must bring us back again and again to what the gospel has at its center: the person and work of Jesus Christ."[32] Both T. F. and J. B. Torrance would have wholeheartedly agreed!

---

32. Purves, *Exploring Christology and Atonement*, 254.

Bibliography

Anderson, Ray S. *The Soul of Ministry: Forming Leaders for God's People.* Louisville, KY: Westminster John Knox, 1997.
———. *Theological Foundations for Ministry.* Grand Rapids: Eerdmans, 1979.
Athanasius. *The Incarnation of the Word of God.* New York: Macmillan, 1946.
Ayo, Nicholas. *Gloria Patri: The History and Theology of the Lesser Doxology.* Notre Dame, IN: University of Notre Dame, 2007.
Baillie, Donald. *The Theology of the Sacraments.* New York: Scribner's Sons, 1957.
Baillie, John. *Baptism and Conversion.* New York: Scribner's Sons, 1963
Baker, Matthew, and Todd Speidell. *T. F. Torrance and Eastern Orthodoxy: Theology in Reconciliation.* Eugene, OR: Wipf and Stock, 2015.
Barker, Margaret. *The Great High Priest: The Temple Roots of Christian Liturgy.* London: T. & T. Clark, 2003.
Barth, Karl. *The Christian Life: Church Dogmatics Volume IV, Part 4 Lecture Fragments.* Grand Rapids: Eerdmans, 1981.
———. *Church Dogmatics.* Translated by G. W. Bromiley and T. F. Torrance. Edinburgh: T. & T. Clark, 1975.
———. *Credo.* New York: Scribner's Sons, 1962.
———. *Dogmatics in Outline.* New York: Harper and Row, 1959.
———. *The Epistle to the Romans.* London: Oxford University Press, 1933.
———. *Fifty Prayers.* Louisville, KY: Westminster John Knox, 2005.
———. *The Heidelberg Catechism for Today.* Richmond, VA: John Knox, 1964.
———. *Prayer: 50th Anniversary Edition.* Louisville, KY: Westminster John Knox, 2002.
———. *Prayer and Preaching.* London: SCM, 1964.
———. *Theology and Church: Shorter Writings 1920–1928 (with an Introduction by T. F. Torrance, 1962).* New York: Harper & Row, 1962.
———. *The Word of God & the Word of Man.* New York: Harper & Brothers, 1957.
Bauckham, Richard, and Daniel R. Driver, Trevor A. Hart, Nathan MacDonald, eds. *The Epistle to the Hebrews and Christian Theology.* Grand Rapids: Eerdmans, 2009.
Bawulski, Shawn, and Stephen R. Holmes. *Christian Theology: The Classics.* Oxford: Routledge, 2014.
Beale, G. K. *We Become What We Worship: A Biblical Theology of Idolatry.* Downers Grove, IL: IVP Academic, 2008.
Beasley-Murray, G. R. *Baptism in the New Testament.* London: MacMillan, 1974.
Begbie, Jeremy, ed. *Beholding the Glory: Incarnation through the Arts.* Grand Rapids: Baker Academic, 2001.

———. *Music, Modernity, and God: Essays in Listening*. Oxford: Oxford University Press, 2013.
———. *Redeeming Transcendence in the Arts: Bearing Witness to the Triune God*. Grand Rapids: Eerdmans, 2018.
———. *Resounding Truth: Christian Wisdom in the World of Music*. Grand Rapids: Baker Academic, 2007.
———. *Theology, Music and Time*. Cambridge: Cambridge University Press, 2000.
———. *Voicing Creation's Praise: Towards a Theology of the Arts*. Edinburgh: T. & T. Clark, 2000.
Begbie, Jeremy S., and Steven R. Guthrie. *Resonant Witness: Conversations between Music and Theology*. Grand Rapids: Eerdmans, 2011.
Best, Harold M. *Unceasing Worship: Biblical Perspectives on Worship and the Arts*. Downers Grove, IL: InterVarsity, 2003.
Block, Daniel I. *For the Glory of God: Recovering a Biblical Theology of Worship*. Reprint, Grand Rapids: Baker Academic, 2016.
Bonhoeffer, Dietrich. *Christ the Center*. San Francisco: Harper San Francisco, 1978.
Borchert, Gerald L. *Worship in the New Testament: Divine Mystery and Human Response*. Atlanta: Chalice, 2008.
Boulton, Matthew Myer. *God against Religion: Rethinking Christian Theology through Worship*. Grand Rapids: Eerdmans, 2008.
Bradshaw, Paul F. *Early Christian Worship: A Basic Introduction to Ideas and Practice*. Collegeville, MN: Liturgical, 2005.
———. *The Search for the Origins of Christian Worship: Sources and Methods for the Study of Early Liturgy*. New York: Oxford University Press, 2007.
Bromiley, Geoffrey W. *Introduction to the Theology of Karl Barth*. Edinburgh: T. & T. Clark, 1979.
Brower, Sandra Fach. "Extending the Sacraments to Children: Insights from the Theology of T. F. Torrance." *Participatio* 6 (2016) 151–77.
Brown, Colin. *Philosophy & The Christian Faith*. Downers Grove, IL: InterVarsity, 1968.
Bruce, Robert, and Thomas F. Torrance. *The Mystery of the Lord's Supper: Sermons on the Sacrament Preached in the Kirk of Edinburgh*. Edinburgh: Rutherford House, 2005.
Bunyan, John. *Prayer*. Edinburgh: Banner of Truth Trust, 1965.
Byars, Ronald P. *What Language Shall I Borrow? The Bible and Christian Worship*. Grand Rapids: Eerdmans, 2008.
Calvin, John. *The Institutes of Christian Religion*. Edited by Tony Lane and Hilary Osborne. Grand Rapids: Baker Books, 1992.
———. *Institutes of the Christian Religion*. Edited by John T. McNeill; translated by Ford Lewis Battles. Philadelphia: Westminster, 1960.
———. *New Testament Commentaries: A New Translation*. 12 vols. Edited by David W. Torrance and Thomas F. Torrance; translated by A. W. Morrison. Grand Rapids: Eerdmans, 1972.
Cameron, Daniel J. *Flesh and Blood: A Dogmatic Sketch concerning the Fallen Nature View of Christ's Human Nature*. Eugene, OR: Wipf and Stock, 2016.
Camfield, F. W. *Reformation Old and New: A Tribute to Karl Barth*. Eugene, OR: Wipf and Stock, 2009.
Campbell, John McLeod. *Christ the Bread of Life*. Danvers, MA: General Books LLC, 2009.

Campbell, John McLeod, James Torrance, and Jock Stein. *Nature of the Atonement.* Eugene, OR: Wipf and Stock, 1999.

Canlis, Julie. *Calvin's Ladder: A Spiritual Theology of Ascent and Ascension.* Grand Rapids: Eerdmans, 2010.

Cass, Peter. *Christ Condemned Sin in the Flesh: Thomas F. Torrance's Doctrine of Soteriology and Its Ecumenical Significance.* Saarbrucken, Germany: VDM Verlag Dr. Muller Aktiengesellschaft & Co., 2009.

Chan, Simon. *Liturgical Theology: The Church as Worshiping Community.* Downers Grove, IL: IVP Academic, 2006.

Chapell, Bryan. *Christ-Centered Worship: Letting the Gospel Shape Our Practice.* Grand Rapids: Baker Academic, 2009.

Cherry, Constance M. *The Worship Architect: A Blueprint for Designing Culturally Relevant and Biblically Faithful Services.* Grand Rapids: Baker Academic, 2010.

Cheyne, A. C. "New College, Edinburgh, 1846–1996." In *Studies in Scottish Church History,* edited by Alex Cheung, 287–312. Edinburgh: T. & T. Clark, 1999.

Chiarot, Kevin. *Unassumed in the Unhealed: The Humanity of Christ in the Christology of T. F. Torrance.* Eugene, OR: Pickwick, 2013.

Chung, Titus. *Thomas Torrance's Mediations and Revelation.* Farnham, UK: Ashgate, 2011.

Colyer, Elmer M. *Evangelical Theology in Transition: Theologians in Dialogue with Donald Bloesch.* Downers Grove, IL: InterVarsity, 2007.

———. *How To Read T. F. Torrance: Understanding His Trinitarian & Scientific Theology.* Downers Grove, IL: InterVarsity, 2001.

———. *The Nature of Doctrine in T. F. Torrance's Theology.* Eugene, OR: Wipf and Stock, 2001.

———. *The Promise of Trinitarian Theology: Theologians in Dialogue with T. F. Torrance.* Lanham, MD: Rowman & Littlefield, 2001.

Crisp, Oliver. "Did Christ have a Fallen Human Nature?" *International Journal of Systematic Theology* 6.3 (2004) 270–88.

Cullmann, Oscar. *Early Christian Worship.* London: SCM, 1953.

Davie, Martin. *New Dictionary of Theology: Historical and Systematic.* Downers Grove, IL: IVP Academic, 2016.

Davies, J. G. *The New Westminster Dictionary of Liturgy and Worship.* Philadelphia: Westminster, 1986.

Dawn, Marva J. *Reaching out without Dumbing Down: A Theology of Worship for the Turn-of-the-Century Culture.* Grand Rapids: Eerdmans, 1995.

———. *A Royal Waste of Time: The Splendor of Worshiping God and Being Church for the World.* Grand Rapids: Eerdmans, 1999.

Dawson, Gerrit Scott. *An Introduction to Torrance Theology: Discovering the Incarnate Saviour.* London: T. & T. Clark, 2007.

———. *Jesus Ascended: The Meaning of Christ's Continuing Incarnation.* London: T. & T. Clark, 2004.

Day, Juliette J. *Reading the Liturgy: An Exploration of Texts in Christian Worship.* Edinburgh: T. & T. Clark, 2014.

Dearborn, Kerry. "Fifteen Years of Teaching Worship, Community and the Triune God of Grace." *Participatio* Supp. Vol. 3 (2014) 50–57

Deddo, Gary W. *Karl Barth's Theology of Relations: Trinitarian, Christological and Human. Towards and Ethic of the Family.* 2 vols. Eugene, OR: Wipf & Stock, 1999.

Denney, James. *Studies in Theology*. London: Hodder and Stoughton, 1895.
Dix, Gregory. *The Shape of the Liturgy*. Glasgow: Dacre, 1943.
Dyk, Leanne Van. *A More Profound Alleluia: Theology and Worship in Harmony*. Grand Rapids: Eerdmans, 2011.
Dyrness, William A. *A Primer on Christian Worship*. Grand Rapids: Eerdmans, 2009.
Engle, Paul E., and Paul A. Basden. *Six Views on Exploring the Worship Spectrum*. Grand Rapids: Zondervan, 2004.
Erler, Rolf Joachim, and Reiner Marquard. *A Karl Barth Reader*. Grand Rapids: Eerdmans, 1986.
Eugenio, Dick O. *Communion with the Triune God: The Trinitarian Soteriology of T. F. Torrance*. Eugene, OR: Pickwick, 2014.
Fach, Sandra. "Answering the Upwards Call: The Ascended Christ, Mediator of Our Worship." PhD thesis, King's College, London, 2008.
———. "Worship as Thanksgiving: The Offering of Life." *Theology in Scotland* XVI Special Issue (2011) 41–60
Fergusson, David. "The Ascension of Christ: Its Significance in the Theology of T. F. Torrance." *Participatio* 3 (2012) 92–107
Ford, David, and Daniel W. Hardy. *Living in Praise: Worshipping and Knowing God*. Grand Rapids: Baker Academic, 2005.
Forsyth, P. T. *The Soul of Prayer*. Vancouver, BC: Regent College, 2002.
Fransen, Piet, and T. F. Torrance. *Intelligent Theology. Volume 3*. Chicago: Franciscan Herald, 1969.
Gillquist, Peter E. *The Physical Side of Being Spiritual*. Grand Rapids: Zondervan, 1979.
Grogan, Geoffrey. *The Faith Once Entrusted to the Saints: Engaging with Issues and Trends in Evangelical Theology*. Nottingham, UK: InterVarsity, 2010.
Gunton, Colin E. *The Theologian as Preacher*. London: T. & T. Clark, 2007.
Habets, Myk. *Theology in Transposition: A Constructive Appraisal of T. F. Torrance*. Minneapolis, MN: Fortress, 2013.
———. *Theosis in the Theology of Thomas Torrance*. Ashgate New Critical Thinking in Religion, Theology, and Biblical Studies. Farnham, UK: Ashgate, 2009.
Habets, Myk, and Bobby Grow. *Evangelical Calvinism: Essays Resourcing the Continuing Reformation of the Church*. Eugene, OR: Pickwick, 2012.
Habets, Myk, Bobby Grow, and Oliver Crisp. *Evangelical Calvinism, Volume 2*. Eugene, OR: Pickwick, 2017.
Hale, Philip. "Eating and Drinking Damnation to Oneself: The Place of 1 Corinthians 11:27–29 in the Lord's Supper." Nebraska Lutherans for Confessional Study, February 17, 2011.
Hammond, Geordan, *John Wesley in America: Restoring Primitive Christianity*. Oxford: Oxford University Press, 2014.
Harnack, Adolf. *What Is Christianity?* New York: Harper & Brothers, 1957.
Hart, Trevor A. *Between the Image and the Word*. Farnham, UK: Ashgate, 2013.
———. *Faith Thinking: The Dynamics of Christian Theology*. 1995. Reprint, Eugene, OR: Wipf and Stock, 2005. (2nd ed. Eugene, OR: Cascade, 2020)
———. *Making Good: Creation, Creativity and Artistry*. Waco, TX: Baylor University Press, 2014.
Hart, Trevor A., Gavin Hopps, and Jeremy Begbie. *Art, Imagination and Christian Hope: Patterns of Promise*. Farnham, UK: Ashgate, 2012.

Hart, Trevor A., Daniel P. Thimell, and James B. Torrance. *Christ in Our Place: The Humanity of God in Christ for the Reconciliation of the World: Essays Presented to James Torrance*. Exeter, UK: Paternoster, 1989.
Hays, Richard B. *The Faith of Jesus Christ: The Narrative Substructure of Galatians 3:1— 4:11*. Grand Rapids: Eerdmans, 2002.
Heaney, Maeve Louise. *Music as Theology: What Music Says about the Word*. Princeton Theological Monograph. Eugene, OR: Pickwick, 2012.
Heron, Alasdair I. *Table and Tradition: Toward an Ecumenical Understanding of the Eucharist*. Philadelphia: Westminster, 1983.
Ho, Man Kei. *A Critical Study on T. F. Torrance's Theology of Incarnation*. Bern, Switzerland: Lang, 2008.
Holcomb, Justin S., and David A. Johnson. *Christian Theologies of the Sacraments: A Comparative Introduction*. New York: New York University Press, 2017.
Horton, Michael Scott. *A Better Way: Rediscovering the Drama of God-Centered Worship*. Grand Rapids: Baker, 2003.
Houston, James, and James B. Torrance. "Prayer and the Trinitarian Faith in the Life of the Church." Vancouver, BC: Regent Audio, 1997. https://www.regentaudio.com/products/prayer-and-the-trinitarian-faith-in-the-life-of-the-church
Humphrey, Edith McEwan. *Grand Entrance: Worship on Earth as in Heaven*. Grand Rapids: Brazos, 2011.
Hunsinger, George. "The Dimension of Depth: Thomas F. Torrance on the Sacraments of Baptism and the Lord's Supper." *Scottish Journal of Theology* 54.2 (2001) 155–76.
———. *Eucharist and Ecumenism: Let Us Keep the Feast*. Current Issues in Theology. Cambridge: Cambridge University Press, 2008.
Hurtado, Larry W. *At the Origins of Christian Worship: The Context and Character of Earliest Christian Devotion*. Didsbury Lectures. Carlisle, UK: Paternoster, 1999.
Jenson, Robert. "The Church and the Sacraments." In *The Cambridge Companion to Christian Doctrine*, edited by Colin Gunton, 207–25. Cambridge Companions to Religion. Cambridge: Cambridge University Press, 1997.
Jungmann, Josef A. *The Early Liturgy: To the Time of Gregory the Great*. Notre Dame, IN: University of Notre Dame Press, 1959.
———. *The Place of Christ in Liturgical Prayer*. Translated by A. Peeler. Staten Island, NY: Alba House, 1965.
Kauflin, Bob. *Worship Matters: Leading Others to Encounter the Greatness of God*. Wheaton, IL: Crossway, 2008.
Kelly, Douglas F. *Systematic Theology*. 2 vols. Fearn, UK: Mentor, 2008.
Kettler, Christian D. *The Breadth and Depth of the Atonement: The Vicarious Humanity of Christ in the Church, the World, and the Self*. Essays, 1990–2015. Eugene, OR: Wipf & Stock, 2017.
———. *The God Who Believes: Faith, Doubt, and the Vicarious Humanity of Christ*. Eugene, OR: Cascade, 2005.
———. *The God Who Rejoices: Joy, Despair, and the Vicarious Humanity of Christ*. Eugene, OR: Cascade, 2010.
———. *The Vicarious Humanity of Christ and the Reality of Salvation*. Eugene, OR: Wipf & Stock, 1991.
Kettler, Christian D., and Todd H. Speidell, eds. *Incarnational Ministry: The Presence of Christ in Church, Society, and Family*. Colorado Springs, CO: Helmers & Howard, 1990.

Knowles, Michael P. *We Preach Not Ourselves: Paul on Proclamation*. Grand Rapids: Brazos, 2008.

Kuyper, Abraham, and Harry Boonstra. *Our Worship*. Grand Rapids: Eerdmans, 2009.

LaCugna, Catherine. *God for Us: The Trinity and Christian Life*. San Francisco: Harper, 1991.

Lamont, Daniel. *Christ and the World of Thought*. Edinburgh: T. & T. Clark, 1999.

Lang, Bernhard. *Sacred Games: A History of Christian Worship*. New Haven, CT: Yale University Press, 1997.

Lee, Kye Won. *Living in Union with Christ: The Practical Theology of Thomas F. Torrance*. New York: Lang, 2003.

Letham, Robert. *The Lord's Supper: Eternal Word in Broken Bread*. Phillipsburg, NJ: P&R, 2001.

Luoma, Tapio. *Incarnation and Physics: Natural Science in the Theology of Thomas F. Torrance*. New York: Oxford University Press, 2002.

Mackintosh, H. R. *The Christian Apprehension of God*. 1929. Reprint, Eugene, OR: Wipf & Stock, 2008.

———. *The Christian Experience of Forgiveness*. New York: Harper and Brothers, 1927.

———. *The Doctrine of the Person of Jesus Christ*. New York: Scribner's Sons, 1928.

———. *Immortality and the Future*. London: Hodder and Stoughton, 1915.

MacLean, Stanley Stephen. *Resurrection, Apocalypse, and the Kingdom of Christ: The Eschatology of Thomas F. Torrance*. Eugene, OR: Pickwick, 2012.

Macmurray, John. *Freedom in the Modern World*. Amherst, NY: Humanity, 1992.

———. *Reason and Emotion*. Amherst, NY: Humanity, 1992.

———. *The Self as Agent*. Amherst: Humanity, 1999.

Marshall, I. Howard. *Last Supper and Lord's Supper*. Didsbury Lectures. Exeter, UK: Paternoster, 1980.

Martin Ralph P. *Worship in the Early Church*. Grand Rapids: Eerdmans, 1964.

———. *The Worship of God: Some Theological, Pastoral, and Practical Reflection*. Grand Rapids: Eerdmans, 1982.

Mathison, Keith A. *Given for You: Reclaiming Calvin's Doctrine of the Lord's Supper*. Phillipsburg, NJ: P&R, 2002.

Maxwell, James Clerk, and Thomas F. Torrance. *A Dynamical Theory of the Electromagnetic Field*. Reprint, Eugene, OR: Wipf and Stock, 1996.

May, Stephen. "Thrown Back upon Ourselves: James Torrance's Christian Life and Worship." *Participatio* Supplement 3 (2014) 220–43

McGowan, Andrew B. *Ancient Christian Worship: Early Church Practices in Social, Historical, and Theological Perspective*. Grand Rapids: Baker Academic, 2014.

McGowan, A. T. B. *Adam, Christ and Covenant: Exploring Headship Theology*. London: Apollos, 2016.

McGrath, Alister E. *The Christian Theology Reader*. Chichester, UK: Wiley Blackwell, 2017.

———. *T. F. Torrance: An Intellectual Biography*. Edinburgh: T. & T. Clark, 1999.

McKim, Donald K. *Westminster Dictionary of Theological Terms*. Louisville, KY: Westminster John Knox, 2000.

McKinney, Richard W. A. *Creation, Christ and Culture: Studies in Honour of T. F. Torrance*. Edinburgh: T. & T. Clark, 1976.

McLelland, Joseph C., and Thomas F. Torrance. *The Visible Words of God: An Exposition of the Sacramental Theology of Peter Martyr Vermigli, A.D. 1500–1562.* Grand Rapids: Eerdmans, 1957.

McMaken, W. Travis. *The Sign of the Gospel: Toward an Evangelical Doctrine of Infant Baptism after Karl Barth.* Minneapolis, MN: Fortress, 2013.

McKim, Donald K., ed. *Major Themes in the Reformed Tradition.* Grand Rapids: Eerdmans, 1992.

McSwain, Jeff, and Jeremy Begbie. *Movements of Grace: The Dynamic Christo-Realism of Barth, Bonhoeffer, and the Torrances.* Eugene, OR: Wipf and Stock, 2010.

Milligan, William. *The Ascension of Christ.* London: MacMillan, 1891.

———. *The Resurrection of Our Lord.* London: MacMillan, 1881.

Molnar, Paul D. *Faith, Freedom, and the Spirit: The Economic Trinity in Barth, Torrance and Contemporary Theology.* Downers Grove: IVP Academic, 2015.

———. "God's Self-Communication in Christ: A Comparison of Thomas F. Torrance and Karl Rahner." *Scottish Journal of Theology* 50.3 (1997) 288–320

———. "The Obedience of the Son in the Theology of Karl Barth and of Thomas F. Torrance." *Scottish Journal of Theology* 67.1 (2014) 50–69

———. *Thomas F. Torrance: Theologian of the Trinity.* Farnham, UK: Ashgate, 2009.

Morrison, Angus. "The Eucharist and Renewal in the Church." *Participatio* 6 (2016) 247–68

Morrison, John Douglas. *Knowledge of the Self-Revealing God in the Thought of Thomas Forsyth Torrance.* New York: Lang, 1997.

Moule, C. F. D. "The Biblical Conception of Faith." *The Expository Times* 68 (October 1956–September 1957) 157.

Munchin, David. *Is Theology a Science? The Nature of the Scientific Enterprise in the Scientific Theology of Thomas Forsyth Torrance and the Anarchic Epistemology of Paul Feyerabend.* Studies in Systematic Theology. Leiden, Netherlands: Koninklijke Brill NV, 2011.

Murray, Andrew. *Collected Works on Prayer.* New Kensington, PA: Whitaker House, 2013.

Myers, Ben. "The Stratification of Knowledge in the Thought of T. F. Torrance." *Scottish Journal of Theology* 61.1 (2018) 1–15.

Need, Stephen W. *Truly Divine and Truly Human: The Story of Christ and the Seven Ecumenical Councils.* Grand Rapids: Baker Academic, 2008.

Newell, Roger. "Apollinarianism in Worship Revisited: Torrance's Contribution to the Renewal of Reformed Worship." (2008). Faculty Publications—College of Christian Studies. Paper 148. http://digitalcommons.georgefox.edu/ccs/148

Neyrey, Jerome H. *Give God the Glory: Ancient Prayer and Worship in Cultural Perspective.* Grand Rapids: Eerdmans, 2007.

Ngien, Dennis. *Gifted Response: The Triune God as the Causative Agency of Our Responsive Worship.* Milton Keynes, UK: Paternoster, 2008.

Noble, Thomas A. *Holy Trinity: Holy People: The Theology of Christian Perfecting.* Didsbury Lectures. Eugene, OR: Cascade, 2013.

———. *Tyndale House and Fellowship: The First Sixty Years.* Leicester, UK: InterVarsity, 2006.

Old, Hughes Oliphant. *Themes & Variations for a Christian Doxology: Some Thoughts on the Theology of Worship.* Grand Rapids: Eerdmans, 1992.

Packer, J. I. *Fundamentalism and the Word of God.* Grand Rapids: Eerdmans, 1958.

Parry, Robin A. *Worshipping Trinity: Coming Back to the Heart of Worship*. Milton Keynes, UK: Paternoster, 2005.

———. *Worshipping Trinity: Coming Back to the Heart of Worship*. 2nd ed. Eugene, OR: Cascade, 2012.

Peterson, David. *Engaging with God: A Biblical Theology of Worship*. Grand Rapids: Eerdmans, 1992.

Pierce, Timothy M. *Enthroned on Our Praise: An Old Testament Theology of Worship*. Nashville, TN: B&H Academic, 2008.

Plantinga Jr., Cornelius, and Sue A. Rozeboom. *Discerning the Spirits: A Guide to Thinking about Christian Worship Today*. Grand Rapids: Eerdmans, 2003.

Polayni, Michael. *Personal Knowledge: Toward a Post-Critical Philosophy*. Chicago: University of Chicago Press, 1974.

———. *The Tacit Dimension*. Gloucester, MA: Peter Smith, 1966.

Purves, Andrew, and Charles Partee. *Encountering God: Christian Faith in Turbulent Times*. Louisville, KY: Westminster John Knox, 2000.

Purves, Andrew. *The Crucifixion of Ministry: Surrendering Our Ambitions to the Service of Christ*. Downers Grove, IL: IVP, 2007.

———. *Exploring Christology & Atonement: Conversations with John McLeod Campbell, H. R. Mackintosh and T. F. Torrance*. Downers Grove, IL: IVP Academic, 2015.

———. *Reconstructing Pastoral Theology: A Christological Foundation*. Louisville, KY: Westminster John Knox, 2004.

———. *The Resurrection of Ministry: Serving in the Hope of the Risen Lord*. Downers Grove, IL: IVP, 2010.

Radcliff, Alexandra S. *The Claim of Humanity in Christ: Salvation and Sanctification in the Theology of T. F. and J. B. Torrance*. Eugene, OR: Pickwick, 2016.

Radcliff, Jason. *Thomas F. Torrance and the Church Fathers: A Reformed, Evangelical, and Ecumenical Reconstruction of the Patristic Tradition*. Eugene, OR: Pickwick, 2014.

Ratzinger, Joseph Cardinal. *God Is Near Us: The Eucharist, The Heart of Life*. San Francisco: Ignatius, 2003.

Redding, Graham. "Prayer and the Priesthood of Christ." *Participatio* Supp. Vol. 3 (2014) 64–72

———. *Prayer and the Priesthood of Christ: In the Reformed Tradition*. London: T. & T. Clark, 2003.

Redman, Robb. *The Great Worship Awakening: Singing a New Song in the Postmodern Church*. San Francisco: Jossey-Bass, 2002.

Riches, Aaron. *Ecce Homo: On the Divine Unity of Christ*. Grand Rapids: Eerdmans, 2006.

Schleiermacher, Friedrich. *The Christian Faith* edited by H. R. Mackintosh and J. S. Stewart. Philadelphia: Fortress, 1976.

Schmemann, Alexander. *For the Life of the World*. Rev. and exp. ed. Crestwood, NY: St. Vladimir's Seminary, 1973.

Schmit, Clayton J. *Sent and Gathered: A Worship Manual for the Missional Church*. Grand Rapids: Baker Academic, 2009.

Senn, Frank C. *Introduction to Christian Liturgy*. Minneapolis, MN: Fortress, 2012.

———. *The People's Work: A Social History of the Liturgy*. Minneapolis, MN: Fortress, 2010.

Smail, Thomas A. *The Forgotten Father*. London: Hodder & Stoughton, 1980.

———. *The Giving Gift: The Holy Spirit in Person*. London: Hodder & Stoughton, 1988.
———. *Once and for All: A Confession of the Cross*. Eugene, OR: Wipf & Stock, 2005.
Smith, Gordon T. *A Holy Meal: The Lord's Supper in the Life of the Church*. Grand Rapids: Baker Academic, 2005.
Smith, James K.A. *Awaiting the King: Reforming Public Theology*. Grand Rapids: Baker Academic, 2017.
———. *Desiring the Kingdom: Worship, Worldview, and Cultural Formation*. Grand Rapids: Baker Academic, 2009.
———. *You Are What You Love: The Spiritual Power of Habit*. Grand Rapids: Brazos, 2016.
Speidell, Todd. *Fully Human in Christ: The Incarnation as the End of Christian Ethics*. Eugene, OR: Wipf and Stock, 2016.
———. *Trinity and Transformation: J. B. Torrance's Vision of Worship, Mission, and Society*. Eugene, OR: Wipf and Stock, 2016.
Spinks, Bryan D. *The Place of Christ in Liturgical Prayer: Christology, Trinity, and Liturgical Theology*. Collegeville, MN: Liturgical, 2009.
Spinks, Bryan D., and Iain R. Torrance. *To Glorify God: Essays on Modern Reformed Liturgy*. Edinburgh: T. & T. Clark, 1999.
Stamps, Robert Julian. *The Sacrament of the Word Made Flesh: The Eucharistic Theology of Thomas F. Torrance*. Eugene, OR: Wipf and Stock, 2013.
Stein, Jock, and Howard Taylor. *In Christ All Things Hold Together: An Introduction to Christian Doctrine*. Eugene, OR: Wipf and Stock, 2010.
Stewart, James S. *A Faith to Proclaim*. London: Hodder and Stoughton, 1953.
———. *Heralds of God*. Grand Rapids: Baker Book House, 1972.
———. *A Man in Christ*. London: Hodder and Stoughton, 1935.
Thiemann, Ronald. *Revelation and Theology: The Gospel as Narrated Promise*. Notre Dame, IN: University of Notre Dame Press, 1985.
Thomson, James G. S. S. *The Praying Christ: Jesus' Doctrine and Practice of Prayer*. Grand Rapids: Eerdmans, 1959.
Torrance, Alan J. *Persons in Communion: An Essay on Trinitarian Description and Human Participation, with Special Reference to Volume One of Karl Barth's Church Dogmatics*. Edinburgh: T. & T. Clark, 2011.
Torrance, Alexis. "The Theology of Baptism in T. F. Torrance and Its Ascetic Correlate in St. Mark the Monk." *Participatio* 4 (2013) 147–61
Torrance, David W., and George Taylor. *Israel, God's Servant: God's Key to the Redemption of the World*. Edinburgh: Handsel, 2007.
Torrance, David W. *The Reluctant Minister: Memoirs by David W. Torrance*. Haddington, UK: Handsel, 2015.
———. *Witness of the Jews to God*. Eugene, OR: Wipf and Stock, 2011.
Torrance, Iain R. "A Particular Reformed Piety: John Knox and the Posture at Communion." *Scottish Journal of Theology* 67.4 (2014) 400–413.
Torrance, James B. "The Covenant Concept in Scottish Theology in Politics and Its Legacy." *Scottish Journal of Theology* 34.3 (1981) 225–43.
———. "Covenant or Contract? A Study of the Theological Background of Worship in Seventeenth-Century Scotland." *Scottish Journal of Theology* 23.1 (1970) 51–76.
———. "The Forgotten Trinity." Vancouver, BC: Regent Audio, 1994. https://www.regentaudio.com/products/the-forgotten-trinity-the-way-of-worship

———. "Interpretation and Understanding in Schleiermacher's Theology: Some Critical Questions." *Scottish Journal of Theology* 21.3 (1968) 268–82.

———. "The Nature of the Problem." In *Where Science and Faith Meet*, edited by Oliver Barclay, James B. Torrance, et al., 7–13. London: Inter-Varsity Fellowship, 1953.

———. "The Priesthood of Jesus." In *Essays in Christology for Karl Barth*, edited by T. H. L. Parker, 153–73. London, Lutterworth, 1956.

———. "The Vicarious Humanity and the Priesthood of Christ in the Theology of John Calvin." In *Calvinus Ecclesiae Doctor*, edited by W. Neuser, 69–84. Kampen: Kok, 1978.

———. "Worship and the Gospel." Vancouver, BC: Regent Audio, 1984. https://www.regentaudio.com/products/worship-and-the-gospel

———. *Worship, Community, and the Triune God of Grace*. Carlisle, UK: Paternoster, 1996.

———. *Worship, Community & the Triune God of Grace*. Downers Grove, IL: InterVarsity, 1997.

———. "Worship in the Reformed Church: The Purpose and Principles of Public Worship." Note: This document is the text of a student 'handout' from J. B Torrance at New College, Edinburgh. Minor editing has involved the italicizing of words underlined and the use of non-gender specific language, with the use of capitals being left mostly untouched [Robert T. Walker—April, 2014].

Torrance, James B., et al. *The Forgotten Trinity 1: The Report of the BCC Study Commission on Trinitarian Doctrine Today*. London: The British Council of Churches, Inter-Church House, 1989.

———. *The Forgotten Trinity 2: A Study Guide Contained in the Report of the BCC Study Commission on Trinitarian Doctrine Today*. London: The British Council of Churches, Inter-Church House, 1989.

———. *The Forgotten Trinity 3: A Selection of Papers Presented to the BCC Study Commission on Trinitarian Doctrine Today*. London: The British Council of Churches, Inter-Church House, 1991.

Torrance, Thomas Forsyth. *The Apocalypse Today: Sermons on Revelation*. London: James Clarke, 1960.

———. *Atonement: The Person and Work of Christ*. Edited and introduced by Robert T. Walker. Milton Keynes, UK: Paternoster, 2009.

———. *Belief in Science and in Christian Life: The Relevance of Michael Polanyi's Thought for Christian Faith and Life*. Eugene, OR: Wipf and Stock, 1998.

———. *The Biblical Doctrine of Baptism*. Edinburgh: Saint Andrews, 1958.

———. *Calvin's Doctrine of Man*. Reprint, Eugene, OR: Wipf and Stock, 2001.

———. *The Christian Doctrine of God: One Being Three Persons*. London: T. & T. Clark, 2006.

———. *The Christian Frame of Mind: Reason, Order, and Openness in Theology and Natural Science*. Colorado Springs, CO: Helmers & Howard, 1989.

———. *Christian Theology & Scientific Culture*. New York: Oxford University Press, 1981.

———. *Christian Theology and Scientific Culture*. Reprint, Eugene, OR: Wipf and Stock, 1998.

———. *Conflict & Agreement in the Church Vol. 1&2*. Eugene, OR: Wipf and Stock, 1996.

———. *Divine and Contingent Order*. Edinburgh, Scotland: T. & T. Clark, 1998.

———. *Divine Meaning: Studies in Patristic Hermeneutics*. Edinburgh: T. & T. Clark, 1995.

———. *The Doctrine of Grace in the Apostolic Fathers*. Grand Rapids: Eerdmans, 1959.

———. *The Doctrine of Jesus Christ*. Reprint, Eugene, OR: Wipf and Stock, 2002.

———. *God and Rationality*. Edinburgh: T. & T. Clark, 1997.

———. *Gospel, Church, and Ministry*. Edited by Jock Stein. Eugene, OR: Pickwick, 2012.

———. *The Ground and Grammar of Theology: Consonance between Theology and Science*. Edinburgh: T. & T. Clark, 2001.

———. *The Hermeneutics of John Calvin*. Edinburgh: Scottish Academic, 1988.

———. *Incarnation: The Person and Life of Christ*. Edited and introduced by Robert T. Walker. Milton Keynes, UK: Paternoster, 2008.

———. *The Incarnation: Ecumenical Studies in the Nicene-Constantinopolitan Creed A.D. 381*. Reprint, Eugene, OR: Wipf and Stock, 1998.

———. *Juridical Law and Physical Law: Toward a Realist Foundation for Human Law*. Reprint, Eugene, OR: Wipf and Stock, 1997.

———. *Karl Barth: An Introduction to His Early Theology 1910–1931*. Edinburgh: T. & T. Clark, 1962.

———. *Karl Barth, Biblical and Evangelical Theologian*. Edinburgh: T. & T. Clark, 1990.

———. *Kingdom and Church: A Study in the Theology of the Reformation*. Eugene, OR: Wipf and Stock, 1996.

———. *The Mediation of Christ*. Colorado Springs, CO: Helmers & Howard, 1992.

———. "The Mediation of Christ." Vancouver, BC: Regent Audio, 2002. https://www.regentaudio.com/products/the-mediation-of-christ

———. *Preaching Christ Today: The Gospel and Scientific Thinking*. Grand Rapids: Eerdmans, 1994.

———. *Reality and Evangelical Theology: A Fresh and Challenging Approach to Christian Revelation*. Philadelphia: Westminster, 1982.

———. *Reality & Evangelical Theology the Realism of Christian Revelation*. Downers Grove, IL: InterVarsity, 1999.

———. *Reality and Scientific Theology*. Eugene, OR: Wipf and Stock, 2002.

———. *Royal Priesthood: A Theology of Ordained Ministry*. Edinburgh: T. & T. Clark, 1993.

———. *The School of Faith: The Catechisms of the Reformed Church*. Reprint, Eugene, OR: Wipf and Stock, 1996.

———. *Scottish Theology: From John Knox to John McLeod Campbell*. Edinburgh: T. & T. Clark, 1996.

———. *The Soul and Person of the Unborn Child*. Edinburgh: The Scottish Order of Christian Unity—Handsel, 1999.

———. *Space, Time, and Incarnation*. Edinburgh: T. & T. Clark, 1997.

———. *Space, Time, and Resurrection*. Edinburgh: T. & T. Clark, 2001.

———. *Theology in Reconstruction*. London: SCM, 1965.

———. *Theological and Natural Science*. Eugene, OR: Wipf and Stock, 2002.

———. "Theological Instinct." Vancouver, BC: Regent Audio, 2002. https://www.regentaudio.com/products/theological-instinct

———. *Theological Science*. Edinburgh: T. & T. Clark, 1996.

———. *Theology in Reconciliation: Essays towards Evangelical and Catholic Unity in East and West*. 1975. Reprint, Eugene, OR: Wipf and Stock, 1996.

———. *Transformation & Convergence in the Frame of Knowledge: Explorations in the Interrelations of Scientific and Theological Enterprise*. Reprint, Eugene, OR: Wipf and Stock, 1998.

———. *The Trinitarian Faith: The Evangelical Theology of the Ancient Catholic Church*. Edinburgh: T. & T. Clark, 2006.

———. *Trinitarian Perspectives: Toward Doctrinal Agreement*. Edinburgh: T. & T. Clark, 1994.

———. *When Christ Comes and Comes Again*. Reprint, Eugene, OR: Wipf and Stock, 1957.

Thomas Forsyth Torrance. The unpublished works listed are found in The Thomas F. Torrance Manuscript Collection. Special Collections, Princeton Theological Seminary Library. Items in brackets indicate illegible words and/or missing information.

Box 38 Sermons, Lectures, and Addresses, in Scotland and Abroad

Untitled sermon preached at Beechgrove Church, Aberdeen, 2 November 1997. Similar sermons: Untitled sermon at Penicuik, Midlothian, 5 September 1993; Untitled sermon at Cluny Parish, Edinburgh, 17 October 1993; Untitled sermon at MacDonald Memorial Church, Bellshill, 7 June 1998. B39 "He that spared not his own Son"; "The Cross—A Window into the Heart of the Father," First Presbyterian Church in Dillon, 2 February 1997.

Untitled sermon on John 1:6-9 (no page or date). Similar sermons: Untitled sermon on 1 John 1:5; "I am the light of the World'; "The Real Light"; B38 Untitled sermon on John 1:34; B39 "A Faith for Hard Times: The Living Light"; B39 "Light: Its Theology and Physics"; B39 "Light"; B41 "Christ the Light of the World"; B41 "The Christian Faith and the Physics of Light"; B43 Untitled Sermon on Isaiah 50:11, 1-8; and B45 Untitled Sermon on 1 John 1:1-10; 2:1-11. For a discussion of light in relation to daily Christian life, see B47 "If we walk in the light," 1-8.

Box 39 Sermons, Lectures, and Addresses, in Scotland and Abroad

"Ecumenical Service—Kirk of the Greyfriars," Sermon on Acts 2:41-47. Edinburgh, Trinity Sunday, 24 May 1970.

Box 43, Folder "Sermons on Daniel"

"Oh man greatly beloved—be stronger." Sermon on Daniel 10:19. Alyth, 22 March 1942.

Box 44, Folder "Sermons on Mark"

"Communion Sermon." Sermon on Mark 10:38; Alyth, June 1940; Blairgrove, May [__]; Beechgrove, 18 January 1948.

Box 44, Folder "Sermons on Luke"

"The Pharisee and the Publican at Prayer." Sermon on Luke 18:10f. Alyth, 18 January 1942.

Box 46, Folder "Sermons on Romans 8-16"

"God commendeth his love toward us." Sermon on Romans 6:7-8. Alyth, 6 September 1942.

Box 47, Folder "Sermons on 1 John"

"The Condemning Heart." Sermon on 1 John 3:20. Alyth, April 1940; Blair [__], May 1940; Edinburgh, October 1940; Beechgrove, 14 December 1947; Queen's [__], 6 June 1948; Bla [__], 4 May 1952; M [__] High Church, Edinburgh, 13 September 1952.

Torrance, Thomas F., James Torrance, David W. Torrance, Gerrit Scott Dawson, and Jock Stein. *A Passion for Christ: The Vision That Ignites Ministry*. Edinburgh: Handsel, 1999.
Underhill, Evelyn. *Worship*. New York: Harper & Brothers, 1937.
Vander Lugt, Wesley, and Trevor A. Hart, eds. *Theatrical Theology: Explorations in Performing the Faith*. Eugene, OR: Cascade, 2014.
Vander Zee, Leonard J. *Christ, Baptism, and the Lord's Supper: Recovering the Sacraments for Evangelical Worship*. Downers Grove, IL: InterVarsity, 2004.
Van Kuiken, E. Jerome. *Christ's Humanity in Current and Ancient Controversy: Fallen or Not?* London: Bloomsbury T. & T. Clark, 2017.
Wainwright, Geoffrey. *Doxology: The Praise of God in Worship, Doctrine and Life; A Systematic Theology*. Oxford: Oxford University Press, 1984.
———. *Eucharist and Eschatology*. Peterborough, UK: Epworth, 2003.
Wainwright, Geoffrey, and Karen B. Westerfield Tucker. *The Oxford History of Christian Worship*. Oxford: Oxford University Press, 2006.
Wallace, Ronald S. *The Atoning Death of Christ*. Reprint, Eugene, OR: Wipf and Stock, 1997.
———. *Calvin's Doctrine of the Word & Sacrament*. Grand Rapids: Eerdmans, 1953.
Warren, Trish Harrison. *Liturgy of the Ordinary: Sacred Practices in Everyday Life*. Downers Grove, IL: InterVarsity, 2016.
Webber, Robert E. *Ancient-Future Time: Forming Spirituality through the Christian Year*. Grand Rapids: Baker, 2004.
———. *Ancient-Future Worship: Proclaiming and Enacting God's Narrative*. Grand Rapids, Baker, 2008.
———. *Evangelicals on the Canterbury Trail: Why Evangelicals Are Attracted to the Liturgical Church*. Harrisburg, PA: Morehouse, 1985.
———. *Worship Is a Verb*. Nashville, TN: Star Song, 1992.
Webster, John. "T. F. Torrance on Scripture." *Scottish Journal of Theology* 65.1 (2012) 34–63.
Weightman, Colin. *Theology in a Polanyian Universe: The Theology of Thomas Torrance*. New York: Lang, 1994.
Welker, Michael. *What Happens in Holy Communion?* Grand Rapids: Eerdmans, 2000.
White, James F. *A Brief History of Christian Worship*. Nashville, TN: Abingdon, 1993.
———. *Christian Worship in North America: A Retrospective, 1955–1995*. Collegeville, MN: Liturgical, 1997.
———. *Christian Worship in Transition*. Nashville, TN: Abingdon, 1976.
———. *Introduction to Christian Worship*. 3rd ed. Nashville, TN: Abingdon, 2000.
———. *New Forms of Worship*. Nashville, TN: Abingdon, 1971.
———. *Protestant Worship: Traditions in Transition*. Louisville, KY: Westminster/John Knox, 1989.
White, Susan J. *Christian Worship and Technological Change*. Nashville, TN: Abingdon, 1994.
Willimon, William H. *The Service of God: How Worship and Ethics are Related*. Nashville, TN: Abingdon, 1983.
———. *Worship as Pastoral Care*. Nashville, TN: Abingdon, 1990.
Witvliet, John D. *Worship Seeking Understanding: Windows into Christian Practice*. Grand Rapids: Baker Academic, 2003.

Wright, N. T. *The Kingdom New Testament: A Contemporary Translation*. New York: Harper One, 2011.

Ziegler, Geordie W. *Trinitarian Grace and Participation: An Entry into the Theology of T. F. Torrance*. Minneapolis, MN: Fortress, 2017.

www.ingramcontent.com/pod-product-compliance
Lightning Source LLC
Chambersburg PA
CBHW062025220426
43662CB00010B/1474